Aspects of
Pentecostal-Charismatic
Origins

Aspects of
Pentecostal-Charismatic
Origins

VINSON SYNAN, Editor

LOGOS INTERNATIONAL
Plainfield, New Jersey

All Scripture quotations are from the King James version of the Bible unless otherwise identified:

NEB = New English Bible.
RSV = Revised Standard Version.

ASPECTS OF PENTECOSTAL-CHARISMATIC ORIGINS

Copyright © 1975 Logos International
Plainfield, NJ 07060

All Rights Reserved
Printed in the United States of America

Library of Congress Catalog Card Number: 75-2802
International Standard Book Number: 0-88270-110-X (hardcover)
0-88270-111-8 (softcover)

To my one and only twin brother
VERNON SYNAN

Contents

Contents

Aspects of
Pentecostal-Charismatic
Origins

Introduction

VINSON SYNAN

RECENT years have been especially exciting ones for pentecostal people around the world. Since World War II it has become apparent that the pentecostal churches are the fastest-growing ones in Christendom. In most of the developing countries of the world, young pentecostal movements have left their older Catholic, Baptist, Methodist, and Presbyterian counterparts far behind in church growth. Pentecostalism seems now to constitute the wave of the future for Christianity. Some experts have predicted that after another generation or so, the majority of all the Christians in the world will probably be nonwhite, from the southern hemisphere, and *pentecostal*. Exciting reports of explosive growth among indigenous pentecostal movements in Chile, Brazil, Africa, Korea, and Indonesia stagger the imagination. The third force in the third world is where the cutting edge of future Christian growth will be.

In the midst of rejoicing, however, there has also been perplexity for pentecostals and nonpentecostals at the rise of the charismatic movement since 1960. This word comes from the Greek *charismata*, gifts of grace, and refers to the gifts of the Holy Spirit. As it is now used, the word "charismatic" refers to those persons in the main-line denominations who have received the Baptism in the Holy Spirit and have chosen to stay within their own churches or to find fellowship in nondenominational charismatic bodies rather than to join the organized pentecostal denominations such as the Assemblies of God, the Church of God (Cleveland, Tennessee), the International Church of the Foursquare Gospel, the Pentecostal Holiness Church, and the Church of God in Christ. The latter groups are now called "classical pentecostal" churches, for want of a better term.

The charismatic movement is actually the latest of several phases in the development of pentecostalism in the United States. The following phases can now be clearly identified as variations of one Holy Spirit movement with one common factor of Spirit Baptism accompanied by glossolalia and/or other gifts of the Spirit:

1. *The holiness-pentecostal movement* began with Charles Parham in 1901 and included the Azusa Street revival with William Seymour from 1906 to 1909. This original phase in the United States was essentially Wesleyan in its theology, worship, and hymnody. Most of the holiness terminology and piety of the classical pentecostals was handed down from the earlier holiness movement.

In this book, the chapters by Melvin Dieter and Donald Dayton specifically examine Wesleyan aspects of pentecostal origins. Since practically all of the black pentecostals in the United States are in the holiness-pentecostal wing of the movement, Leonard Lovett's contribution on black pentecostalism also deals with this aspect of pentecostal beginnings.

2. *The "Finished Work" pentecostal movement* began with Chicagoan William Durham in 1910 and includes the Assemblies of God and most of the pentecostal groups organized after 1914. The streams that flowed into this theological camp are examined by Larry Christenson in his study of the Irvingites, and by William Menzies in his chapter on non-Wesleyan influences on the development of modern pentecostalism.

The chapter by Thomas Zimmerman, head of the Assemblies of God, is written from the perspective of a veteran administrator of the largest pentecostal denomination in the United States. His perspective on the growth of pentecostalism shows the great importance classical pentecostals attribute to doctrine as the basis of their success.

3. *The "oneness" or pentecostal unitarian movement* began in 1913 and caused a major schism in the Assemblies of God in 1916. Many charismatics are unaware of this development among the pentecostals which once nearly took over the mainstream of the movement in the United States. Although this movement has existed for over sixty years, it is probably the least-understood aspect of our subject.

David Reed's chapter sheds new light on the thinking and theology of the oneness pioneers.

4. *The Protestant "neo-pentecostal" movement* dates from about 1960. After sixty years, the traditional denominations learned to tolerate pentecostals among their members rather than excommunicating them. Most observers point to the experience of Father Dennis Bennett in his Episcopal parish in Van Nuys, California, as the beginning of this phase, although untold thousands had received the pentecostal experience and remained in their churches *sub rosa* before this time.

The social and theological implications of this movement are examined by Martin Marty in his perceptive chapter near the end of the book. The often bitter opposition of the traditional churches to the early pentecostal movement is covered in the chapter by Horace Ward. Its current success among some of the main-line Protestant churches contrasts sharply with earlier vitriolic opposition.

5. *The "Catholic charismatic" pentecostal movement* traces its beginning to 1966. This latest phase of the Spirit's outpouring caught the church world by surprise. "Catholic pentecostalism" seemed a contradiction in terms to many, yet by 1974 over 30,000 Catholic pentecostals gathered at Notre Dame to celebrate the eighth year of the movement's progress.

Many people have assumed that the Catholic pentecostal movement appeared out of thin air as a radical departure from traditional Catholicism. Yet there had been a great deal of

groundwork laid for this astounding development as far back as the
latter part of the nineteenth century. In fact, the convening of
Vatican I and the founding of the National Holiness Association
both occurred in 1867. In His own way, the Lord was preparing
two mighty streams that began to converge a century later in the
pentecostal outpouring in Pittsburgh and South Bend.

The chapter by Edward O'Connor gives valuable insights into
the lesser-known events and personalities which preceded the
current Catholic charismatic renewal.

Each passing year demonstrates anew the importance of understanding the phenomenon of pentecostalism. Perhaps we are seeing
only the beginnings of what will rank as a major revival on the
order of the Lutheran and Wesleyan renewals of the sixteenth and
eighteenth centuries. If this be so, then a book exploring in depth
the origins of the movement in the United States will be a great
service to the entire Church.

It has been a distinct pleasure to work with each of the men
whose papers appear in the following chapters. They delivered
them to the assembled members and guests of the third annual
meeting of the Society for Pentecostal Studies at Lee College,
Cleveland, Tennessee, late in 1973. One of the miracles of that
meeting was that people from each of the five phases mentioned
above, along with many friends and observers from non-pentecostal backgrounds, met together in friendly and sanctified dialogue
without the bitterness and suspicion that would have made such a
meeting impossible just a few years ago.

The Reason for the Rise of the Pentecostal Movement

THOMAS F. ZIMMERMAN

Since 1960, Thomas F. Zimmerman has served as the General Superintendent of the Assemblies of God, largest of the American pentecostal denominations. Born in Indianapolis, Indiana, in 1912, he was ordained in 1932 and rose through the ranks as pastor and district superintendent until his call to lead the entire church in 1960.

Since that time, Zimmerman has established himself as one of the leading spokesmen for world pentecostalism. His leadership has been especially notable in the field of religious broadcasting, in the National Association of Evangelicals, the Pentecostal Fellowship of North America, and the World Pentecostal Conference. He serves also as president of the recently formed Assemblies of God Graduate School in Springfield, Missouri.

For the past decade, Zimmerman has been the single most influential pentecostal leader on the world scene. His evaluation of the rise of pentecostalism in the following chapter is one which most classical pentecostals would agree faithfully describes the forces that brought their movement into existence. Of significant interest are the reasons he, a prominent insider, adduces for the phenomenal growth of the movement in recent years.

5

LATE in 1969, Jessyca Russell Gaver received a clipping from the September 6, 1969, edition of the *New York Times* sent by her publisher, Arnold Abramson. The headline read, "Pentecostal Movement Rapidly Finding New Adherents."

Abramson wanted Mrs. Gaver to write a book about this phenomenon, and to encourage her to accept the assignment, he included the story of the growth of pentecostals. She accepted, and the result was an almost 300-page paperback entitled *Pentecostalism*.

While there were certainly other considerations which caused Mrs. Gaver to take the assignment, a prominent motivating factor was one sentence in the newspaper article:

> Pentecostalism has developed into the world's fastest-growing denomination at a time when membership in most other churches is declining as a proportion of the population.

Like the initial outpouring of the Holy Spirit on the day of Pentecost, the pentecostal movement today has received widespread attention. It has been referred to by various designations—both kind and unkind. Possibly one of the most appropriate descriptions from a biblical point of view is the term "revival." The rise of the pentecostal movement came under conditions which existed prior to revivals both in Bible times and in later Church history. The rise of the present-day move of the Spirit is directly attributable to believers who fulfilled God's conditions for revival.

Great revivals have often begun in times of spiritual and moral darkness. Conditions of gross darkness prevailed before revivals under such leaders as Asa (II Chron. 15:1–15), Joash (II Kings 11, 12), Hezekiah (II Chron. 29–31), Josiah (II Kings 22, 23), Zerubbabel (Ezra 5, 6), and Nehemiah (Neh. 8:9; 12:44–47). The people and leaders were guilty of idolatry, neglect of and in some cases

7

contempt for the house of God, unjust and sometimes cruel treatment of fellow Israelites, entangling alliances and associations with heathen nations, and the practice of spiritism and other forms of the occult.

Against this backdrop of ungodliness, there were always those who were earnestly looking to the Lord for His intervention. These people were never disappointed, for when God's people sought the Lord with the whole heart, a spiritual and moral revival always followed.

A quick perusal of history books makes it very evident that conditions prior to the present pentecostal revival were deplorable. Post–Civil War America was fraught with sectional hostility and financial turmoil. Increasing population movements into the cities were accompanied by the usual moral decay—crime, gambling, alcoholism, and prostitution grew rampant. Corruption reached high levels of federal and state governments, and many became rich quickly at the expense of the taxpayers. In the business world, those who became wealthy through stock manipulations, oil speculations, and other fraudulent means often outnumbered those who succeeded through honesty.

Nor was the church exempt from the spirit of the times. American seminaries exchanged professors with the German universities where liberal theology and higher criticism of the Bible were in vogue. It wasn't long until pulpits were being populated by literal apostles of unbelief. They ridiculed the deity of Christ, the virgin birth, and the substitutionary atonement. The social gospel was supplanting the supernatural Gospel, and the theory of Christian nurture preempted the necessity of repentance.

But still there were many devout believers in every denomination who continued to "contend for the faith which was once delivered unto the saints." As these people began to pray more earnestly because of deteriorating world conditions, it was not long until God began to pour out His Spirit and to restore to the remnant Church the gifts of His Spirit, notably speaking in tongues.

Not all these people upon whom the Spirit fell realized, at first, the biblical precedent for the experiences they were having. But soon, from many different places, they began to declare that the Holy Spirit was being outpoured as during the first days of the Church age. Once again God had honored His ancient promise in a time of deep darkness.

This, then, is the explanation for the remarkable growth of the pentecostal movement. Men have tried to adduce all kinds of reasons for it in terms of sociology, psychology, ecology, and economics. But nothing short of the almighty power of God responding to the contrition of His faithful remnant could have produced such results.

Let us then review the essential elements in the lives of these people on whom the Spirit fell. First, they revered the Word of God, the Bible. And so it always was. The revivals under Asa (II Chron. 15:8–19), Joash (II Chron. 24:6), and Hezekiah (II Kings 18:6), as well as those under Josiah, Zerubbabel, and Nehemiah, were attributable largely to the fact that these Old Testament leaders insisted on a renewed commitment to the Mosaic documents, especially to Deuteronomy.

Evan Roberts, leader of the famous Welsh revival at the turn of this century, exemplified this same dedication to the priority of Scripture. A contemporary observer said of him, "He is no orator, he is not widely read. The only book he knows from cover to cover is the Bible." George T. B. Davis, in his book *When the Fire Fell*, reported that a religious paper in Chicago made this observation of Evan Roberts: "First he worked in a coal mine, then became an apprentice in a forge, then a student for the ministry. But all his life he has yearned to preach."

The Bible was given priority in Bethel College, Topeka, Kansas, where about forty students came together primarily to study the Word of God. It was after exhaustive study of the Bible that the students unanimously agreed that speaking in tongues is the initial evidence of the Baptism in the Spirit. What they believed the Word of God taught, they soon began to experience, and so the modern pentecostal movement was launched.

Secondly, these people on whom the Spirit fell lived holy lives. They studied to avoid sin and to shun the very appearance of evil.

Since the pentecostal movement is strongly biblical, its emphasis on holiness is not surprising. It might have seemed that such an emphasis would inhibit its growth, but the opposite has been true. The committed life with all its attendant blessings came to be appreciated by people who recognized the greater price which had to be paid for selfish and sinful living. Holiness was not to them a cross to be borne, but a cherished delight.

While there have been different doctrinal positions on the matter of sanctification, all pentecostal fellowships have emphasized holiness. A careful study of the past seventy years would show that this has certainly been a factor in the growth of these bodies.

A third prominent feature of all revivals of Bible and church history has been a strong emphasis on the truth of substitutionary atonement. Sin is a reality which can only be taken care of through the transfer of the offender's guilt to Christ, and the transfer of Christ's righteousness to the believer.

The work of the Holy Spirit is to glorify Christ (John 16:14). This is why, when pentecostal believers have emphasized the atoning work of Christ, lost souls have responded with joy. Persuasive human eloquence did not produce these many conversions, but the convicting power of the Holy Spirit who honored the cross-centered preaching of the pentecostals.

Perhaps one of the most significant and widely observed phenomena of the pentecostal revival is its emphasis upon free and exuberant worship. Man is a worshiping creature. He will worship something. If he doesn't worship God, he is surely an idolater.

When people are filled with the Holy Spirit, they are indwelt by the One who glorifies Christ and who also empowers authentic worship. This Spirit of worship which has attracted so many in the past will certainly continue to do so.

Dr. Leland R. Keys, a retired minister who has served many years with distinction both as a pastor and educator, was introduced to pentecost in a mission in an eastern city in the early years of this century. He said there was one custom of that mission which attracted his attention most: a lady would play the pump organ before the service and sometimes would sing familiar choruses and hymns. Without waiting for the service to commence formally, the people as they gathered would join in, and God's presence would become wonderfully real.

Dr. Keys continued, "A Spirit-baptized body of believers, loving the Lord with all their hearts, singing and making melody to the Lord, expressing their joy in the public assembly, prepared the way for what was called a 'Holy Ghost meeting.' The gifts of the Spirit were manifested, and the Word of God was proclaimed with power. The result was that the altars were filled with those who were hungry for God."

Much more could be said about the numerous features which attracted people into the pentecostal ranks from every walk of life. The joy of salvation, their irrepressible happiness, miraculous healings and deliverances, transformed homes—all had great appeal.

Less appealing was the persecution. It happened in the home, in the community, in the schoolhouse. Wary onlookers quickly coined epithets to describe these people whose behavior they considered bizarre. As in the early church, however, persecution didn't hinder the work of God—it helped.

The final characteristic of the early pentecostals which accounts for much of their success was their consuming evangelistic zeal. In spite of charges to the contrary, pentecostals do not spend all their time talking in or about tongues. They have instead consistently sought to bring people to Christ. Like the people described in the Book of Acts, they have gone everywhere, earnestly proclaiming the message of salvation.

A. W. Orwig, who attended some of the Azusa Street meetings in Los Angeles, later wrote:

> One thing that somewhat surprised me was the presence of so many from different churches. Some were pastors, evangelists, or foreign missionaries. Persons of many nationalities were present. Sometimes

these, many of them unsaved, would be seized with deep conviction of sin under the burning testimony of one of their own nationality, and at once heartily turn to the Lord. Occasionally some foreigner would hear a testimony or earnest exhortation in his native tongue from a person not at all acquainted with that language, and thereby be pungently convicted that it was a call from God to repent of sin.

W. J. Seymour, a leader in the Azusa Street mission, was often heard to say, "Now, do not go from this meeting and talk about tongues, but try to get people saved."

In conclusion, we must not overlook the prophetic and eschatological implications of the pentecostal movement. When the multitude gathered at the first pentecostal outpouring, some were angered, some were in doubt, and some mocked. It was then Peter offered an explanation in terms of the prophecy of Joel:

> And it shall come to pass in the last days, saith God, I will pour out of my Spirit upon all flesh: and your sons and your daughters shall prophesy, and your young men shall see visions, and your old men shall dream dreams: and on my servants and on my handmaidens I will pour out in those days of my Spirit; and they shall prophesy: and I will show wonders in heaven above, and signs in the earth beneath; blood, and fire, and vapour of smoke: the sun shall be turned into darkness, and the moon into blood, before that great and notable day of the Lord come: and it shall come to pass, that whosoever shall call on the name of the Lord shall be saved. (Acts 2:17–21)

The pentecostal revival is a fulfillment of prophecy—a sign of the last days.

Paul made a less buoyant forecast about those days: "This know also, that in the last days perilous times shall come" (II Tim. 3:1). He followed that with a dreary catalog of evils which would characterize the last days—a list that convinces believers more than ever of the imminence of the end of the age. But pentecostals know that where sin abounds, grace is even more plentiful, and they are optimistic. They expect an outpouring of the Spirit greater than ever.

Thank God for what happened on the day of Pentecost! Thank God for the rise of the twentieth-century pentecostal movement.

But let us especially thank God that the best days are not in the past. They are in the future.

Convinced of this, we will continue to sensitively follow the leadership of the Holy Spirit; we will continue in dedicated service to Christ; and we shall continue to pray, "Even so, come, Lord Jesus! Maranatha!"

Pentecostalism's Forgotten Forerunner

LARRY CHRISTENSON

Larry Christenson is an ordained minister in the American Lutheran church and since 1960 has served as pastor of the Trinity Lutheran Church in San Pedro, California. Author of the bestseller The Christian Family, *Christenson has also written* A Message to the Charismatic Movement *and* A Charismatic Approach to Social Action. *In addition to these works, he is a talented composer and dramatist.*

As an active participant in the charismatic renewal, Christenson has been instrumental in bringing pentecostalism to his fellow Lutherans in Germany as well as in the United States. Through his efforts, many members of the German nobility have received the pentecostal experience.

In the following chapter, Christenson examines the little-known nineteenth-century British forerunner of modern pentecostalism, the Catholic Apostolic church, founded by followers of Edward Irving.

IN the first three decades of the twentieth century, pentecostalism, with its tongue-speaking, prophecy, healings, and miracles, spread outward from a revival on Azusa Street in Los Angeles to encircle the globe and become a "third force" in Christendom.[1] In the train of earlier revivals in the Wesleyan-holiness tradition, pentecostalism stressed the importance of the Baptism with the Holy Spirit as a second or third work of grace.[2] It linked this experience to palpable manifestations of the Holy Spirit, especially speaking in tongues. The experience of charismatic phenomena formed a part of the central core of the pentecostal proclamation, and was heralded as evidence of a new breakthrough of the Holy Spirit.

Yet during this same period, charismatic manifestations were a commonplace occurrence in a body of churches outside pentecostalism. In congregations scattered around the world, but predominantly in Europe and North America, members of the Catholic Apostolic church recorded their experience of tongues, prophecy, and healings—as they had quietly been doing for more than half a century previous.[3]

The Catholic Apostolic church has represented something of an enigma to churchmen, rather like "a beautiful Church built from the roof downwards, coming down from above, like New Jerusalem," as one Anglo-Catholic cleric has rather quaintly put it. It was in essence—and this is its most striking feature—a revival of Catholicism out of Protestantism. It was described by an influential writer of the day as "answering to the great religious desideratum of the age—a simple creed, a gorgeous ritual, and a devoted priesthood." Its liturgy is incomparable, described by Dr. David Hislop, in his Kerr Lectures, as "containing all the virtues and escaping all the blemishes of the Book of Common Prayer." Its Book of Regulations describes a quality of spiritual nurture and

17

care for its members which could well serve as a primer in Pastoral Theology. It grew out of a charismatic awakening in Great Britain in the 1830s, founded churches throughout Europe and America, and produced a not insignificant literature. Yet it is, today, almost totally unknown in Christendom. And where it is known, it is most often misunderstood.

Though the movement as it began was diffuse, growing spontaneously without organization or direction, it came to a certain focus in the public mind in the person of the minister of the National Scottish Church in Regent Square, London, the most famous preacher of his day, Edward Irving.

The name of Edward Irving is inextricably linked with the history and development of the Catholic Apostolic church. Adherents to the movement were dubbed Irvingites, a designation which Irving himself protested bitterly. Yet to this day, "Irvingism" is the convenient handle by which many people dispose of the movement, often in a pejorative sense, as when foreigners dispose of all Americans with the designation "Yankee." The fact of the matter is that the name of Edward Irving, for all the notability which it enjoyed during his own lifetime, is today little more than a name to most students of church history, somewhat vaguely identified with speaking in tongues, prophecy, and other sundry fanaticisms.

How far this is from an accurate estimate of the man and his ministry may be discovered by the most cursory reading of his life. Irving had arrived in London in 1822, unknown, newly ordained, to minister to a handful of Scotsmen at the little Caledonian Chapel in Hatton Garden. In a matter of months, that little chapel had become the center of attraction in the great metropolis. High society and low flocked to hear the Scotsman preach. Orators, scholars, and nobles hung upon his lips as he discoursed of righteousness, temperance, and judgment to come, with the boldness and power of one of the old prophets. Within two years, the congregation had outgrown the tiny chapel, and a large new church was built in Regent Square.

Yet impressive as was his power in the pulpit, Irving's gifts as a pastor—a shepherd of souls—were more impressive still, and stood somewhat in contrast to his flamboyant oratorical style. Before ordination, he had worked as an assistant to the great Reverend Chalmers in the slums of Glasgow, where he acquired a lifelong sympathy, rapport, and pastoral concern for the "simple poor of the earth." When fame visited upon him the adulation of the mighty, with ever-increasing demands upon his time, and later, when storm clouds of controversy lowered about him, he never ceased his quiet and faithful shepherding of the flock entrusted to his care. "He was," wrote Thomas Carlyle after Irving's death, "the freest, brotherliest, bravest human soul mine ever came in contact with. I call him on the whole the best man I have ever, after trial enough, found in this world or now hope to find."

In July of 1831, Irving mentioned in a letter to a friend, "Two of my flock have received the gift of tongues and prophecy." Two years earlier, in his "Homilies on Baptism," Irving had taken the established position of the Church of Scotland at that time, that the supernatural gifts of the Spirit had disappeared in the Church.

As firm and highly reflected as were his theological views, his sensitivity as a pastor would not allow him to remain shackled to a stated theological position where the spiritual care of one of his members was at stake. He counseled extensively with the individuals involved, and slowly satisfied himself that these were indeed genuine manifestations of the Holy Spirit. Having come to this conclusion, with the single-minded sincerity which was his characteristic, Irving spoke out in favor of the movement, lending it the not inconsiderable weight of his reputation and pastoral office. In this regard, it is worth noting that Irving himself never spoke in tongues, or interpreted, or prophesied. Thus it was no light-headed enthusiasm which led Irving into the movement, but a sober theological reflection and pastoral concern, based on the opportunity to test the spiritual validity of these manifestations at first hand.

Though he did not at first permit it, Irving felt constrained at last to allow the utterance of tongues and prophecy in the regular worship service. The trustees of the congregation took exception to this, and on Communion Sunday, May 6, 1832, Irving found himself locked out of his church. The trustees refused to deal with the substantive issue of the manifestations themselves—whether they were genuine or not—but moved against Irving on the purely technical grounds that he had allowed persons not ordained by the Church of Scotland to "minister" (speak in tongues and prophesy) in the church building.

The greater part of Irving's congregation followed him. Before long, they had located a large picture gallery on Newman Street, and remodeled it into a meeting place for their church, which then continued to be one of the focal points of the movement.

Irving lived scarcely more than two years from the founding of the church in Newman Street. In December of 1834, during a trip to Scotland in a weakened state of health, he succumbed to pneumonia and died, at the age of forty-two. Already, however, the leadership of the movement had passed to other hands. After the initial spread of the movement, Irving, despite his fame and his not inconsiderable gifts, was destined to play a less prominent role.

A recent student of Irving's life states that his writings during his last years reveal a lucid and ordered mind, unfolding a complete theological system. A sober reading of the evidence, in the light of the Church's experience with the pentecostal movement, renders possible a new understanding of Irving's place in Church history: He was a man ahead of his time, pointing to things yet future for the great body of the Church. He was a forerunner not only of the Catholic Apostolic church in a direct sense, but of the entire pentecostal phenomenon of the twentieth century. The things he said and did, his emphases and concerns, largely rejected in his own day, have become commonplace in the pentecostal movement of our time.

Near the outbreak of the movement in Great Britain, certain words of prophecy were spoken which had little apparent meaning for the immediate hearers, but which portended a significant development in the future of the Catholic Apostolic church. In

1830, at a prayer meeting in the MacDonald household in Port Glasgow, the word was spoken, "Send us *apostles.*" In Bavaria, two years earlier, in a Roman Catholic cottage meeting, came the word, "Thus saith the Lord, I will again send you *apostles* and *prophets,* as at the beginning." The promise that God would restore the ancient ordinances of the Church continued to be voiced in words of prophecy, though it seems that no clear idea of what this meant or would involve was prevalent in the movement.

On October 31, 1832, at a prayer meeting in Irving's home, Henry Drummond, a wealthy businessman and sometime member of Parliament, who was deeply committed to the movement, approached John Bates Cardale, a prominent London lawyer who was kneeling, and had just finished praying for the Church, that she might be clothed with power from on high. Drummond spoke with what was later remembered as "indescribable power and dignity," naming Cardale to the office of apostle. A week later, on November 7, the call was repeated, this time through Edward Taplin, later to be named the chief prophet of the movement. Thus emerged into view that which was to become the signal characteristic and claim of the Catholic Apostolic church, the restoration of the charismatic offices in the Church.

Over the next two years, eleven other men were called, by prophetic utterance, to complete the college of apostles. Men were called to numerous other offices as well: prophets, evangelists, pastors and teachers, "Angels" (their term for local bishop, or chief pastor of a congregation), elders, deacons, and miscellaneous assisting ministries. On July 14, 1835, the twelve apostles were formally set apart for their calling.

The first action of the apostles was to remain quiet for twelve months, an accomplishment so uncharacteristic of ecclesiastical officials in general, and of newly appointed clerics in particular, that it must be remarked as one of the more compelling evidences of divine inspiration.

Together with seven of the prophets, they lived in seclusion at Albury, where daily they prayed and studied through the Bible together. Their study and concern came to center upon the nature and destiny of the Church. Through prophetic revelation, the Mosaic Tabernacle was set forth as a type of the Christian Church, in considerable detail. The history, worship, order, ministry, and present condition of the Church were considered with great thoroughness.

The great bulk of Catholic Apostolic literature has to do with the nature and structure of the Church. This is rooted in their conviction that the Church has a certain God-given constitution, and only as the eternal ordinances of God are put into effect can the Church become that spiritual dwelling place of God in which He makes Himself known.

The Catholic Apostolic church's understanding of the Church proceeds along these lines: What is the Church? It is the Body of Christ, an *organism:*

> As the body of a man was so fashioned by God that its life should find full expression through its several organs, so was it with the body of Christ; through its several ministries this new and supernatural life is to find its full expression. If man can add no new organ to his own body, much less can he add a new ministry to the Church. Nor can he enlarge or diminish the function of any. He can, indeed, refuse to use the means by which his own bodily life is nourished and strengthened, and so bring in a state of weakness in which all the organs shall be unable to perform their full functions; and he can mutilate his body by the destruction of an organ, but the organic structure remains. The eye-ball may perish, the empty socket remains to tell where it has been, and where, if vision is restored, it must be set again. The Holy Ghost may be unable, for a time, to use all the Church's ministries as the instruments of His operation, but they abide as structural parts, ready to be used by Him when He can again put forth the fulness of His power.[4]

Despite marked similarities between the Catholic Apostolic church and the pentecostal movement, one searches in vain for any historical link. Whereas a spark-over point from classical pentecostalism to neo-pentecostalism is clearly discernible,[5] no such historical connection is evident between the Catholic Apostolic church and classical pentecostalism. The Catholic Apostolic church took but little note of the rise of pentecostalism, and the pentecostal movement appears to have been largely ignorant of, and historically unaffected by, the Catholic Apostolic church.[6] One is faced, at last, with the mystery of two movements existing side by side in history, sharing in considerable measure a unique religious outlook and experience, yet historically unrelated to one another.

No serious study of the beginnings of the pentecostal movement will want to ignore the Catholic Apostolic church. For the story of the Catholic Apostolic church, precisely because of the absence of any historical connection between the two movements, sheds a particular light on the origins of pentecostalism.

One way to relate two events to each other is to note their historical-causal connection. Mr. T tells Mr. C about an article he read which pointed up the dangers of excessive coffee drinking. Two weeks later, Mrs. C mentions to Mrs. T that her husband has cut down on his coffee drinking. When they look into it, they discover that this change came about as a result of his conversation with Mr. T two weeks previous. A clear historical-causal connection links the two events.

This, however, is not the only way in which two events may relate to one another. A red fire engine races down Maple Street, siren screaming. Little Johnny races into the house and interrupts his father's exegetical studies to report the event.

Three blocks down Maple Street, little Peggy sees the same red fire engine. Later in the day she encounters Johnny's parents at the market, and tells them about the red fire engine.

"Oh," says Johnny's father, "you must have been talking to Johnny."

"No, I haven't seen him all day," Peggy replies.

Johnny's father furrows his brow and squints his eyes together the way theologians do when they go searching for the connection between two seemingly unrelated events. At the check-out counter, his face suddenly lights up, and he reports to his wife that the story of the red fire engine passed from Johnny to some unknown third party, who in turn reported it to Peggy.

"Is that so?" she inquires. "How do you know?"

"The assured results of scientific scholarship," he reports sagely.

The two reports of the red fire engine which reached Johnny's father were not unrelated to one another. But the relationship was not historical-causal. The two reports originated from two different moments of history, and had no direct, causal effect upon one another. The reports were similar not because Johnny and Peggy had direct or indirect contact with one another, but because each had a separate encounter with the same essential reality—the trip of the red fire engine down Maple Street. As distinguished from an historical-causal relationship, this kind of relationship might be called existential-independent, i.e., independent encounter with the same essential reality.

The significance of an historical-causal relationship is established by discovering the direct influence of one event upon another. The significance of an existential-independent relationship, on the other hand, is established by noting the *correlation* between two otherwise unrelated events. Where the level or the nature of correlation appears to be more than coincidental, one forms hypotheses about the event or reality to which the two reports bear independent witness.

We engage in this kind of thought and evaluation every day, of course. You read two newspaper accounts which, independently of one another, report the same incident. From the two reports, you put together an impression of the event. Some of the details may differ, but the overall correlation is high. Without any conscious thought, you accept the hypothesis that the two reporters have been in touch with the same event, even though they may have had no personal contact with one another.

Some thoughtful interpreters of religious experience have suggested that this everyday mode of thinking has application not only for man's experience of physical reality, but also for his encounter with nonphysical reality.[7] A similarity of religious insight, expression, or ritual *may* point to a causal influence of one person or group upon another. But it may also point *beyond* any such influence, to a spiritual reality which has been communicated independently to more than a single individual or group.

The correlation between pentecostalism and the Catholic Apostolic church suggests the possibility that both movements, independently of one another, apprehended a common area of truth. The points of comparison between the two movements do not root out of a connection in history, but out of a common origin beyond history. The cluster of similarities is neither causally related nor is it accidental; it is a leitmotif which accompanies the historical manifestation of certain characteristics or potentialities which lie resident in Christ and His Body.

There are distinct differences between the orchestration of events which make up the history of the Catholic Apostolic church and that of the pentecostal movement. But threaded through both is a leitmotif which characterizes what we might call pentecostal or charismatic Christianity. A consideration of some of the elements of correlation which make up the leitmotif can help give us an impression of the general shape and texture of the pentecostal reality which found expression in these two movements.

1. *The priority of "event."* Pentecostal Christianity tends to find its rise in events which are heralded as a demonstration of supernatural power and activity. These events are inseparably linked to biblical types and patterns, which gives a distinct focus to one's reading of Scripture. The focus is upon the realistic, even the empirical, results of the Christian faith. One notes, for instance, the affinity of pentecostal Christianity for the historical portions of the Bible. The focus is not merely upon a God who *is*, but upon a God who *does*. For the charismatic, the record of happenings which we find in *Acts* becomes paradigmatic of the Christian life as it ought to be experienced.

The movement which eventually took the form of the Catholic Apostolic church may be dated from the first day of spring, 1830.

On that day, a pious, uneducated girl named Mary Campbell lay close to death in Fernicarry, Scotland. For weeks, she had been unable even to sit up in bed. Suddenly she raised up, stood out of bed, and began to speak melodiously in an unknown tongue, and to prophesy. She continued for a quarter of an hour, then returned to her bed in her former weakness. Word of this event spread, and not long afterward, similar occurrences took place in the Mac-Donald home in Port Glasgow, a few miles distant. Margaret MacDonald, also lying on her deathbed, was healed at the command of her brother, James. On that same day, James wrote a letter to Mary Campbell, encouraging her, also, to stand up and walk. Upon reading the letter, Mary rose up from her bed well, and walked to Port Glasgow to meet the MacDonalds.

Word of these events stirred great interest, both in Scotland and in England. Men from London, who had long prayed for an outpouring of the Holy Spirit, sent several of their number to Scotland to investigate. They returned convinced that what they had seen and heard was a true work of the Holy Spirit. They established meetings in various houses to pray for a restoration of the spiritual gifts. About a year later, on April 30, 1831, the first manifestation took place in London: Mrs. John Cardale, wife of a prominent Anglican lawyer, spoke in tongues. During the course of that year, tongues and prophecy were experienced by several other persons, from various religious denominations. These manifestations, accompanied by a number of healings, continued to increase and spread throughout 1832.[8]

The modern pentecostal movement is usually dated from New Year's Day, 1901, the day when Agnes Ozman, a student at Bethel Bible School in Topeka, Kansas, first spoke in tongues.[9] From Kansas, the tongue-speaking experience spread to surrounding states, down into Texas, then out to Los Angeles. There the famous Azusa Street revival broke out and became the launching pad for what was to become the worldwide pentecostal movement.

It is true that a significant doctrinal aspect of the modern pentecostal movement was set forth by Charles Parham when he singled out speaking in tongues as the only evidence of one's having received the Baptism with the Holy Ghost.[10] Yet it was not the doctrine, but the *event* of speaking in tongues, which midwifed the birth of modern-day pentecostalism. The reports of the early days of the pentecostal movement, both in secular and religious press, were very much a report of happenings. Nor were the happenings restricted to speaking in tongues. Healings, prophecies, and miracles were a part of the charismatic panorama that broke upon the scene.

The congregation which grew out of the Azusa Street meetings, still active today as the Apostolic Faith Church on West Adams Boulevard in Los Angeles, has one member still living who participated in the Azusa Street revival—Sarah Covington, now well past ninety. Her recounting of that historic three year non-stop prayer meeting is all event—prophecies that came true, healings, revelations, miracles. One word, more than any other, interlaces her recounting of those days: *power.* "We had the *power* in those days, and I haven't seen anything like it since!" [11]

Pentecostal Christianity appears to find its rise in a dramatic breakthrough of supernatural power, a display of charismatic phenomena. It is not the case of a teaching that gains a hearing, but events that attract a following.

2. *A mood of expectancy.* Pentecostal Christianity is Christianity standing on tiptoe, expecting something to happen. The focus of expectancy is very precise: It is upon what *God* will do. It is what Emil Brunner called, "the 'pneumatic factor,' the non-theological, the purely dynamic. Outsiders," said Brunner,

> were attracted—the story of a Pentecost already shows us this quite plainly—not primarily by what was said, but by the element of mystery—what happened simply. People draw near the Christian community because they are irresistibly attracted by its supernatural power. They would like to share in this new dimension of life and power. . . . There is a sort of fascination which is exercised mostly without any reference to the Word, comparable rather to the attractive force of a magnet or the spread of an infectious disease.[12]

The Catholic Apostolic church lived with a keen sense of expectancy during the early decades of its existence. Even after it had begun to wane as a movement, the flow of prophetic utterance in the many congregations, and the seriousness with which this was weighed, indicated how fundamental to their religious outlook was this mood of expectancy.[13]

In explaining the value of the public use of tongues, Edward Irving focused on this very issue of expectancy:

> The unknown utterance (in tongues) is for us a prevenient sign that the words addressed to our understanding are a message from God, a prophecy in the power of the Spirit, an utterance impelled by the Holy Ghost, and not the utterance of an enlightened and pious human intellect.[14]

In 1847, the chief spokesman of the Catholic Apostolic church, John Cardale, shared with some of his fellow leaders a "crisis of apathy" which had been reported to him by a number of the bishops. A feeling of deadness, a lack of conscious spiritual life and power, seemed to pervade the churches. Their answer to this crisis was to institute the Rite of Sealing, whereby the Holy Spirit should be conveyed through the laying on of hands. For, "assuming that the churches were instructed and built upon the foundations, the mode of going on to perfection was clearly the giving of the Holy Ghost by an outward act of laying on of hands."[15] This had been hinted at in prophecy twelve years earlier, but only now did they grasp its significance. Thus faced with a dwindling of spiritual life, the leadership recalled the people to the initial revelation which had given rise to the movement, that *power for the Church is to be sought nowhere else than in a fresh outpouring of the Holy Spirit.*[16]

The Rite of Sealing itself assumed a highly liturgical form, in keeping with the worship forms of the Catholic Apostolic church, and was not accompanied by the manifestation of spiritual gifts.[17] In the subsequent experience of the member, however, the exercise of spiritual gifts was commonly expected. The typical congregation had regular evening services specifically for the exercise and development of spiritual gifts.[18] Even when the movement dwindled and appeared to have lost much of its verve, the focus upon divine initiative persisted, so deeply ingrained was this mood of expectancy.

Many reports of the later Azusa Street revival highlighted the emotional excesses, the apparent extravagances and fanaticism. But closer investigation reveals that an awesome sense of the Divine Presence also pervaded the meetings. The people were so expectant of God's visitation that a kind of holy fear rested on them.

W. J. Seymour, the "Apostle of Azusa Street" and nominal leader of the meetings, often sat at the front behind two empty shoe boxes, one on top of the other. He kept his head inside the top one during the meeting, in prayer.

> The services ran almost continuously, [writes Frank Bartleman in the account of the revival compiled from his own diary]. The place was never closed nor empty. The people came to meet God. The meeting did not depend on the human leader. God's presence became more and more wonderful. Pride and self-assertion, self-importance and self-esteem, could not survive there. The religious ego preached its own funeral sermon quickly.[19]

Sarah Covington recounts incidents of a similar nature. When a policeman came in to break up the meeting, or a rich man came in "dressed like a peacock, and strutted around," Seymour simply motioned the people to pray, and the people waited until the intruders "went down under the power." [20] This kind of thing could happen only where expectation of divine action was a matter of practical reckoning.

> The dynamics of the charismatic-pentecostal spirituality [writes Kilian McDonnell], expand the expectations and awareness of the initiated believer. If we come with limited expectations, then that is all we take away. The charismatic-pentecostal movement expands expectations. When this occurs, the fullness of life in the Spirit is released in the measure of those expectations.[21]

3. *Fullness of Life in the Holy Spirit.* Whereas for Catholic

Christianity the Holy Spirit is the authenticator of ecclesiastical order, and for Protestant Christianity the illuminator of Scripture, and for the average men in the pew a vague, oblong blur, for pentecostal Christianity the Holy Spirit is the initiator of rich and varied Christian experience. No personal testimony is adequate, no worship service complete, without clear-cut evidence of the presence and activity of the Holy Spirit. This finds expression in a variety of ways, but most noticeably in the practice of spiritual gifts.

The Catholic Apostolic church, as we have noted, instituted the Rite of Sealing for the specific purpose of strengthening its members in the power of the Holy Spirit. John Cardale, in his two-volume work, *Readings Upon the Liturgy*, which is the definitive theological work of the movement, elaborates the view that a distinct operation of the Holy Spirit is involved:

> There is a gift of the Holy Ghost which Christ sends down and imparts after Baptism, and to those already baptized . . . to be distinguished from baptism with water.

The effect or purpose of this experience was to equip the believer for service in the Body of Christ:

> To the reception of the promised Gift of the Holy Ghost, every baptized man is bound to press forward. He that is baptized into Christ, and is not filled with the Spirit of Christ dwelling in him, so that he may be ready at all times to speak the words and do the works of God, according to God's good pleasure and his place in the Body of Christ—that man fails of the grace in which every baptized man should stand. And when this failure is not confined to individuals, but extends to the whole community . . . it is impossible that God's people should continue to realize their calling.[22]

Here is the teaching of a "second work of grace" which, as far as we can determine, was historically uninfluenced by Wesleyanism, and in any case has a somewhat different focus. Yet despite the lack of an historical connection, the similarity to pentecostal doctrine is striking. Here, under slightly different terminology, we see pentecostalism's doctrine of the Baptism with the Holy Spirit.

"According to Pentecostalism," writes Walter Hollenweger in his extensive survey of the movement, "the traditional churches are still stuck between Easter and Pentecost." His citing of an Assemblies of God publication in Italy as typical of the pentecostal teaching stands in substantial agreement with the view of the Catholic Apostolic church:

> We believe in the baptism of the Holy Spirit, as in a mighty divine power which penetrates into man after salvation.[23]

Pentecostal Christianity does not merely *assume* the presence and activity of the Holy Spirit in the Church. It expects it, plans for it, and depends upon it.

4. *The Paradox of Ecumenism and Exclusivism.* Pentecostal Christianity in its formative period had strong ecumenical tendencies. The spontaneity and vitality of its experience spread without too much regard for denominational boundaries. Either by intuition, or by conscious reflection, or both, one sees the unity of the Body of Christ as a necessary correlate to the outpouring of the Holy Spirit. Yet a charismatic movement, as it develops, exhibits distinct exclusivistic tendencies.

The paradox of these two contrasting motifs both finding expression in pentecostal Christianity must be understood as part of a typical—though not intrinsically necessary—historical rhythm. The essence of ecumenism is *acceptance*; the essence of exclusivism is *rejection*.

During the initial phase of a charismatic outpouring, the focus of rejection within the movement is diffuse and generalized, loosely embracing abstract or cultural categories such as "the world," "dead religion," "formalism." The heavier accent falls on acceptance. Regardless of background or station, one is welcomed into the charismatic arena. While the focus of acceptance is direct and personal, it embodies clear ecumenical overtones. One looks beyond the awakened and renewed individual to an awakened and renewed Church. While sin and error will be roundly denounced, the overall mood which dominates a charismatic awakening is expansive, positive, accepting.

From the time of the Montanists, charismatic movements have tended to be rejected by ecclesiastical authorities and structures. Hand-in-hand with this has been the tendency of charismatics to reject ecclesiastical authority.[24] As the confrontation between a loosely structured movement and formal religious authority shapes up, the ecumenical horizon of a charismatic awakening begins to narrow down. The fellowship and outlook become more exclusive. The hope of renewing the Church gives way to a defensive posture against "Babylon."

The charismatic happenings which gave rise to the Catholic Apostolic church ignored denominational boundaries. From 1830 to 1833 in England, the movement located in churches or home groups wherever a clergyman or influential layman had stepped out to embrace the new phenomena: an Anglican parish in Albury, an independent congregation in Bishopsgate, a nondenominational fellowship in Southwark, an Anglican parish in Park-Chapel, a Baptist congregation in Oxford. And in Scotland, people gathered together in home groups, or in churches, to share a fellowship and a freedom of worship which stirred the dour Scotch religious temperament like a bracing wind. In southern Germany, somewhat earlier than these events, there had been tongues and prophesying in a Roman Catholic parish, which later made contact with the movement in Great Britain.[25]

An early evidence of the ecumenical vision of the Catholic Apostolic church was their "Testimony Addressed to the Rulers in Church and State in Christian Lands," one of the most remarkable documents in the literature of the movement.[26] In this document, the evils pervading society are traced to their spiritual source, in the Church's departure from God's essential ordinances (both in Church and in state); and God's means for restoring the same are set forth. The leaders of the movement were sent out to the various countries of Christendom. They were to seek contact with Pope, with bishops, with kings, presenting their testimony wherever it would be received. Yet the greater burden of their commission was to "mine for gold," i.e., to go out in the character of private individuals, as learners and observers, rather than as teachers; to discover in the various countries of Christendom those elements of worship, church order, and spiritual life which belonged to the Church universal.[27]

The Catholic Apostolic church's generally fair and balanced evaluation of the various historical streams in Christendom remains remarkably free of the sectarian spirit which one has come to expect from exclusivistic revival movements. An Anglo-Catholic clergyman who made a lifelong study of the movement and was adviser to the Archbishop of Canterbury on the subject stated,

> There was no breakaway from the Historic Church (by the Catholic Apostolic Church). It was not and is not Dissent at all, because before you can dissent you must have first assented, before you can break away you must have first been joined. *It was a Movement from without the Historic Church towards it* . . . [italics mine]. By its century of witness to many under-valued or forgotten truths . . . its beauty of worship . . . and its power of forming Christian character of primitive but Catholic type . . . it reveals the abiding of the Holy Spirit.[28]

Despite the ecumenical vision of the Catholic Apostolic church, which may be judged exceptional by virtually any standard, in practice and in fellowship they moved toward exclusivism as the years went by. They eschewed contact with other Christians, hoarded their spiritual treasures, and looked on other Christians who claimed a measure of spiritual life with the bemusement of adults watching children at their make-believe games.[29] From time to time, the ecumenical vision would reassert itself, as when a strong word of prophecy was spoken in the 1920s, rebuking the people for supposing that God could not be doing a renewing work among even "the most despised," a reference that seemed to point quite clearly to the pentecostal movement.[30] But in practice, the ecumenical motif found only sporadic and largely theoretical expression. The surviving remnant of the Catholic Apostolic church remains in the clutch of a stultifying exclusivism.

Kilian McDonnell points out that the first beginnings of classical pentecostalism were decidedly ecumenical:

At the beginning of the movement, at the turn of the century, many classical Pentecostals thought in ecumenical categories. The intention was not to form a new church, but to be an interdenominational movement whose purposes were "to bring unity and union to Christians everywhere." This ecumenical dimension was evident not only in the United States but also for example in Scandinavia.[31]

Vinson Synan sees this same ecumenical tendency in some of the early mergers of pentecostal groupings.[32] The fact that the pentecostal movement was interracial in its early years also demonstrates the general spirit of openness and ecumenism which characterizes pentecostal Christianity.[33]

"The ecumenical beginnings of Pentecostalism, however, were soon forgotten," McDonnell points out.[34] As the historic denominations hardened in their resistance to pentecostalism, the movement itself moved progressively toward exclusivism.

> The early history of the pentecostals in society was in reality a story of mutual rejection [writes Synan]. The pentecostals rejected society because they believed it to be corrupt, wicked, hostile, and hopelessly lost, while society rejected the pentecostals because it believed them to be insanely fanatical, self-righteous, doctrinally in error, and emotionally unstable.[35]

The pattern of ecumenism leading to exclusivism is not inherent in pentecostal Christianity as such; it is simply the way that things have usually gone with charismatic movements, dating back to one of the very first charismatic renewals, namely the Montanists. Kilian McDonnell's evaluation at this point is especially noteworthy.

> The church [he says] reacted to the excesses (of Montanism) with such extreme vigor that all charismatic manifestations were looked upon as near heresy. *The church never really recovered its balance after it rejected Montanism* [italics mine].[36]

The neo-pentecostal movement, since its beginnings in the 1960s has been *de facto* ecumenical. "There was no conscious effort to be ecumenical," notes McDonnell. "People who had a deep religious experience gathered to share—and the sharing knew no denomina-

tional boundaries." [37] One hopes that the discordant note of
exclusivism may finally be dropped from the score, and that in
receiving the present-day manifestation of pentecostal Christianity,
the church may recover that balance between charismatic power
and ecclesiastical authority which characterized the apostolic and
sub-apostolic era.[38]

In 1901, the last of the original leaders of the Catholic Apostolic
church died, portending a dying out of the movement itself. For
according to their order, only these men could ordain priests, and
only ordained priests could celebrate the Eucharist.

Yet in that very expectation of death, there was a new hope. For
several decades there had been prophecies concerning the "Mission
of the 70"—a second, and greater work, which God would raise up
in due time. Their own was the "Mission of the 12," corresponding
to Jesus' appointment of the twelve apostles near the beginning of
His ministry; the new work would correspond to the appointment
of the seventy (Luke 10:1), near the end of His ministry. If their
work were to end as a seed, dropped into the ground to die, then
God, in His own time and way, would bring forth new life.[39]

That same year, halfway around the world, in a little Bible
school in Topeka, Kansas, a faint offstage melody was heard. A
group of students prayed for an outpouring of the Holy Spirit; one
of them began to speak in tongues. The melody spread to Houston,
Texas, then to Los Angeles. It had a familiar lilt. It was the
leitmotif announcing a new entrance onto the stage of history of
pentecostal Christianity!

NOTES

1. Vinson Synan, *The Holiness-Pentecostal Movement in the United States*
   (Grand Rapids, Mich.: Eerdmans, 1971), p. 215.
2. *Ibid.*, p. 162.
3. The many congregations of the Catholic Apostolic church kept
   stenographic records of all charismatic manifestations which took

place in their midst. These were periodically transmitted to the Central Church, in London, where they were compiled and compared with records received from other congregations. When something was deemed important for the church as a whole, it was included in the published "Record" which was sent to the chief pastor of every congregation.
4. Larry Christenson, *A Message to the Charismatic Movement* (East Weymouth, Mass.: Dimension, 1972), pp. 30–46. (This historical summary of the Catholic Apostolic church is adapted from the author's book on the subject; a detailed summary of sources is included in the book.)
5. Michael Harper, *As at the Beginning* (Plainfield, N.J.: Logos, 1971), p. 57. See also Walter J. Hollenweger, *The Pentecostals: The Charismatic Movement in the Church* (Minneapolis: Augsburg, 1972), p. 4.
6. Christenson, *op. cit.*, p. 15. (The author's own research could not turn up any evidence of historical influence of the Catholic Apostolic church upon classical or neo-pentecostalism. This judgment was confirmed in private conversation with an authority on classical pentecostalism, Vinson Synan; and in private conversation with an authority on the Catholic Apostolic church, Gordon Strachan.)
7. Morton Kelsey, *Encounter With God* (Minneapolis: Bethany Fellowship, 1972), p. 49.
8. Dr. Ernst Adolph Rossteuscher, *Der Aufbau der Kirche Christi auf den Urspuenglichen Grundlagen. Eine Geschichtliche Darstellung Seiner Anfaenge*, pp. 195, 199, 200. Verlag Hermann Neier Nachf., Siegen (1871, reprinted, 1969); A. L. Drummond, *Edward Irving and His Circle* (London: James Clarke and Co., 1934), p. 153; W. W. Andrews, *The History and Claims of the Body of Christians Known as the Catholic Apostolic Church* (Wembley, Middlesex, England: H. B. Copinger, 1950), pp. 15–16.
9. Synan, *op. cit.*, p. 101–102.
10. *Ibid.*, p. 99.
11. Sarah Covington, Private conversation with the author.
12. Emil Brunner, *The Misunderstanding of the Church* (London: Lutterworth Press, 1954), pp. 51–52.
13. See the careful attention given to such things as prophetic utterance, note #3 above. The author has seen these records dating into the 1920s, long after the movement had begun to decline.
14. Rossteuscher, *op. cit.*, p. 258.
15. F. W. Woodehouse, *A Narrative of Events Affecting the Position and Prospects of the Whole Christian Church* (10 Tavistock Place, London: Bedford Bookshop, 1938), p. 123.
16. Christenson, *op. cit.*, p. 56.
17. Woodehouse, *op. cit.*, pp. 130–31.
18. See note #3 above. A number of references in these volumes are to

the service which was designated for the "Exercise of Spiritual Gifts." The author has talked with a member of the Catholic Apostolic church who attended such services regularly as a young man.

19. Frank Bartleman, *What Really Happened at 'Azusa Street'?* (Northridge, Calif.: Voice Christian Publications, 1968), p. 3.
20. Covington, *loc. cit.*
21. Kilian McDonnell, *The Baptism in the Holy Spirit as an Ecumenical Problem* (Notre Dame, Ind.: Charismatic Renewal Services, 1972), p. 47.
22. John Bates Cardale, *Readings upon the Liturgy* (London: Thomas Bosworth, 1878), p. 441.
23. Hollenweger, *op. cit.*, p. 330.
24. Christenson, *op. cit.*, pp. 105–106.
25. Rossteuscher, *op. cit.*, pp. 278–307.
26. Dr. Reiner-Friedemann Edel, *Heinrich Thiersch als Oekumenische Gestalt*, p. 80. See his reference to the German scholar Kurt Hutten's evaluation of the "Testimony" as "a serious document, worthy of high regard." See also Morse-Boycott (note #28), p. 307: "A supreme literary achievement, instinct with a beautiful Christian spirit, informed from depths of wisdom and redolent with an unction equal to their claims which, we must note, were modestly put forward, without any show."
27. Woodehouse, *op. cit.*, pp. 58–59.
28. Desmond Morse-Boycott, *They Shine Like Stars* (London: Skeffington and Son, 1947), pp. 407, 308.
29. Private correspondence with members of the Catholic Apostolic church.
30. Private information obtained in conversation with a student of the movement who has had access to the "Records." (See note #3 above.)
31. McDonnell, *op. cit.*, p. 29.
32. Synan, *op. cit.*, p. 133.
33. *Ibid.*, pp. 137, 158.
34. McDonnell, *op. cit.*, p. 29.
35. Synan, *op. cit.*, p. 185.
36. McDonnell, *op. cit.*, p. 44.
37. *Ibid.*, p. 29.
38. Hans von Campenhausen, *Ecclesiastical Authority and Spiritual Power in the Church of the First Three Centuries* (Stanford, Calif.: Stanford University Press, 1969), p. 178.
39. Christenson, *op. cit.*, p. 109.

From "Christian Perfection" to the "Baptism of the Holy Ghost"

DONALD W. DAYTON

Donald W. Dayton is a graduate student in the Department of Christian Theology at the Divinity School of the University of Chicago. Prior to going to Chicago, Dayton served on the staff of the B. L. Fisher Library at Asbury Theological Seminary, Wilmore, Kentucky.

A member of the Wesleyan church, Dayton comes from a family prominent in the holiness movement for many years.

The following paper is the result of research done with Jerald Brauer and Martin Marty on "Nineteenth Century American Religious Thought." This excellent paper won the student prize at the third annual meeting of the Society for Pentecostal Studies which convened at Lee College in Cleveland, Tennessee, in 1973. The key work of William Arthur, Phoebe Palmer, and in particular Asa Mahan of Oberlin College in moving toward a modern pentecostal terminology is outlined in this chapter.

IN spite of extensive recent scholarship devoted to the history of pentecostalism, the origins and background of the movement are still obscure. Earlier history has been combed for occurrences of glossolalia, but there has been little attempt to delineate carefully the development of the complex of theological and religious ideas that culminated in pentecostalism.

Most students of pentecostalism have noticed the holiness movement as an immediate antecedent. This has been defended and developed most extensively by Vinson Synan, whose stance within the holiness-pentecostal tradition has enabled him to see this connection more clearly.[1] But as Synan himself admits,[2] his delineation of the development of the holiness movement is based largely on secondary sources prepared by representatives of Methodism and the classical holiness tradition who have not given particular attention to those features that have led more directly into pentecostalism. Much of this work needs to be redone with new questions in mind. I will offer here only a sample probe into this literature; a close tracing of the development of the doctrine of the Baptism of the Holy Spirit will indicate the lines that need to be followed up.

Some students of pentecostalism have assumed that this doctrine derives ultimately from early Methodism and the Wesleys. Hollenweger comments, for example, that "John Wesley . . . had already made a distinction between the sanctified, or those who had been baptized in the Spirit, and ordinary Christians."[3] But such a statement is at best oversimplified and at worst completely misleading. Wesley taught a doctrine of Christian perfection and not a Baptism of the Holy Spirit. Indeed, if we may trust the recent study of Herbert McGonigle, Wesley seems not even to have put major emphasis on the place of the Holy Spirit in the work of sanctification. His development of the doctrine in the *Plain Account*

41

of Christian Perfection is almost entirely Christocentric in character. Wesley does use the expression "Baptism of the Holy Spirit" a very few times, but always, McGonigle concludes, in reference to conversion or "justifying grace." [4]

This pattern holds true also for other early British Methodists. Wesley's preachers (whose lives and testimonies are collected in *The Lives of Early Methodist Preachers*) were not inclined to describe their experience in terms of a Baptism of the Holy Spirit. Nor is the expression characteristic of early Methodist hymnody. Adam Clarke does not speak in this manner in either his exegetical or his theological works. John Fletcher, however, does use the expression a very few times, but, according to McGonigle, ambiguously, applying it equally to the new birth and sanctification. Perhaps of more significance is the fact that at one point Wesley found it necessary to reprimand Joseph Benson, who was the editor of Fletcher's works, for speaking of sanctification as a "receiving of the Holy Ghost." [5] But it does seem clear, nonetheless, that there was no developed doctrine of a Baptism of the Holy Spirit in early Methodism.

Further study of these questions needs to be undertaken. There seem to have been developments in England that climaxed by the mid-nineteenth century in William Arthur's *The Tongue of Fire*, which will be discussed below. My study has concentrated on the American scene, and there the situation is much like that described above for early British Methodism. By 1830 or so, American Methodism had begun to neglect its crowning doctrine, and there arose in the following decade forces to reassert it. Particularly important were *The Guide to Christian Perfection* under the editorship of Timothy Merritt, the "Tuesday Meeting" for the "promotion of holiness" under the leadership of Phoebe Palmer and her sister Sarah Lankford, and perhaps most interesting of all, the school of Oberlin perfectionism that arose among Congregationalists and Presbyterians. In all of these, the emphasis was on Christian perfection developed along classical Wesleyan lines.

There was occasional reference to a Baptism of the Holy Spirit, but with little precision in its application.

As nearly as I can determine, the first sustained development of this doctrine took place, at least in America, in Oberlin perfectionism. Many students of pentecostalism have noticed this movement and especially its two greatest leaders, evangelist Charles Grandison Finney, who became the first theology professor at Oberlin, and Asa Mahan, the school's first president. But it is very difficult to trace the development of Oberlin theology. Frederick Dale Bruner emphasizes Finney's Baptism of the Holy Spirit language in his *Autobiography*.[6] But Finney uses the term very generally, referring to both his conversion of 1821 and the spiritual unction which he claimed was the *sine qua non* of an effective ministry. The *Autobiography*, moreover, was not published until 1876, when the teaching was relatively common. It plays no part in such earlier statements as his *Views of Sanctification*[7] or his systematic theology (the relevant section was first published in 1847). Though he may well have made earlier statements, the first I have discovered is his address on the "Baptism of the Holy Spirit" before the Oberlin Council of Congregationalism in 1871.[8]

Greater emphasis should perhaps be placed on Asa Mahan, who was in many ways the major architect of Oberlin perfectionism and much closer to Wesleyanism and the growing holiness movement within Methodism.[9] But Mahan reveals a pattern similar to that of Finney. The expression "Baptism of the Holy Ghost" dominates his *Autobiography*[10] and the more spiritually oriented *Out of Darkness into Light*.[11] Mahan himself refers to those "two great doctrines [i.e., "Christian Perfection" and "Baptism of the Holy Ghost"] which have been the theme of my life during the past forty-six years." [12] This statement would date his interest in the subject to at least as early as 1836. But this is the date of his sanctification, and there is no evidence that he described his experience at the time in terms of a Baptism of the Holy Ghost. The expression plays no part in his *Christian Perfection*[13] or other early writings. Mahan's full development of the doctrine was not published until 1870,[14] but we do know from Mahan's correspondence with Phoebe Palmer that the content of this book was first given as lectures at Adrian College six to eight years before publication.[15] Other indications in Mahan's writings would suggest that his thought did not turn to this doctrine until 1855 or so. This period (the late 1850s and early 1860s) seems to coincide, as we shall see, with broader interest in the doctrine.

But there does appear to have been at Oberlin an even earlier development of the doctrine among the other two members of the theological faculty. A third figure, Henry Cowles, placed greater emphasis on the place of the Holy Spirit in effecting sanctification, though usually without using the expression "Baptism of the Holy Spirit." [16] But two short sermons by Cowles do make the identification. The second of these concludes that "the plan of salvation contemplates as its prime object, the sanctification of the church; and relies on the baptism of the Holy Spirit as the great efficient power for accomplishing the work." [17]

Even more significant is the work of John Morgan who published in the first volume of the *Oberlin Quarterly Review* (1845—then under the editorship of Mahan) two essays to bolster Oberlin perfectionism. One of these, "The Holiness Acceptable to God," develops the nature of holiness without identifying it as a work of the Holy Spirit, but the second essay, "The Gift of the Holy Spirit," is a sustained argument that "the baptism of the Holy Ghost, then, in its Pentecostal fullness, was not to be confined to the Primitive Church, but is the common privilege of all believers." [18]

These essays are important for several reasons. In the first place, they illustrate the tension that must always exist between a doctrine of Christian perfection and one of the Baptism of the Holy Spirit. (This tension will be spelled out shortly.) The first essay has almost no reference to the Holy Spirit, while in the second, "perfection" and "holiness" fade almost entirely into the background. Asa Mahan was later to attempt to bring the two into more of a synthesis, but even there, one may detect problems. It is difficult, however, to trace any impact of Morgan's essays (though the former was published as a pamphlet in 1848 and the latter was serialized in the *Oberlin Evangelist*) until after the publication of Mahan's book on the subject in 1870. *The Gift of the Holy Spirit* was reprinted in 1875,[19] when it had major impact on A. J. Gordon, identified by Bruner as a major figure on the way to pentecostalism.[20] Gordon found Morgan's essay "a decided advance in the way of thorough scriptural discussion of this important subject." [21]

But Oberlin perfectionism was already by this time taking new directions and losing its earlier impact and influence. Apparently Morgan's works were largely buried in this decline, and one must look elsewhere for the continued development of the doctrine. Our study of Mahan has already drawn attention to the years of the late 1850s and early 1860s. Several other important developments seem to have taken place during this period. Eighteen fifty-six saw the publication of *The Tongue of Fire* by English Methodist William Arthur. This book develops the work of the Holy Spirit in terms of Pentecost and ends with the prayer:

> And now, adorable Spirit, proceeding from the Father and the Son, descend upon all the churches, renew the Pentecost in this our age, and baptize thy people generally—O, baptize them yet again with the tongues of fire! Crown this 19th century with a revival of "pure and undefiled religion" greater than that of the last century, greater than that of the first, greater than any "demonstration of the Spirit" ever yet vouchsafed to men! [22]

There is a sense in which this prayer found immediate fulfillment. The next two years (1857–58) saw the "layman's revival" which "spread abroad the ideals of the holiness and perfectionist movements." [23] A cursory overview of this revival reveals that contemporary reports often described it as a new Pentecost and spoke of the Baptism of the Holy Spirit. Phoebe Palmer, who had by this time become the most important advocate of holiness, also played an important part in this revival. She had been engaged in evangelism in Canada where the revival broke out, and she was present at the first stirrings. She also spent several years in the British Isles in the wake of this revival, continuing its spirit in vigorous evangelistic work.[24]

Though the language is not characteristic of her earlier works, Phoebe Palmer was by this time very committed to speaking of the Baptism of the Holy Spirit. In her letters home, printed in the *Guide to Holiness*,[25] she commented that the importance of this doctrine had just recently been impressed upon her. Perhaps it was William Arthur's book that produced this impact. It had been published in New York (1856), and Phoebe Palmer's terminology seems at times to reflect Arthur's. But whatever the source of the teaching, she sent back from England such reports as "we talked about the endowment of power, the full baptism of the Holy Ghost, as the indispensable, ay, *absolute* necessity of all the disciples of Jesus." [26] By this she meant "holiness," for which she seems to have discovered a new language. And this new language now permeates her work.

But it was still left to an Oberlin theologian to give the doctrine its final formulation. In 1870, Asa Mahan approached Phoebe Palmer about publishing his *Baptism of the Holy Ghost* under the auspices of the *Guide to Holiness* which she now edited. From their correspondence at the time, it is apparent that the doctrine was still controversial (Phoebe Palmer was reluctant to publish the book) but that it was already widely discussed (Mahan was able to argue that such discussion was the major reason that his "non-controversial" and "experiential" treatment was needed). In the end, the book was published and soon both generated and rode the crest of a wave of interest in the Baptism of the Holy Ghost. Within a dozen years, Mahan could report that his book had been "very extensively circulated in America, in Great Britain and in all missionary lands; and has been translated into the Dutch and German languages." [27] Mahan carried the message to the Oxford (1874) and Brighton (1875) meetings from which the Keswick movement emerged. At both conventions, he spoke and led very popular seminars on the subject. Revivalist D. L. Moody had wrestled with the doctrine in 1871, achieving a spiritual resolution that has seemed to a number of his biographers more important than his conversion in launching his evangelistic campaigns. At any rate, the doctrine was picked up by Moody and his followers, and Keswick was introduced back into the United States by Moody's Northfield Conventions.

But our interest lies still more with the impact of the new view on the Methodist and holiness traditions. Within a year, the *Guide to Holiness* could quote rave reviews from Methodist periodicals, while in 1874, Daniel Steele, then of Syracuse and later of Boston University, described his own experience in terms of a Baptism of the Spirit and appealed to his brethren to "cease to discuss the subtleties and endless questions arising from entire sanctification or Christian Perfection and all cry mightily to God for the baptism of the Holy Spirit." [28] The cumulative effect of this doctrine can be traced in the pages of the *Guide* until it climaxed in 1897 with a title change. In that year, the words "and Revival Miscellany" (dating from Phoebe Palmer's days) were dropped in favor of "and Pentecostal Life" in response to "signs of the times, which indicate inquiry, research, and ardent pursuit of the gifts, graces and power of the Holy Spirit. 'The Pentecostal idea' is pervading Christian thought and aspirations more than ever before." [29] The same issue includes a testimony to Mahan's continuing impact. The inside front cover announces a new edition of that "Great Pentecostal Gift," the *Baptism of the Holy Ghost*, "this truly magnificent work of Dr. Mahan on the Great Theme of the Period."

By the turn of the century, *everything* from camp meetings to choirs is described in the *Guide* as "pentecostal." Sermons are published under the heading "Pentecostal Pulpit"; women's reports under "Pentecostal Womanhood"; personal experiences are reported as "Pentecostal Testimonies"; and so on. Even devotional periods take place in the "pentecostal closet." What took place on the pages of the *Guide to Holiness* was typical of what happened in

most holiness traditions in the 1880s and 1890s. By 1900, the shift
from Christian perfection to Baptism of the Holy Spirit was nearly
universal.

The usual holiness interpretations of this shift, where it has even
been noticed, have minimized its significance. It has been seen as a
valid extension of Wesleyan doctrine and primarily a terminologi-
cal shift. But it is much more than that. It is a profound
transformation of theological ideas and associated concepts. The
significance of this theological shift can best be understood by
comparing the two books by Asa Mahan. His earlier *Scripture
Doctrine of Christian Perfection* stands very much in the classical
Wesleyan tradition (though differing in a few nuances) while his
Baptism of the Holy Ghost represents later developments and
includes most of the seed of what followed. Both books were
published under the auspices of the Methodistic holiness movement. The first was published by D. S. King, who soon thereafter
became the publisher and then an editor of the *Guide to Christian
Perfection*. The later book was published by the Palmers, after
Phoebe Palmer had become editor of the same journal, now
renamed the *Guide to Holiness*.

The shift in terminology involved, in the first place, a shift from
Christocentrism to an emphasis on the Holy Spirit. Mahan's
Christian Perfection, like Wesley's *Plain Account*, is basically
oriented to Christ for the work of sanctification; thus he says, "The
Spirit shows not himself, but Christ to our minds." [30] Mahan
likewise gave the Spirit no autonomy in guidance and advised
ignoring "undefined impressions" to "testify" or follow a particular
course of action. But in the *Baptism of the Holy Ghost*, the Spirit
becomes primary. Christ Himself was dependent upon the "indwelling, and influence, and baptism of the Holy Spirit, the same in
all essential particulars as in us." [31] This shift in emphasis
underlined an interesting shift in terminology. In the earlier book,
salvation history is divided into two covenants (law/grace) whose
line of demarcation is Christ, especially His atonement. But in the
later book, the division is into dispensations (the Spirit is "the

crowning glory and promise of the New Dispensation")[32] and Pentecost is the new fulcrum.

This shift involves, in the second place, a movement away from the goal and nature of Christian perfection to an emphasis on the event in which it is instantaneously achieved. Wesley was clearest in his statement of the ideal but vacillated somewhat as to whether this was to be achieved in crisis or in process. Mahan's basic definition of perfection was, "a full and perfect discharge of our entire duty, of all existing obligations in respect to God and all other beings. It is perfect obedience to the moral law." [33] In the second book, Mahan emphasizes the method by which this is to be achieved and explicates it in terms of the Baptism of the Holy Ghost. This necessarily involves an emphasis on the "eventness" of the experience, perhaps to the detriment of a concern for ethics, particularly social ethics. It may be that the ground was prepared for this new teaching by the impact of revivalism in reshaping Wesleyanism on the American scene. Particularly with Phoebe Palmer, there was an emphasis on "claiming the blessing *now*" without the struggle sometimes characteristic of early Methodism.[34]

In the third place, there is an almost complete shift in the exegetical foundations of the doctrine. In *Christian Perfection*, Mahan, like Wesley before him, hardly ever appeals to the Book of Acts. Use is made instead of passages that refer to cleansing and perfection (such as Ezek. 36:25; Mat. 5:48; II Cor. 7:1; I Thess. 5:23–24; John 17:20–23, etc.). In the *Baptism of the Holy Ghost*, most of the crucial texts are taken from the Book of Acts. Basic, of course, is the account of Pentecost, but also important is Acts 19, especially verse 2: "Have ye received the Holy Ghost since ye believed?" as well as other passages speaking of a reception of the Holy Spirit. Of particular interest is the appeal to Joel 2:28, "And it shall come to pass in the last days . . . I will pour out of my Spirit upon all flesh; and your sons and daughters shall prophesy" (Acts 2:17), Zechariah 13:1, "In that day there shall be a fountain opened to the house of David," and a few other Old Testament prophetic passages.

This exegetical shift involves an intensification of the sense of eschatology and the use of predictive prophecy. Wesley's relative lack of interest in eschatology is well-known. In Oberlin perfectionism this was somewhat altered by American millennialism, though it plays little part in Mahan's *Christian Perfection.* His later book, however, picks up the theme and assigns to Methodism a special place in the divine drama:

> The central article of her creed is the great central Truth of the Gospel. If she will be true to her calling, she will not only enable "the fountain to be opened" in her own midst, but also in other communions. When this takes place, "then is the millennium near, even at the door." [35]

In this quotation, we may also see the seed of an idea that gained importance. Mahan was troubled by the meaning of the expression "in that day" which occurs in a number of the prophecies that he utilized. In *Baptism of the Holy Ghost*, he devotes several pages to this problem and concludes that the "fountain" is to be opened in these *latter days*.[36] But we may see here the hermeneutical problem that resulted in the distinction between the earlier and latter rains of the Spirit's blessing which became so important in later holiness and pentecostal thought. In Mahan this is all, of course, still expressed in terms of the postmillennial framework of his thought, but we can see how these patterns of thought and interest would find much in common with the prophecy conferences which were to begin in America in 1878. And it was not until 1883, for example, that A. T. Pierson capitulated to premillennialism.[37]

This shift in exegetical foundations, finally, turns attention to a new set of ideas and associated contexts. A new emphasis falls on the empowering of the Holy Spirit. Following such passages as Acts 1:8 ("But ye shall receive power, after that the Holy Ghost is come upon you"), Mahan noted that at Pentecost "*power* was one of the most striking characteristics of this baptism." [38] Another emergent emphasis is on prophecy, usually interpreted as "testifying" or "speaking as the Spirit giveth utterance." Mahan finds this now "the common privilege of all believers." [39] It is also very significant that the gifts of the Spirit move into the center of attention. Mahan, like many holiness writers, attempted to emphasize not the gifts but the fruit of the Spirit, and not "the miraculous, but common influence of the Spirit." [40] This concern is, of course, somewhat weakened by the development in the second book. And one can quite easily trace in the latter third of the nineteenth century a rising interest in such things as "divine healing."

One may go on. I am convinced that one can find in late nineteenth century holiness thought and life every significant feature of pentecostalism. The major exception would be the gift of tongues, but even there the ground had been well prepared. Once attention had been focused on the Book of Acts, on Pentecost as an event in the life of each believer, and on the gifts of the Spirit, the question inevitably arose.

Mahan's later book also reveals a strong concern for "assurance." This, of course, has its antecedents in the Wesleyan doctrine of the witness of the Spirit, but appears intensified in the *Baptism of the Holy Ghost*. Mahan was convinced that the Baptism of the Spirit would have a conscious and perhaps even a physical effect. "Where the Holy Ghost is received, such a change is wrought in the subject that he himself will become distinctly conscious of the change . . . a change also observable to others around." [41] Hannah Whitall Smith's posthumously published papers on religious fanaticism also report, from 1871 or so on, several cases of people desperately seeking a "conscious" Baptism of the Holy Spirit that would even result in "physical thrills." [42] It is easy to see how the gift of tongues would fill this longing.

Indeed, in the last quarter of the nineteenth century, one can trace a number of incidents in which tongues did break out. Relying on the work of Stanley Frodsham *(With Signs Following)*, William Menzies mentions several such instances which "occurred principally in Holiness revival and camp meetings," particularly in southeastern United States.[43] I have come across other incidents that could be added to this list. One of them took place in 1881 at a holiness camp and reveals the sort of development that naturally took place.

> One day right in the midst of a great sermon, a woman from Carrol County, a holiness professor, sprawled out at full length in the aisle. This, in itself, was not much to be thought of, for to tumble over now and then was to be expected. But the unexpected happened in this case. It kept some of the sisters busy to keep her with a measurably decent appearance. Directly she began to compose a jargon of words in rhyme and sing them with a weird tune. She persisted till the service was spoiled and the camp was thrown into a hubbub. Strange to say, the camp was divided thereby. Some said it was a wonderful manifestation of divine power, some said it was a repetition of speaking in unknown tongues as at Pentecost. But every preacher on the ground without exception declared it to be of the devil. But the camp was so divided in opinion that it had to be handled with the greatest of care.[44]

We see in this passage how this sort of event could occur, how the interpretation naturally developed, and also an example of the antagonism that characterized the response of holiness people to the practice, particularly in the early part of the twentieth century.

With all of this in the background, the emergence of pentecostalism in the next century may be seen as a natural development of forces that had been set in motion much earlier. And when we turn to those events usually identified as the beginnings of the pentecostal movement, these connections are very apparent. It was a *holiness* evangelist, Charles Fox Parham, who after founding Bethel Bible School near Topeka, suggested that his students during his absence continue a study of Acts 2 to discover the "evidence" of the Baptism of the Holy Spirit. He returned to discover that the students had concluded that the evidence is speaking in tongues. And in 1906, it was W. J. Seymour, a Negro *holiness* evangelist and a student of Parham, who had come to Azusa to speak in a *Nazarene* Negro mission, but found himself locked out when he preached from Acts 2:4 his pentecostal doctrine. The Azusa Street revival that launched pentecostalism was then held in an abandoned Methodist church. It is, therefore, not surprising that pentecostalism swept through many holiness churches, particularly in the south; nor that for a decade most pentecostals claimed to be holiness in theology; nor that a large number of pentecostals today view themselves as standing in the Wesleyan tradition.

NOTES

1. Cf. his *The Holiness-Pentecostal Movement in the United States* (Grand Rapids, Mich.: Eerdmans, 1971), especially chaps. 1–4.
2. *Ibid.,* p. 8.
3. Walter J. Hollenweger, *The Pentecostals* (Minneapolis: Augsburg, 1972), p. 21.
4. "Pneumatological Nomenclature in Early Methodism," *Wesleyan Theological Journal* 8 (Spring 1973), 61–72.
5. Cf. The *Works* (1872 edition or the Grand Rapids, Mich.: Zondervan, 1959 reprint), 7:416.
6. Frederick Dale Bruner, *A Theology of the Holy Spirit* (Grand Rapids, Mich.: Eerdmans, 1970), pp. 40–42, 332–35, etc.
7. (Oberlin: James Steele, 1840).
8. This apparently formed the kernel of *The Enduement with Power* published as an appendix to the British edition of Mahan's *Baptism of the Holy Ghost.*
9. The literature on Mahan is growing. Important for our purposes are the older works by Paul Fleisch, *Zur Geschichte der Heiligungsbewegung. Erstes Heft: Die Heiligungsbewegung von Wesley bis Boardman* (Leipzig: Wallmann, 1910) and Benjamin B. Warfield in articles in the *Princeton Theological Review* (1921), later incorporated into vol. 2 of *Perfectionism* (New York: Oxford University Press, 1931) and the abridged reprint by Presbyterian and Reformed Publishing Co., 1958. Cf. also Barbara Zikmund, "Asa Mahan and Oberlin Perfectionism" (Ph.D. dissertation, Duke University, 1969) and my essay on Mahan in *Wesleyan Theological Journal* 9 (Spring 1974, 60–69), which amplifies some points of this essay.
10. *Autobiography, Intellectual, Moral and Spiritual* (London: Woolmer, 1882).
11. (London: Wesleyan Conference Office, 1877).
12. *Autobiography,* p. 321.
13. *Scripture Doctrine of Christian Perfection* (Boston: D. S. King, 1839).
14. *Baptism of the Holy Ghost* (New York: W. C. Palmer, Jr., 1870).
15. This correspondence (two letters from Mahan) is available among the Phoebe Palmer papers held by Drew University Library.
16. Cf. his *Holiness of Christians in the Present Life* (Oberlin: Steele, 1840), first serialized in the *Oberlin Evangelist.*

17. *Oberlin Evangelist* 2 (1840), 93.
18. *Oberlin Quarterly Review* 1 (August 1845), 115.
19. *The Gift of the Holy Spirit*, with an introduction by Finney (Oberlin: E. J. Goodrich, 1875).
20. Bruner, *op. cit.*, pp. 44–45, 340.
21. Cf. the preface to the second edition of his *The Twofold Life* (Chicago: Bible Colportage Association, n.d.). The preface is dated 1884.
22. (New York: Harper, 1856), p. 354. This work has always been regarded as a holiness classic and remains in print today (published by the Free Methodists).
23. Nelson R. Burr, *A Critical Bibliography of Religion in America*, Religion in America, vol. 4 (Princeton: Princeton University Press, 1961), p. 165.
24. Cf. the several works on this revival by J. Edwin Orr, and for the place of Phoebe Palmer, Melvin E. Dieter, "Revivalism and Holiness" (Ph.D. dissertation, Temple University, 1973).
25. These letters (from 1859 and following) were reprinted in *Four Years in the Old World* (New York: W. C. Palmer, Jr., 1870).
26. *Ibid.*, p. 96. The letter is dated Sept. 16, 1859.
27. Mahan, *Autobiography*, p. 414.
28. "Baptism of the Spirit," *Guide to Holiness* 20 (February 1874), 1.
29. "Pentecost—What Is It?" *Guide to Holiness* 66 (January 1897), 37.
30. *Christian Perfection*, pp. 158–59.
31. *Baptism of the Holy Ghost*, p. 21.
32. *Ibid.*, p. 50.
33. *Christian Perfection*, p. 7.
34. On this point, see Melvin Dieter, "Revivalism and Holiness," already cited above in note 24.
35. *Baptism of the Holy Ghost*, p. 150.
36. *Ibid.*, pp. 138–43.
37. *D. L. Moody at Home* (Chicago: Revell, 1886), p. 168.
38. *Baptism of the Holy Ghost*, p. 78.
39. *Ibid.*, p. 47.
40. *Christian Perfection*, p. 166. Cf. *Baptism of the Holy Ghost*, p. 113.
41. *Baptism of the Holy Ghost*, p. 39.
42. Ray Strachey, ed., *Religious Fanaticism: Extracts from the Papers of Hannah Whitall Smith* (London: Faber & Gwyer, 1928).
43. *Anointed to Serve: The Story of the Assemblies of God* (Springfield, Mo.: Gospel Publishing House, 1971), p. 31.
44. A. M. Kiergan, *Historical Sketches of the Revival of True Holiness and Local Church Polity from 1865–1916* (Fort Scott, Kans.: Board of Publication of the *Church Advocate and Good Way*, 1971), p. 31.

Wesleyan-Holiness Aspects of Pentecostal Origins: As Mediated through the Nineteenth-Century Holiness Revival

MELVIN E. DIETER

Melvin E. Dieter is an ordained minister in the Wesleyan church with headquarters in Marion, Indiana. He now serves his denomination as General Secretary of Educational Institutions. The Wesleyan church represents a merger between the Wesleyan Methodist church, which began as a holiness body before the Civil War, and the Pilgrim Holiness church, a product of the National Holiness Association movement. Dieter thus writes about this aspect of holiness history from a unique perspective.

This paper is based on research done at Temple University on the doctoral level in the field of American religious history. The title of Dieter's dissertation is "Revivalism and Holiness" (Temple University, 1973).

The following work offers keen insights into the holiness milieu at the turn of the century out of which the mainstream of American pentecostalism sprang.

IN 1885, William Jones, a holiness evangelist, attempted to locate the mission of the holiness movement within the prevailing *Zeitgeist.** In a tone reminiscent of Josiah Strong's oft-quoted analysis of the American nation and churches (*viz.*, that they were divinely commissioned to bring civil liberty and spiritual Christianity to the whole world) at that same period, Jones spoke to questions only infrequently raised by revivalists.[1] He discussed the churches' responsibilities to such diverse groups as the immigrants who were pouring onto the nation's shores like an "ever-increasing flood"; "the fetid Indians" that lingered "in squalor and filth" on the country's "Western borders"; and the millions of "illiterate and imbruted ex-slaves." The magnitude of these responsibilities, he observed, raised serious doubts about the power and the will of the churches to meet them.

However, woven into the often tawdry fabric of the age, Jones saw the clear pattern of a divine plan which promised a rapidly approaching "ultimate victory" over these obstacles. The expectancy of that victory filled the revivalist and many of his holiness colleagues with "inexpressible pleasure." To them, the divine destiny was manifest. Everywhere they looked, they saw God at work in new ways. Crowns and thrones, they said, were "falling like stars in an apocalyptic vision"; "conservatism" was being startled from its "death of sleep." Technology, moreover, had become the Lord's handmaiden. In the ever-deepening thrusts of the railroad builders into the heart of Africa, they heard "the footsteps of Jehovah." It was as if a "tremor of . . . invisible forces" were pervading all lands and thrilling and agitating all peoples.

Jones likened the whole to the manner in which engineers had destroyed the massive outcrop of rock which once restricted the

---

* Spirit of the age.

entrance to the New York harbor. In that instance, workers had painstakingly tunneled into the bedrock, quietly and carefully set their explosive charges, and then in one instant had "loosed the electric spark that converted the potential energy into actual energy." In a similar manner, Jones reckoned, God was now "tunneling into the world and packing it with His truth. . . ." When "the church" got "ready," and "the ministry" believed in "the Holy Ghost" and accepted "his fiery baptism," God would let slip "one spark of Pentecostal fire," and the whole earth would become His kingdom.[2]

It is probably within the context of this kind of late nineteenth century holiness rhetoric about "crumbling thrones," "dissolving empires," and the world-changing potential of "one spark of Pentecostal fire" that one must search for some of the main roots of the pentecostal movement of the twentieth century. In this brief study, we shall also consider the earlier theological roots in Wesleyan theology and experience and the later roots channeled through individuals and organizations who moved from the Wesleyan holiness movement to the pentecostal movement around the world; but central to the whole was the change in the evangelical mood created in large measure by the American holiness revival.

The attempt of the revival to restore primitive Christianity to the churches through a renewal of pentecostal experience and an accompanying "new age of the Holy Spirit" created a spiritual expectancy unequaled in prior Protestant history. By the turn of the century, some in the "left wing"[3] of the holiness movement began to define these pentecostal hopes for worldwide revival in doctrinal and experiential terms which became unacceptable to the mainstream of the older National Holiness Association movement; a separation resulted which formed the dynamic nucleus of the pentecostal revival.

In brief then, the American holiness movement of the nineteenth century mediated Wesleyan theology and experience through American revivalism to almost the whole of evangelicalism around the world. It won broad acceptance of a "second blessing" leading to spiritual power and fullness in the Holy Ghost. New concepts of Christian experience were generated; methodologies for the promotion of those concepts were developed; expectancies of a new age of pentecostal power were aroused; tensions were created in the holiness movement which seemed to some to demand better answers than were being given; and finally, in the nineteenth century holiness revival, the pentecostal movement found a large number of its founding leaders and organizations. Frederick Bruner has swept it all into one brief summary: "Out of the world-wide Holiness movements the Pentecostal movement was born." [4]

Wesley's Contribution—"The Second Blessing"

The indebtedness of the pentecostal movement to Wesley had been recognized in studies of pentecostal history from the very early work of the German scholar, Paul Fleisch, to that of recent scholars such as Fredrick Bruner, Walter Hollenweger, and Vinson Synan.[5] Only a few years after the effects of the Azusa Street revival had begun to spread around the world, Fleisch wrote that it was worthy of note that the holiness teaching of a clean heart as it was then being espoused by the tongues-speakers was a return "to the point of origin of the whole Holiness movement—Wesley's teaching on holiness." [6] Therefore, in the sense that Wesley's teachings on Christian perfection, experienced as a second blessing distinct from justification, represent the major introduction of this thought into Protestant Christianity, all modern holiness movements—the pentecostal movement among them—may be said to stem down from him.[7]

The enduring nature of the centrality of this relationship between Wesley's second-blessing experience and the holiness, Keswick, pentecostal, and charismatic movements is indicated in that this is the one common point at which they frequently have come under questions by both friendly and unfriendly critics from within the Reformed tradition.[8] Their conjunction of the life in the fullness of the Holy Spirit with a definite crisis experience of faith and grace subsequent to evangelical justification constitutes the one unacceptable aspect of their teaching.

The Modifying Influences
of the American Holiness Revival

The Development of the Revival

Wesley, himself, believed that the teaching and propagation of scriptural holiness had been made the peculiar responsibility of the people called Methodists. However, within less than one hundred years after Wesley's followers had first transplanted Methodism in America, responsibility for this grand depositum of spiritual truth did not appear to be widely acknowledged by its trustees. In the early decades of the nineteenth century, Methodism spoke of the doctrine in muted tones, and the witnesses of the experience were sparse. In the late 1830s, however, a new twin-pronged and yet coordinated holiness revival movement began to stir. The espousal of an essentially Wesleyan doctrine of Christian perfection, or a second conversion, by Charles G. Finney and Asa Mahan at Oberlin College paralleled and soon reinforced an awakening to the experience within Methodism in the home of Walter and Phoebe Palmer, prominent laymen of New York City.[9]

The subsequent wedding of the mainstream of American revivalism under its most able leader, Finney, with Methodist perfectionism as represented by the Palmers, was most significant for the future of both revivalism and perfectionism. The new methods of the revivalists were soon used to call Christians to an immediate response to God's provision of a life of present Christian holiness just as effectively as they had previously been used to call sinners to an instantaneous new birth at the penitent bench. The revival of the promotion of the Methodist doctrine and the upsurge of testimonies to the experience which ensued seemed to more than fulfill Wesley's own prophecy that the day would come when sanctifications would become as numerous as conversions.[10] On the other hand, the acceptance by many revivalistic Congregationalists, Presbyterians, Baptists, Episcopalians, and others of the need for a further work of grace in the life of the born-again Christian greatly expedited the Methodization of American revivalism. Methodism's evangelical Arminianism appeared to be essential to the general appeal of the revivalist, and the desire for a quality of Christian experience more stable than that which frequently accompanied continual revivalism culminated in a broad acceptance of the Methodist teaching of a second-blessing experience or some adaptation of it by the end of the century.[11] The Arminianization of revivalism has been rather widely acknowledged; but it has yet to be as fully recognized how widespread was the shift to an emphasis on a second blessing and the subsequent turn to a new interest in the work of the Holy Spirit and the significance of the meaning of Pentecost in the experience of the Church.

For almost thirty years after the revival of Christian perfection began, evangelists of the movement such as Finney, Mahan, Caughey, and the Palmers dominated American revivalism. Their work—particularly that of the Palmers—was especially important to the revival of 1857–58. That revival marked a significant point in American evangelicalism; by then, the Arminianizing of the American churches was almost complete, and the perfectionist leanings were strongly evident. The involvement of the holiness evangelists in the spread of this "layman's revival" to Europe in the beginnings of what J. Edwin Orr has called the "Second Evangelical Awakening" clearly indicates that trend.[12] Their ministry in the British Isles prepared the way for the burst of holiness evangelism a decade later under Robert Pearsall and Hannah Whitall Smith, lay evangelists of the National Association for the Promotion of Holiness. Out of Smith's whirlwind campaign, his essentially American Wesleyan teaching on the second blessing was introduced to many evangelicals who might have rejected the revivalism of the Methodists because of doctrinal or denominational prejudices. Those influences were preserved by the ongoing work of the Keswick Conventions for the Promotion of Holiness and the *Gemeinshaftsbewegung*—both of which deeply penetrated the fabric of the life of the established churches in England and Germany.[13]

The Character of the American Holiness Revival

The Palmer Influences. A brief review of the characteristics of Mrs. Palmer's promotion of holiness may give some indication of the changes which were taking place in the American holiness movement by the beginning of the Civil War period—changes which illustrate shifts in mood which possibly helped to prepare the way for the rise of the pentecostal movement forty years later.

It should be noted first of all that Mrs. Palmer's teaching on the doctrine of entire sanctification vis-à-vis that of Wesley greatly enhanced the distinctiveness of the second blessing from that of the initial experience of regeneration. Wesley generally regarded entire sanctification as a definite experience, but nevertheless a point in a process of growth and gradualism, and therefore, a maturity following considerable experience in the Christian life. Mrs. Palmer, however, tended to make the experience "the beginning of days" for the Christian.[14] The definiteness of her urgent revivalism called upon every believer to recognize the biblical promise of the fullness of the Spirit and to receive the experience by consecration and faith—now. The result was that the American holiness revival came to emphasize crisis stages of salvation at the expense of an emphasis on growth in grace. Dramatic and even revolutionary experience frequently became the hallmark of Christian life and witness. This distinctive eventually became a vital element of pentecostalism.[15]

The Witness Controversy. As a result of this strong emphasis upon the crisis experiences, the verification of the authenticity of the experiences became critical. They were the touchstones of one's standing before God; one had to have a firm witness to their reality. Moreover, Mrs. Palmer also insisted on the believer's regular public testimony to what God had done. One could neglect such testimony only to the detriment and eventual loss of his spiritual relationship. The place and meaning of "the witness" consequently created considerable controversy in the movement. Phoebe Palmer taught, in what has become known as her "altar theology" or "terminology," that the Bible revealed that Christ was the Christian's sanctifying altar; when a believer received that truth and by faith placed his wholly consecrated life upon that altar, the altar immediately sanctified the gift, cleansing the believer from inbred sin and filling him with perfect love.

. As a good Methodist, Mrs. Palmer believed that the Wesleys' "witness of the Spirit" would surely come to the believer at some point, but whether that was immediate or not, complete consecration and implicit faith in God's Word were the key to the genuineness of the finished work of entire sanctification. Many Methodists—both friends and foes of her special holiness promotion—challenged what they regarded as this "easy believism." The venerable Methodist Nathan Bangs, otherwise a firm supporter of the holiness movement, cautioned her against what he believed was a non-Wesleyan tack. Bangs warned that the blessing should not be claimed until at the same time the Holy Spirit testified that the work in the soul was complete. The subsequent history of the holiness movement shows that both positions continued to prevail.[16]

The persistence of the issue and its importance to an experience-centered movement undoubtedly agitated interest in alternate definitions of the nature of the witness. That these led some to emphasize a sensate evidence of the Spirit's presence followed from a consistent tendency to stress the importance of emotional and physical evidences throughout the history of the revival. Although the holiness camp meeting movement only rarely exhibited the emotional excesses which were common to the older frontier camp meetings, revivalistic Methodist enthusiasm or "getting blessed" was very much a part of holiness worship. The "holy" shout, dance, jump, or the trance "under the power of the Spirit" were so common that in many areas if one did not visibly "demonstrate," his spirituality might be called into question.

The importance which the movement attached to this is pointed up sharply in the experience of Hannah Whitall Smith, author of the holiness classic, *The Christian's Secret*.[17] In her autobiography, she tells of her anguish of soul over the lack of the same kind of dramatic emotional witness to her own sanctification experience which her husband, Robert Pearsall Smith, had had to his; he had gotten the blessing in good Methodist style. She finally had to conclude that the blessing apparently came to each according to his own nature.[18] But the problem apparently continued to plague her as she worked as an evangelist in the movement. In 1871, she says that she was introduced to a Dr. R. who revealed to her that when he had received the Baptism of the Spirit, physical thrills had gone through him from "head to feet." "No one," he told her, "could really know what the baptism of the spirit was who did not experience these thrills." He urged Hannah Whitall Smith to pray for this Baptism. His enthusiasm for the experience and her own "hunger and thirst for some tangible Baptism that would give . . . the enrapturing thrills of bliss others seemed to enjoy, and would," she said, "assure me that I had really received the Baptism of the Holy Spirit," led her to seek it; she never claimed to have found it.[19]

Such ambivalence on the witness questions, vocalized perhaps by only a small part of the total holiness movement, nevertheless indicates the kind of climate which persisted and continued to prevail in the movement worldwide when the pentecostal revival sprang up with its distinguishing witness of tongues. Other factors such as the inherited ultraistic tendencies of a perfectionist movement and the influence of the spiritual raptures in the experiences of the Quietists and other Catholic mystics who had been widely accepted as part of the true holiness movement probably contributed to this turn as well.[20] For some, the tensions between Mr. Wesley and Mrs. Palmer were erased in the new and fully evident witness of tongues. The acceptance or rejection of "the sign" quickly became the "watershed" which gave identity to the pentecostal movement as a whole and just as quickly set into two distinct camps those who claimed to be Wesleyans and yet stood on either side of that watershed.[21]

The Development of Pentecostal Semantics. The Palmer movement also prepared the stage for the rise of the pentecostal mind by helping to popularize new terminology for describing the revival and the experiences it promoted. At about the same time that William Arthur's influential holiness classic, *The Tongue of Fire*, emphasizing the Holy Spirit's pentecostal activity was first published just before the Civil War,[22] Phoebe Palmer began using similar Pentecost language in reporting the results of her and her husband's evangelism in Canada. Her 1857 reports are filled with language and expressions which heralded a major change in the semantics and maybe even the theology of the American holiness movement. An account of a talk on holiness which she gave at the Millbrook, Canada, Methodist camp meeting (she would never allow that she preached) clearly illustrates this shift. "We live," she said,

> under the dispensation of the spirit. If the ushering in of the dispensation of the spirit [at Pentecost] was so glorious, what ought we to expect now?—Surely not a *decrease* in power. [Italics hers.]

She continued the address by asking whether everyone might not now receive a Baptism of the Holy Ghost similar to that received by the believers at Pentecost. She urged upon the congregation that such a Baptism was every Christian believer's privilege and therefore his duty. "The question now before us is," she concluded, "May we ask in faith . . . that we may be endued with power from on high, baptized with the Holy Ghost and with fire?" Mrs. Palmer testified that the meeting closed with many receiving "the baptism of fire," and the rest "in expectation of receiving a Pentecostal Baptism." [23]

Similar language permeates her reports of her wartime ministry in the British Isles. Amazed at what she saw happening there, she concluded, "Surely now as in the early days of the Spirit's dispensation, Pentecostal blessings bring Pentecostal power." Again, she reports that a young local preacher who received "the tongue of fire," testified "as the Spirit gave utterance." [24] In the county of Antrim in Ireland she encountered instances of trances, visions, sleeps, dreams, and miracles, "such as that persons who never knew a letter of the alphabet when awake could read the Bible distinctly [and] sing Psalms and hymns . . . with eloquence and fluency." [25] In Scotland, a minister observed that the people who were being filled with the Spirit in the Palmers' meetings reminded him of the apostles at pentecost. "Clapping his hand, [the minister] . . . leaped and shouted for joy," crying that they were surely "being blessed with the return of Pentecostal power." [26]

The emphasis on the Baptism of the Spirit and the use of pentecostal references also arose early in the Oberlin movement.[27] The emphasis steadily intensified throughout the development of the revival following the Civil War. It was also evident in the large camp meetings of that period of the National Association for the Promotion of Holiness. Adam Wallace, editor of the accounts of the National Committee's sixteenth camp at Landisville, Pennsylvania, was inclined at first to title the work "Pentecost Repeated"; finally, however, he titled it, *A Modern Pentecost*.[28] At the second National Camp Meeting in 1868 at Manheim, Pennsylvania, in a prayer meeting at which two thousand were in attendance, "all at once, as sudden as if a flash of lightning had fallen upon the people, one . . . burst of agony and then of glory was heard in all parts of the congregation. . . ." The article continued that many of the people present "declared that the sensation was as if a strong wind had moved from the stand over the congregation." [29] In the third National Camp Meeting at Round Lake, New York, following "a most powerful sermon" by Bishop Peck of the Methodist Episcopal Church, one of the ministers stood and declared that the meeting had "rolled the world a hundred years towards the millennium.

. . . It was," he said, "the outflow of God's great Amazon" which would eventually flow around the globe.[30]

These common experiences of the developing holiness revival are merely illustrative of a steadily growing emphasis. They tend to prove that whether surrounded by the optimism of the postmillennialism which commonly dominated the movement's eschatology during most of this period or whether deeply involved in the premillennialism which ruled it later, the place of Pentecost in the preaching, thinking, and experience of the movement took on a prominence never before seen in Protestantism. It resulted in a strong belief that the coming of a new age of the Spirit would restore primitive Christianity to the churches; they, in turn, would recover the purity and the power to overcome the forces of formalism, wordliness, materialism, higher criticism, and all the other "isms" which increasingly seemed to threaten everything that the first Pentecost had promised.[31] Delegates to the Evangelical Alliance Meeting in New York in 1873 heard that as long as "Pentecostal effusions" continued to manifest themselves, "primitive Christianity survives in one of its chief characteristics and will . . . vindicate its reality and potency. . . ."[32]

By the turn of the century—one of those points in time at which men become especially conscious both of what has been and what may yet be—Pentecost as past proof of God's power, Pentecost as the present pattern for the renewal of the churches, and Pentecost as the portent of fulfillment of all things in the restoration of God's kingdom among men became the pervading atmosphere of the holiness movement.[33] It all blended very well with what Russell Nye has called the "American Sense of Mission" and expressed that mission in religious terms: a nation rebaptized with pentecostal power would serve as an example to the rest of the world of God's plan for all nations.[34]

The Significance of the Healing Movement.   In addition to this sense of the renewed activity of the Holy Spirit in deepening the

personal experience of Christian believers, many holiness adherents
saw the increased incidence of miraculous physical healing as
another demonstration of the new dispensation of the Spirit. The
belief in and the witness to miraculous divine healings attended the
holiness movement at every turn. The healing testimony of John
Inskip, president of the National Camp Meeting Association, was
widely publicized in National Association circles. Inskip had
suffered from a variety of ailments as a result of a slight sunstroke.
Dr. Charles Cullis, founder of a Boston home for consumptives and
an Episcopalian lay evangelist of the holiness movement, had
prayed for Inskip's healing.[35] Cullis' pioneer healing emphasis was
furthered by evangelists such as W. E. Boardman, author of *The
Higher Christian Life*, who ended his days in a healing ministry in
England and Europe following the great holiness crusades there in
1874–75.[36] Later in the century, Jennie Smith, known as the
"railroad evangelist" because of her work among railroad men,
spread the story of her claims to miraculous healing (she had been
an invalid for decades) all across the country in personal witnessing
and in the effective public forums which the numerous and
vigorous holiness camp meetings afforded.[37] The involvement of
other holiness leaders such as A. B. Simpson of the Christian and
Missionary Alliance is well-known.

Within the holiness movement, the developing "healing question" was thoroughly debated and the teaching propagated in spite
of the fact that the National Association eventually proscribed
preaching in their meetings on that and the other so-called side
issues which the national leaders believed to be detrimental to a
singular promotion of Christian holiness.[38] Both sides of the
controversy as to whether or not healing is in the atonement were
espoused in the movement. The more moderate place given to
divine healing in the economy of redemption by most holiness
churches today is best illustrated in the writings of R. Kelso Carter,
professor at Pennsylvania Military College and author of the
well-known Gospel song "Standing on the Promises." In a book
published in 1877, he first supported the "healing in the atone-

ment" concept later espoused by most pentecostal groups and then retracted that position in a work written twenty years later.[39]

The Four-Fold Gospel. The emphasis on healing continued to be a prominent factor in the formative period of the holiness churches organized around the turn of the century. The Pentecostal Church of the Nazarene, as it was originally known, and the Pilgrim Holiness church, the two churches in which the largest groups of converts gathered together out of the holiness camp meeting movement, were typical of the holiness groups who commonly emphasized healing in their statements of faith.[40] With the exception of the Church of the Nazarene, these same groups commonly included an article avowing their commitment to a premillennial position of the Second Coming as well.[41] This "fourfold Gospel" of "salvation, sanctification, healing, and the second-coming," set a pattern of doctrine and a definition of mission which finally became almost universally accepted in the holiness churches—in practice, even by the Church of the Nazarene.

Sanctification and Power. The logic inherent in this renewed emphasis on the restoration of primitive faith and holiness through the revival of the pentecostal experience was outlined by Arthur T. Pierson, a Presbyterian who was strongly influenced by the Keswick holiness movement. At the turn of the century, in discussing the rise of the healing movement, Pierson reasoned,

> If, therefore, supernatural signs have disappeared in consequence of the loss of primitive faith and holiness, a revival of these may bring some new manifestations of the former. . . . If in these degenerate days a new Pentecost would restore primitive faith, worship, unity, and activity, new displays of divine power might surpass those of any previous period.[42]

In the holiness movement, the gap which frequently prevailed between such high spiritual expectations and subsequent spiritual results created questions of the relationship of the sanctifying experience to the power imparted by the sanctifying Spirit. At all periods in the history of the movement, an undertone of tension at this point consistently paralleled the reports of the advances the movement seemed to be making. A few scattered examples from history may outline the pattern of the development of the "power" controversy which ultimately contributed to the rise of the "third blessing" movement and subsequently the pentecostal movement.

In 1873, at the beginning of the Landisville, Pennsylvania, National Camp Meeting, John Inskip, president of the National Association for the Promotion of Holiness, said, "I, as President of this Association, want to be endowed with power from on high, so that I may direct the services aright. I want the deepest baptism of my life." [43] Such statements expressed a dichotomy which the movement fully recognized as thoroughly consistent with a distinct second-blessing experience. They interpreted it according to the recorded prayers of the disciples for special endowments of power subsequent to their own pentecostal experience.[44] That dichotomy did establish the fact, however, that there were some aspects of power for service which were not automatically inherent in the power which accompanied the movement's teaching on the initial Baptism with the Holy Ghost in entire sanctification.[45]

In 1884, J. P. Brooks, a leader of the more radical midwestern holiness movements, expressed the opinion that what the badly divided holiness adherents of his area really needed, was to seek "the baptism of the Holy Ghost." [46] S. B. Shaw, one of the movement's early editors, noted in the same year that "of late it is common to find professors of heart purity bemoaning the lack of fullness." Shaw would not allow that such a condition represented the true experience of the revival. "That anyone should think that we may be entirely sanctified . . . and not possess the fullness of the *Spirit of Grace* is certainly very strange indeed," he observed [italics his].[47] In 1902, C. W. Ruth, an early leader in the Holiness Christian church, the International Apostolic Holiness Union, and finally in the Church of the Nazarene, also defended the traditional stance of the Methodist center of the holiness revival that "the Holy Ghost himself is the power; . . . hence to get sanctified wholly is to get the Pentecostal promise. The negative and the positive side of sanctification occur simultaneously." [48]

But the inherent tension between challenge and achievement persisted. In 1907, a year after the Azusa revival began, an article in the *Nazarene Messenger* decried the shallowness of experience which had crept into the movement and called upon the movement to "tarry for the power," no matter what the past profession may have been. The author continued: "We are not third-blessingites; we have learned better things; but what we want and what our hearts need is a genuine second blessing. We need it to save us from fanaticism that is no doubt a result of superficial work. . . ." [49]

As the above tend to indicate, any lack of spiritual power within the movement was generally attributed to the failure of individuals to enter into the fullness of the sanctification experience, to the failure to take advantage of the means of grace which could keep the soul spiritually strong and alert, or to actual apostasy from sanctifying grace. Apparently, however, some in the movement looked to an alternative answer to the question; their thinking tended to center around the belief that what was lacking was a third experience in grace which would bring the desired Baptism of power. This tendency accelerated with the increasing expectancy of the return of pentecostal power as the revival progressed and with the introduction of the "Baptism" language which we have already noted in the Palmer ministry. It was crystallized across the whole movement by the publication of Asa Mahan's *The Baptism of the Holy Ghost* in 1870. [50]

Within this milieu, an 1869 article on the subject by Dr. Asbury Lowrey is instructive. Lowrey, a stalwart in the Methodist holiness movement and co-editor with Asa Mahan of *Divine Life*, raised the question, "Is the Baptism of the Holy Ghost a Third Blessing?" Lowrey's answer was both yes and no, but definitely tended to separate the cleansing and empowering work of the Holy Ghost in the believer's life. He wrote,

> But if the question be asked, "May we have a dispensation of the Holy Ghost after sanctification and supplementary to that grace, a dispen-

sation greater and more powerful than necessarily belongs to the state of a pure heart?" I unhesitatingly answer, *Yes*. The Gospel evidently promises such accessions. [Italics his.]

Without this "post-sanctification dispensation," he continued, a Christian's "capacities . . . cannot be developed at all. . . ." But with it, "even the weakest believer may do greater works than those wrought by the ministry of Christ, Himself." [51] Distinctions such as this tended to bifurcate what the main movement held were two aspects of a single work of grace and are remarkably similar to those eventually raised by the third-blessing movement.

Such an ambience enveloped those in the movement who began to promote third-blessing teaching toward the end of the nineteenth century. In spite of strong opposition, the teaching quickly caught hold in some areas. Vinson Synan and other historians of the pentecostal movement describe the ministry of Benjamin Hardin Irwin, the establishment of this third-blessing movement, and its consequences for the study of pentecostal origins.[52] Ralph C. Horner, a minister of the Methodist church in Canada, also pursued a third-blessing theology. Horner, the founder of what eventually became the Standard Church of Canada, began to preach in the late 1880s that the Baptism of the Spirit was distinct from His work in sanctification. In 1891, he published his beliefs in his book, *From the Altar to the Upper Room*.[53] He maintained that modern holiness teachers had "muddled Wesley." The latter, he claimed, "had taught holiness by commands, prayers, and promises in the Word. . . . He selected commands from the Old and New Testaments, but didn't use any that were given by the Lord Jesus to the Apostles regarding Pentecost." Horner observed that had Wesley not been convinced that the apostles had already been sanctified and that the Acts passages referred to a "baptism for service," he would most certainly have used those passages, for they would have been his strongest texts. Horner concluded that the experience of the holiness movement of his time was the practical proof that sanctification did not bring spiritual power.[54]

For some it was but a short step from such third-blessing

teaching—especially when cast in the dynamic rhetoric of the Irwin movement—to the pentecostal movement. The scattered remnants of Irwin's Fire-Baptized church eventually took that step. Horner's group did not. They remained on the fringes of the holiness movement whose main leaders and organizations rejected the third-blessing experience as a dangerous aberration at best, and at worst, as heresy and fanaticism.[55] Nevertheless, the developing history of the holiness and pentecostal movements increasingly indicates that the rise of this teaching within the more radical elements of the National Holiness Association movement, encouraged by a renewed awareness of John Fletcher's use of "Spirit baptism" terminology, and the effective dissemination of the Keswick holiness movement's "baptism for service" teachings by R. A. Torrey, all worked together to create the potentiality for the immediate, worldwide response aroused by the Azusa Street meetings in 1906.[56]

Men and Methods—the Final Contribution

The rejection of the Irwin movement by the National Holiness Association and its satellite groups at the turn of the century was an omen of the future; it portended a similar reaction by the center-core holiness leaders to the tongues movement almost from the first stirrings of the Azusa Street revival. There were some early efforts to make caution the key word in judging the new phenomena associated with that Los Angeles center. The radii of the revival which quickly spread across the country and around the world were supported, though briefly, by some of the existing institutions of the continuing holiness revival which had similarly circled the world thirty years previously.[57] However, when Phineas Bresee, founder of the Church of the Nazarene, finally published his first editorial reaction to the revival in his hometown, it exhibited a pattern of reaction and judgment which has characterized the viewpoint of the holiness movement in general since that time. Bresee said that, at first, he had quietly ignored the nearby meetings at Azusa Street where "there began something which was called 'the gift of tongues.' " He judged that all men knew that,

> so far as it was good it was necessarily the same as is being carried on with much success in this city of getting believers sanctified and sinners converted, and so far as it partakes of fanaticism and was fostered by heretical teachings, we did not care to give it the prominence of public discussion.

The Nazarene leader admonished his readers to cautiously and carefully examine anything which varied from the standard teaching of the movement on sanctification and the Baptism of the Holy Ghost. He believed that these people who were seeking "after the hope of exceptional or marvelous things" were "more or less" those whose experience was "unsatisfactory, who have never been sanctified wholly, or have lost the precious work out of their hearts." He said, "People who have . . . Christ revealed in the heart by the Holy Spirit, do not hanker after strange fire. . . . There is rest only in the old paths where the Holy Spirit Himself imparts to the soul directly the witness of the cleansing and the indwelling," he concluded.[58]

But apparently there were significant numbers of people in the holiness movement of Bresee's day who were either dissatisfied or lax, or even apostate in their experiences. Frank Bartleman, a holiness evangelist who had preached his way across the country to Los Angeles in a number of holiness centers, may serve as a typical example of these; he was at least among the dissatisfied. His reactions to Azusa Street were quite the opposite of Bresee's. Stirred by the revival in Wales in 1904, he feared that the awakening might pass the holiness people by. The holiness people, he judged, were "loaded down to the water's edge with a spirit of prejudice and pharisaism." "They were too proud of their standing," he said, and warned that God might "humble them by working in other places." [59]

In 1906, Bartleman quickly became part of the Azusa Street meetings and the new movement; he wrote articles for holiness papers such as the *Way of Faith* and *God's Revivalist*, seeking, he said, to bring the holiness people into the stream of what he believed was the rising tide of the revival they had always sought.[60] Of his eventual separation from the holiness movement, he said that it became necessary because the holiness leaders were old-timers, many of whom had worked faithfully in their time and day, but now would not join the new revival to which he had committed himself. Finally failing in his attempts to win them over, he testified that the Lord told him to leave the holiness people with God. Bartleman, himself, was now to move on with a "new order of Priests." [61]

Thus the holiness revival forces were divided. It was mainly in the south that there were significant shifts of groups of holiness churches to the new movement.[62] However, other holiness bodies were also affected. In April 1909, H. F. Reynolds, General Superintendent of the Pentecostal Church of the Nazarene for the Eastern Division, reported to the *Pentecostal Advocate* that he had not visited Durant, Florida, at that time as he had anticipated, because in Florida, the "so-called Tongue Movement" had swept all the Nazarene churches into its fold except one.[63] Wesleyan Methodist records show that their southern districts were often affected.[64] According to Conn, all the members of the Southern Florida Holiness Association except three became members of the Church of God and the N.H.A. camp meeting at Durant became a pentecostal center.[65]

Much more significant to the actual continuity between the two movements than the organizational crossovers, however, were the numerous individuals—some heralded in the older movement, especially among southern holiness leadership, but most unheralded—who promptly took places of leadership in the pentecostal revival. It was the Kings, the Tomlinsons, the Seymours, the Bartlemans, the Barratts, the Pauls, the Parhams, the Masons, the Ebys—all out of the holiness movement—who set the Wesleyan patterns that dominated the pentecostal revival's formative years and which are still normative for more than half of the movement's

76   MELVIN E. DIETER

members today. These rapidly passed on the theology, the methodology, and the mores of the older movement to the newer. They
adopted for the newer movement from the older, the Gospel songs;
the evangelistic methods; the use of the camp meeting as a center
of celebration, communication, and catechism; the Pietistic concern for personal purity and a separated life; and the concepts of
"faith works," of healing and of premillennialism.

Rooted in these commitments, the two movements have continued to be at the forefront of the growing edge of evangelical
Christianity around the world. Together they form a significant
part of the National Association of Evangelicals. It may do no
violence to the facts nor to human nature to suggest that the
differences, the conflicts, the sometimes bitter recriminations which
have been part of the past relationships of the holiness and
pentecostal movements could be the strongest proof of the
commonality of their origins. It is in one's family that one often has
the most difficulty in establishing his identiy and his role; it is
especially difficult when one is born a twin—even if only fraternal
and not identical.

NOTES

1. William Jones, *From Elim to Carmel* (Boston: Christian Witness Co.,
   1885); Josiah Strong, *The New Era: or the Coming Kingdom* (New
   York: Baker and Taylor, 1893).
2. Jones, *op. cit.*, pp. 78–81.
3. John A. Hardon, *The Protestant Churches of America* (Westminster,
   Md.: Newman Press, 1957), p. 305; John Thomas Nichol, *Pentecostal-
   ism* (New York: Harper and Row, 1966), p. 6.
4. Frederick Dale Bruner, *A Theology of the Holy Spirit: The Pentecostal
   Experience and the New Testament Witness* (Grand Rapids, Mich.:
   Eerdmans, 1970), p. 44. Vinson Synan makes this the "overriding
   thesis" of his *The Holiness-Pentecostal Movement in the United States*
   (Grand Rapids, Mich.: Eerdmans, 1971); see *ibid.*, p. 8. Winthrop
   Hudson, *Religion in America* (New York: Scribner, 1965), p. 345;
   Willard Sperry, *Religion in America* (Cambridge: University Press,
   1946), p. 76; Nils Bloch-Hoell, *The Pentecostal Movement: Its Origin,*

Development, and Distinctive Character (New York: Humanities Press, 1964), pp. 16, 17; *Church of God Minutes, 1962* (Cleveland, Tenn.: Church of God Publishing House, 1962), p. 182; Elmer T. Clark, *The Small Sects in America* (New York: Abingdon, 1949), p. 148; Charles W. Conn, *Like a Mighty Army Moves the Church of God, 1886–1955* (Cleveland, Tenn.: Church of God Publishing House, 1955), p. xix; Klaude Kendrick, *The Promise Fulfilled: a History of the Modern Pentecostal Movement* (Springfield, Mo.: Gospel Publishing House, 1961), pp. 25–36; Nichol, *op. cit.*, pp. 5–7.

5. Paul Fleisch, *Zur Geschichte der Heiligungsbewegung* (Leipzig: Wallmann, 1910), pp. 9–46; Bruner, *op. cit.*, pp. 37–39; W. J. Hollenweger, *The Pentecostals: The Charismatic Movement in the Churches* (Minneapolis: Augsburg, 1972), p. 21; Synan, *op. cit.*, pp. 13–19.

6. Fleisch, *op. cit.*, p. 8.

7. W. E. Sangster, *The Path to Perfection* (London: Epworth Press, 1943), p. 7.

8. "Justification by Faith and the Baptism of the Spirit," *Present Truth*, Special Issue (1972), 9–15; Russell Hitt, "Tongues: Updating Some Old Issues," *Eternity* 24 (March 1973), 8. Also see James W. L. Hill, "The New Charismatics 1973," in *ibid.*, p. 33.

9. General accounts are in Timothy L. Smith, *Called unto Holiness: The Story of the Nazarenes, the Formative Years* (Kansas City, Mo.: Nazarene Publishing House, 1962), pp. 11–26; Synan, *op. cit.*, pp. 25–54. Timothy L. Smith, *Revivalism and Social Reform in Mid-Nineteenth-Century America* (Nashville, Tenn.: Abingdon, 1957), pp. 45–147, gives a more detailed account.

10. *Guide to Christian Perfection*, 1 (July 1839), 13.

11. See Glen C. Atkins, *Religion in Our Times* (New York: Round Table Press, 1932), p. 19; Melvin E. Dieter, "Revivalism and Holiness" (Ph.D. Thesis, Temple University, 1973), pp. 20–23, 210–12.

12. Walter and Phoebe Palmer, *Four Years in the Old World: Comprising the Travels, Incidents, and Evangelistic Labors of Dr. and Mrs. Palmer in England, Ireland, and Wales* (New York: W. C. Palmer, Jr., 1870); James Orr, *The Second Evangelical Awakening in Britain* (London: Marshall, Morgan and Scott, 1949).

13. For a thorough though negative account, see Benjamin B. Warfield, *Perfectionism* (Philadelphia: Presbyterian and Reformed Publishing Co., 1971), pp. 312–464.

14. Charles E. Jones, "Perfectionist Persuasion: a Social Profile of the National Holiness Movement within American Methodism, 1867–1936" (Ph.D. Thesis, University of Wisconsin, 1968), pp. 22–25; John L. Peters, *Christian Perfection and American Methodism* (New York: Abingdon, 1956), pp. 112–13.

15. Bruner, *op. cit.*, p. 20.

16. R. Wheatley, *The Life and Letters of Mrs. Phoebe Palmer* (New York:

78   MELVIN E. DIETER

W. C. Palmer, Jr., 1876), pp. 15–26; Smith, *Revivalism and Social Reform*, pp. 124–29; Dieter, *op. cit.*, pp. 30–37.

17. *The Christian's Secret of a Happy Life* (Westwood, N.J.: Revell, [1870], 1968).

18. Hannah Whitall Smith, *The Unselfishness of God, and How I Discovered It: A Spiritual Autobiography* (New York: Revell, 1903), p. 243.

19. Ray Strachey and Rachel Cossteloe, eds., *Religious Fanaticism: Extracts from the Papers of Hannah Whitall Smith* (London: Faber and Gwyer, 1928), pp. 166–71.

20. Fleisch, *op. cit.*, p. 100.

21. Hollenweger, *op. cit.*, p. 209.

22. William Arthur, *The Tongue of Fire: or the True Power of Christianity* (New York: Harper, 1856).

23. *Beauty of Holiness*, 8 (June 1857), 164–65.

24. Palmer, *Four Years*, p. 96.

25. *Ibid.*, p. 76.

26. *Ibid.*, p. 232.

27. See the *Oberlin Evangelist*, 2 (1840), 93.

28. Adam Wallace, ed., *A Modern Pentecost: Embracing a Record of the Sixteenth National Camp Meeting* . . . (Philadelphia: Methodist Home Journal Publishing House, 1873).

29. William McDonald and John E. Searles, *The Life of Rev. John S. Inskip, President of the National Association for the Promotion of Holiness* (Chicago: Christian Witness Co., 1885), p. 201.

30. *Ibid.*, pp. 203–204.

31. See Dieter, *op. cit.*, pp. 102–104.

32. Philip Schaff and S. Iranaeus Prime, eds., *History, Essays, Orations and Other Documents of the Sixth General Conference of the Evangelical Alliance* . . . (New York: Harper, 1874), p. 351.

33. This "Pentecost line," as it was called in the movement, is best illustrated by the publishing efforts of Martin Wells Knapp, editor of God's Revivalist publications; e.g., Seth Cook Rees, *The Ideal Pentecostal Church* (Cincinnati: God's Revivalist Office, 1897), and Knapp's series of paperbacks called the *Pentecostal Holiness Library*.

34. Russell E. Nye, *This Almost Chosen People: Essays in the History of American Ideas* (n.p.: Michigan State University Press, 1966), pp. 164–207.

35. McDonald and Searles, *op. cit.*, pp. 279–80.

36. Mrs. William E. Boardman, *The Life and Labors of W. E. Boardman* . . . (New York: D. Appleton and Co., 1887), pp. 136–37, 156–60.

37. Jennie Smith, *From Baca To Beulah* (Philadelphia: Garrigues Brothers, 1880).

38. Jones, *Perfectionist Persuasion*, p. 175.

39. Russell Kelso Carter, *The Atonement for Sin and Sickness: or a Full*

Salvation for Soul and Body (Boston: Willard Tract Repository, 1884); idem, *Faith Healing Reviewed after Twenty Years* (Boston: Christian Witness Co., 1897).

40. *Manual of the Church of the Nazarene, 1940* (Kansas City, Mo.: Nazarene Publishing House), p. 31. *Manual of the Pilgrim Holiness Church, 1930* (Indianapolis, Indiana: The Pilgrim Holiness Advocate), p. 20.
41. Cf. above: Pilgrim *Manual*, p. 20, and Nazarene *Manual*, p. 30.
42. Arthur T. Pierson, *Forward Movements of the Last Half Century* (New York: Funk and Wagnalls Co., 1905), p. 401.
43. Wallace, *op. cit.,* p. 75.
44. For example, Acts 4:29–31.
45. See, "Getting the Power," *Nazarene Messenger*, 10 (June 7, 1906), 12.
46. *Good Way*, 6 (April 26, 1884), 2.
47. *Michigan Holiness Record*, 3 (May 1884), 10.
48. *Nazarene Messenger*, 7 (October 2, 1902), 5.
49. *Ibid.,* 12 (October 17, 1907), 2.
50. (New York: W. C. Palmer, Jr., 1870).
51. *Divine Life*, 3 (August 1879), pp. 46–47.
52. Synan, *op. cit.,* pp. 61–64; Kendrick, *op. cit.,* p. 33; Joseph E. Campbell, *The Pentecostal Holiness Church, 1898–1948* (Franklin Springs, Ga.: Publishing House of the Pentecostal Holiness Church, 1951), pp. 191ff.
53. Ralph C. Horner, *From the Altar to the Upper Room* (Toronto: Wm. Briggs, 1891).
54. *Ibid.,* pp. 136–39.
55. See "Minutes of the Fifteenth Session of the Wesleyan Methodist Connection and Church . . . 1899" (Original "Minute Book" in the Wesleyan Church Archives), pp. 146–47; *Weleyan Methodist*, 54 (November 29, 1897), 4: *Nazarene Messenger*, 3 (August 24, 1899), 2.
56. Bruner, *op. cit.,* pp. 44–46.
57. *Pentecostal Herald*, 18 (October 3, 1906), 7; *The Way of Faith*, 25 (July 9, 1914), 6–7. Bloch-Hoell, *op. cit.,* p. 49.
58. "Editorial—The Gift of Tongues," *Nazarene Messenger*, 11 (December 13, 1906), 6.
59. Frank Bartleman, *How Pentecost Came to Los Angeles* (Los Angeles: Frank Bartleman, 1925), p. 21.
60. As late as 1914, letters from Bartleman were still appearing in the *Way of Faith* edited by John Paul with such holiness stalwarts as J. M. Pike (founder and former editor of the paper), J. L. Brasher, and Roy T. Williams as corresponding editors; see 25 (July 9, 1914), 6, 7.
61. *Latter Rain Evangel*, 2 (July 1910), 5.
62. Synan, *op. cit.,* pp. 127–39.
63. *Pentecostal Advocate*, 12 (April 8, 1909), 10.

64. "Minutes of the Seventeenth General Conference of the Wesleyan Methodist Connection and Church . . . 1907" (Original "Minute Book" in the Wesleyan Church Archives), p. 372; *Weleyan Methodist*, 70 (August 12, 1908), 12.

65. Conn, *op. cit.*, pp. 96–97.

The Non-Wesleyan Origins
of the Pentecostal Movement

WILLIAM W. MENZIES

*William W. Menzies serves as Chairman of the Depart-
ment of Biblical Studies at Evangel College in Springfield,
Missouri. He is an ordained minister in the Assemblies of
God church and is widely known as his church's leading
historian. His recently published book,* Anointed to
Serve—The Story of the Assemblies of God, *may be
regarded as the definitive history of the church. He is
author of two other books, entitled,* Understanding the
Times of Christ *and* Understanding Our Doctrine.

*One of the founders of the Society for Pentecostal
Studies, Menzies served as the first president when the
group began in 1970. He did his graduate work at
Wheaton College and the University of Iowa, where he
received his Ph.D. in religion in 1968 under the direction of
Sidney E. Mead.*

*The following paper points out the extremely important
contributions to the development of pentecostalism from
such non-Wesleyan sources as fundamentalism, the Keswick movement, and the "Finished Work" movement.*

THERE is no question that the seedbed of the modern pentecostal movement was the holiness revival of the late nineteenth century. However, not all aspects of the quest for holiness in that period can be identified as Wesleyan. Certainly some of the non-Wesleyan elements of the holiness movement had a profound impact on the shaping of twentieth-century pentecostalism, not only in the United States, but elsewhere in the world as well. Further, there is some evidence of influence from early fundamentalism in the forming of the pentecostal tradition.

To furnish boundaries for our discussion, some definitions and limitations must be established. First, the author understands "Wesleyanism" to be a term distinguishing a doctrine of a second definite work of grace, a crisis experience subsequent to regeneration, in which the sin-principle is eradicated from the believer. The believer is said to enter upon a state of sanctification. Those in the Wesleyan tradition who have also allied themselves to the pentecostal movement speak of three distinct crisis experiences, adding to the Wesleyan teaching a third experience, called the Baptism in the Holy Spirit, evidenced by speaking in other tongues.

Second, the author has taken some liberties with the term "origins." It was not until 1916 that the permanent shape of the traditional pentecostal movement emerged. It was in that year that the Assemblies of God drafted a statement of faith which set it apart, not only from the holiness-pentecostal bodies, but also from the oneness segment of American pentecostalism. The basic configuration of traditional American pentecostalism has remained fairly constant since that time. Thus, the author wishes to include a fifteen-year span under the mantle of the term "pentecostal origins."

By way of limitation, only the American scene is presented here.

Non-Wesleyan Influences
In the Pentecostal Revival from 1901 to 1910

Fundamentalism

The religious forces sweeping into the American church in the late nineteenth century produced consternation among many orthodox believers. Two parallel, sometimes overlapping, movements, fundamentalism and the holiness revival, developed in opposition to what was felt to be an alarming trend in the larger church world. Fundamentalism was the result of a coalition of the "Princeton theology" with dispensational premillennialism. The chief contributions of the Princeton theology lay in the attempt to support the credibility of Christianity by appeal to external evidences and the "citadel view" of biblical inspiration, in which inerrancy was assigned only to the original documents written in the hand of the authors or their amanuenses. (None of these documents exist today, all having presumably been destroyed through excessive use.) Dispensational premillennialism had its origins in the British sect, the Plymouth Brethren, founded about 1830 by J. Nelson Darby. Darby visited the United States on various occasions between 1866 and 1877, evidently with tremendous influence on key American churchmen. His influence is evident in the Bible conference movement which began in 1876. A series of interdenominational conferences, combining a zeal for promoting serious Bible study with a kindred zeal for prophetic themes, culminated in the Niagara Bible Conference, which in 1895 issued the famous five points of fundamentalism.[1] In the years immediately following, fundamentalism became increasingly identified with dispensationalism, chiefly under the direction of A. C. Gaebelein and C. I. Scofield. Those who held to historic premillennialism gradually lost influence, particularly after the Scofield Reference Bible was published in 1909.

In the Assemblies of God alone, more than 200 titles by dispensationalist-fundamentalist writers appear in the catalogs of the Gospel Publishing House during the height of the fundamental-ist-modernist controversy.[2] Further, it is significant that the escha-tology of the Assemblies of God is derived directly from the categories of C. I. Scofield. Frank M. Boyd and Ralph M. Riggs, in effect, gave a pentecostal Baptism to Scofieldian dispensational-ism.[3] It is noteworthy that when Frank Boyd entered the ranks of the pentecostal movement in 1908, he came with his eschatology already fully developed. It is at the point of eschatology that the fundamentalist influence is perhaps most clearly discernible in the pentecostal movement.

From 1909 to 1912, R. A. Torrey and A. C. Dixon edited the famous ten-volume paperback set entitled *The Fundamentals.* Through the resources of two wealthy laymen, 3,000,000 copies of this classic presentation of fundamentalist ideas were published and distributed broadly.[4] It is a matter of speculation to what extent this massive effort affected the emerging theology of the pentecostal people. But for whatever reasons, the strong sense of kinship with fundamentalism remained acute in the pentecostal movement, even after the World Christian Fundamentals Associa-tion at a convention in Chicago in May, 1928, passed a resolution disavowing any connection with the "tongues-talkers and faith healers." The editorial in the *Pentecostal Evangel,* dated August 18, 1928, conveys the wounded spirit of the pentecostals. They allied themselves to the principles for which the fundamentalists had fought so ardently, desiring not to retaliate, but to hold out the olive branch to the fundamentalists, yearning for the day when they would no longer be spurned.

The Keswick Influence

The holiness revival which flowered in post–Civil War America really had two wings. One was the attempt to recover Wesley's original second-blessing eradication doctrine of sanctification. This found expression in the National Holiness Association, which can look to Vineland, New Jersey, for its genesis in 1867. Splinters from the Methodist church, the spawning of new Wesleyan denominations, and interdenominational holiness camp meetings punctuate the period from the Civil War into the early years of the pentecostal revival. But that is a story for others to tell. Our immediate concern is to trace the impact of non-Wesleyan thought on the pentecostal movement.

In the lake district of northern England, in the parish of Keswick, an interdenominational convention developed in the mid-1870s with the specific objective of promoting a deeper Christian life. The American, Robert Pearsall Smith, was instrumental, not only in establishing Keswick as a perennial convention, but also in introducing the Keswick emphases back into the United States. Typical of the new emphasis was the displacement of the concept of eradication by one of an enduement of power. The experience anticipated by ardent believers was cast not so much in terms of cleansing, but of anointing. Further, it was not a state, but a "maintained condition." [5] There were other characteristics which marked the Keswick movement:

> These teachings—the denial of the eradication of inward sin and the emphasis on premillennialism, faith healing, and the "gifts of the Spirit"—opened a wide breach in the holiness ranks. The conflict spread to America when Dwight L. Moody, R. A. Torrey, first president of Moody Bible Institute, Chicago, Adoniram J. Gordon, father of Gordon College, Boston, A. B. Simpson, founder of the Christian and Missionary Alliance, and the evangelist J. Wilbur Chapman began to propagate in this country the Keswick version of the second blessing. [6]

One of the principal early figures who had a direct impact on the pentecostal movement was Alexander Dowie. Donald Gee classifies him as an exponent of Keswick holiness views. [7] Dowie had his roots in Scottish Prebyterianism, but in Australia became a minister of the Congregational Church. In 1888, Dowie emigrated from Australia to the United States. After conducting a series of healing missions, he felt impressed to establish a headquarters for his operations near Chicago, which he chose to call Zion. About this time, he founded the Christian Catholic church.

Among the four articles in the statement of faith of this new organization, there is no clear statement about sanctification. A candidate for membership was expected to be a believer and to "witness a measure of the Holy Spirit." There does not seem to be great emphasis upon a clear-cut sanctification experience, certainly not in Wesleyan terms, at any rate. The big emphasis in the Dowie movement was divine healing. At the time that the Dowie enterprise was crumbling, there were wholesale defections to the new pentecostal movement.

Dowie seems to have suffered a kind of mental breakdown. He set himself up as an apostle and began to behave in an unseemly manner, exhibiting a thirst for unqualified power. His authoritarian stance became so distasteful to his own disciples that they cast him out. This occurred at about the time the great Azusa Street revival was in full bloom. As early as 1904, ardent pentecostalists had sought to penetrate the Christian Catholic church, but were held out by Dowie. A pentecostal assembly was formed in Zion. With Dowie's tragic downfall, many of his followers drifted into pentecostal groups. What influence Dowie had on the young pentecostal movement is uncertain. It is interesting to note that Charles Parham visited Zion City early in 1900, within months of the great Topeka revival. It is possible that he sought to recreate in Topeka a healing center, much as Dowie had done in Zion. This much is clear. Parham had definitely adopted a Wesleyan view of sanctification and Dowie's view on that subject did not dissuade him.[8]

The single most significant influence from the Keswick world which came upon the embryonic pentecostal revival was that of the Christian and Missionary Alliance. A. B. Simpson, Canadian-born Presbyterian minister, adopted a Keswick view of sanctification, experiencing a remarkable personal spiritual and physical renewal in the summer of 1881 at a convention in Old Orchard, Maine. Within a short time, Simpson had left his New York pastorate and was devoting himself to evangelism. Out of his evangelistic and missionary zeal, eventually the "Gospel Tabernacle" was erected, and the Nyack Missionary Training Institute established. By 1887, the Christian and Missionary Alliance was formed, with Simpson as the first director of the society.

The Alliance was a relatively loose federation of churches, which came under the broad banner of Simpson's "fourfold Gospel," featuring Christ as Savior, Healer, Sanctifier, and Coming King. The definition of sanctification which Simpson advocated was in the Keswick tradition, rather than the eradicationist Wesleyan tradition. It was couched in Christocentric terms. The key to distinguishing Simpson's view is the "indwelling Christ." [9] The theologian of the Alliance movement, George Pardington, follows similar Keswickian terminology.[10] In the official biography of Simpson, written shortly after his death by A. E. Thompson, in 1920, a chapter of eulogy is included, furnished by James M. Gray, the dean of Moody Bible Institute. Gray was a long-time friend of Simpson. He recalls the origin of Simpson's "fourfold Gospel," citing the influence of A. J. Gordon on Simpson, remarking that both of these were Spirit-filled men. Evidently Gray saw common theological threads in Gordon and Simpson, emphases to which he himself was sympathetic.[11]

Gordon's view of sanctification, which influenced Simpson, emphasized that sanctification is progressive, but also insisted that the Baptism in the Spirit must be seen as a separate experience from regeneration, and subsequent to it. This Baptism must be appropriated by faith. Gordon said, "We conceive that the great end for which the enduement of the Spirit is bestowed is our qualification for the highest and most effective service in the church of Christ." [12] Thus, the typical emphasis on enduement with power is attached to the experience of the Spirit. The Keswick emphasis was that this Spirit Baptism is received by faith. Therefore, even though the Alliance language speaks of a second blessing called sanctification, upon investigation, the definition of the term is not Wesleyan but Keswickian. For this reason, it is perhaps fair to classify the influences of the Christian and Missionary Alliance upon the pentecostal movement as non-Wesleyan.

Nineteen hundred and seven was the year of crisis for the Christian and Missionary Alliance and its relationship with the pentecostal movement. Entire congregations, some large and important, became pentecostal. Members of the Alliance across the nation, and particularly in the midwest and east, received the pentecostal experience in great numbers. In May, an unusual visitation of God interrupted the Alliance's annual convention at its Nyack Missionary Training Institute. And similar events occurred during the summer at two large camp meetings.

All this unprecedented commotion prompted Dr. Simpson to commission Henry Wilson to examine and study the matter. Wilson's visit that fall to Alliance, Ohio, and his subsequent report provided the basis for Simpson's manifesto which appeared late in the year. It denied the pentecostal teaching that the Baptism of the Holy Spirit is always accompanied by speaking in tongues and advised Alliance leaders and members neither to seek to speak in tongues, nor to forbid it.[13] It was, by comparison with other denominational responses of the period, a remarkably conciliatory document in its refusal to excommunicate pentecostals. This, however, went unnoticed by the offending members who felt themselves being driven from the Alliance fold, and promptly left in great numbers.

The immediate result of this exodus was to provide a fresh infusion of qualified leadership into the burgeoning pentecostal assemblies. Certainly men like Frank Boyd, William Evans, D. W. Kerr, J. Roswell Flower, Noel Perkin, A. G. Ward, and D. W. Myland, all former members of the Alliance, figured importantly in shaping the theology of the Assemblies of God. It is no happenstance the Alliance doctrinal statement was adopted wholesale by the Assemblies—nor that the polity of the new pentecostal denomination showed a heavy reliance on Alliance structure and procedures, even to the extent of calling their places of worship by the same name, "Gospel Tabernacles."

Of all the writers in the Assemblies of God who have written clearly on the doctrine of sanctification, none is more significant than William I. Evans. In a volume of sermons and notes, published posthumously by his son, Paul, Evans outlines a position on sanctification in the classic Keswickian language which reaches through the Alliance, through A. B. Simpson, all the way to A. J. Gordon, Robert Pearsall Smith, F. B. Meyer, and others who traveled the Keswick circuit.[14]

Let me cite an example of what happened to many of the Keswick-type holiness people who encountered the pentecostal message. In 1920, Aimee Semple McPherson held a meeting in Dayton, Ohio, to which she invited ministers of many denominations so that they could judge for themselves whether or not God was in the pentecostal movement. Among those who went was Charles H. Pridgeon, who, like Simpson, was a one-time Presbyterian minister who had left the denomination to strike out on his own. He had opened the Pittsburgh Bible Institute, which featured an Alliance-type sanctification doctrine. Upon his return to Pittsburgh from Dayton, a tremendous revival erupted at the Institute. On one occasion, in the presence of several hundred people, Pridgeon, weeping, confessed that he had been mistaken about the doctrine he had been proclaiming. He told the students that they had been misled. They had not been filled with the Spirit at all! Not until they had a genuine pentecostal experience would they receive what God had for them! From then on, the tongues-experience completely displaced talk of an experience of sanctification. The whole emphasis was on an enduement of power.[15]

1910–1916: Years of Controversy

William H. Durham and the Finished Work of Calvary

A problem began to manifest itself in the ranks of the early pentecostal movement when large numbers of people began to enter the movement from groups who knew neither the Wesleyan nor the Keswickian type of holiness doctrine. Most of these seem to have come from the Baptists. The Baptists generally held to a

Reformed view of sanctification in which the great emphasis was upon process, not crisis. Thus, for them, there were only two works of grace, the regeneration of the believer, and his subsequent filling with the Spirit, evidenced by tongues, as an enduement for service. (Those who espoused this view spoke of "the finished work of Calvary.") The individual most responsible for bringing this conflict into the open was William H. Durham, a Baptist who had received the pentecostal experience, and was pastoring the North Avenue Mission in Chicago. Durham visited the Azusa Street revival in Los Angeles in 1907 where he ran head on into the Parham-Seymour holiness-pentecostal doctrine. Durham rejected their Wesleyan concept of eradication as unscriptural. The vagueness of the experience, the lack of a concrete verification factor, and the disappointment some reported upon discovery that the carnal nature still remained, contributed to the support that Durham received when he launched into his campaign of setting the movement straight.

It was in the year 1910 at a pentecostal convention held in Chicago that Durham really entered the controversy and attempted to discredit the Wesleyan point of view. He felt that it was time for his private convictions to be aired publicly. He said this:

> I began to write against the doctrine that it takes two works of grace to save and cleanse a man. I denied and still deny that God does not deal with the nature of sin at conversion. I deny that a man who is converted or born again is outwardly washed and cleansed but that his heart is left unclean with enmity against God in it.[16]

In February, 1911, Durham carried his crusade to the west coast. By this time, the leading pentecostal center in Los Angeles was the Upper Room Mission, pastored by Elmer Fisher. When Durham unveiled his new message, he was asked not to return. Durham next went to the old Azusa Street Mission, by this time abandoned by the white pentecostals and left in the hands of the blacks, who still held strongly to the Wesleyan views of Parham and Seymour. Durham had considerable success in the mission, until Brother

Seymour returned from the east. When Seymour learned what Durham was proclaiming, he and the trustees agreed to lock Durham out of the mission. Frank Ewart and Frank Bartleman were won over by Durham, however, and Bartleman arranged for Durham to preach in another location, but the crowds were too large to be contained. To accommodate the crowds, which numbered one thousand each Sunday, it became necessary for Durham to rent a sizable auditorium. He conducted some of the meetings in a rented building at the corner of Seventh and Los Angeles Streets, evidently captivating a large part of the Los Angeles pentecostal population.

Feelings became intense. Even Bartleman was disappointed by the vituperation which Durham exhibited in his publication, *The Pentecostal Testimony*.[17] Parham, reflecting sometime later upon the division Durham caused in pentecostalism, also wrote some strong things: "The diabolical end and purpose of his Satanic majesty, in perpetuating Durhamism in the world, in repudiating sanctification, as a definite work of grace, has now been clearly revealed." [18]

However, Durham's influence eventually prevailed among the tiny missions which dotted the countryside and which were not already part of established denominations in the holiness-pentecostal tradition. Frank Ewart makes this observation about the outcome of the struggle between Durham and Parham:

> The struggle was fraught with much bitterness, and Pastor Durham soon found himself in the position of a speckled bird amongst his brethren in the ministry. He stuck to his guns, however, and after a few years the entire movement had swung back and adopted "the Finished Work of Calvary" as orthodox. Sanctification is a progressive work in the development of the Christian graces in the character of the believer. . . . When this view of sanctification was established, the movement was regarded with much more tolerance by the nominal churches, and a great addition from their membership was enjoyed.[19]

The First General Council: Hot Springs, Arkansas, 1914

The situation by 1913 looked much like this. In the southeastern

United States, several great holiness denominations, already in existence by the time of the Azusa Street revival, were swept almost overnight into the pentecostal fold. G. B. Cashwell, Elder C. H. Mason, A. J. Tomlinson, and others exerted a great influence on the regional bodies in that part of the country, and for them, the pentecostal experience was easily defined as a third work of grace. In the Pacific northwest, the Apostolic Faith Mission, a small group, begun in 1907 by Florence Crawford from Azusa Street, likewise followed the Wesleyan viewpoint.[20] Scattered in between was an array of independent pentecostal missions, at best only loosely federated in small clusters, centering in regional camp meetings. It was to this uncommitted group of pentecostals, some of Wesleyan leanings, others inclining to the "Finished Work" theology of Durham, that the call was issued in December, 1913, for a "General Convention of Pentecostal Saints and Churches of God in Christ." The call was signed by M. M. Pinson, A. P. Collins, H. A. Goss, D. C. O. Opperman, and E. N. Bell.[21] It is interesting to note the reaction of Charles Parham to this intention to form an organization of local pentecostal missions.

> Let us cease wasting time at this juncture in systematizing or organizing the work of God. Let each minister go forward doing his work, and leaving local Assemblies under local leaders.[22]

In spite of the controversy that raged around organizing a new church, the meeting was held, and the keynote address was preached by M. M. Pinson, who took as his theme, "The Finished Work of Calvary." Although no formal doctrinal platform was developed in that first meeting, the "Preamble and Resolution on Constitution" which was adopted carries with it the implications of the Durham view on sanctification, for only two experiences are identified—salvation and the Baptism in the Holy Spirit. Sanctification is not mentioned in that document. So, the birth of the Assemblies of God, as the first major attempt to organize the various pentecostal missions in the new revival, carried with it the strong influences of Keswickian and Baptistic theologies. The first chairman, E. N. Bell, was a Baptist who received the pentecostal experience in Durham's North Avenue Mission in Chicago.

Subsequent Developments

The Oneness Controversy

At a pentecostal camp meeting in April, 1913, a fresh revelation seems to have gripped one of the believers, John G. Scheppe. He and others began to proclaim that the only valid baptism is baptism "in the name of Jesus." Many had been baptized according to the formula, "in the name of the Father, Son, and Holy Ghost." Great blessing was assured those who would be rebaptized in the scriptural form set forth in Acts 2:38. This emphasis led quickly to a serious questioning of the orthodox doctrine of the Trinity, and proponents of the Acts 2 formula gained rapidly the title of "Jesus Only" Christians, their doctrine considered by some to be a representation of Sabellianism.

Frank Ewart, a former Baptist minister who fell heir to the church Durham had been pastoring in Los Angeles at his death in 1911, was recognized as one of the leading pentecostal figures in the west. By 1914, Ewart became convinced of the truth of the oneness doctrine and began to proclaim it. A convert to the new message, Glenn A. Cook, an evangelist, soon spread the word throughout the midwest. Called the "new issue," this teaching threatened to disrupt the newly formed General Council.[23] Many of the early leaders of the Assemblies of God were rebaptized. The 1915 General Council was a critical moment in the history of the new organization, then but eighteen months old. It was agreed to reserve judgment for the time.[24]

A year later, at the 1916 General Council, a statement of faith was adopted which was strongly trinitarian, and clearly non-Wesleyan in respect to the doctrine of sanctification.[25] On the committee appointed to draft the statement of faith were T. K.

Leonard, who had been ordained in the Christian church, D. W. Kerr who had come from the Christian and Missionary Alliance, E. N. Bell, a former Baptist minister who had graduated from the Southern Baptist Seminary in Louisville, S. H. Frodsham who came from an Anglican background, and S. A. Jamieson, whose earlier denominational affiliation is uncertain.

The result of the 1916 General Council was the disaffection of the ministers who continued to hold oneness views. Particularly hard hit were the midwest and the west. Growing out of this separation from the Assemblies of God, the oneness people took immediate steps to form their own fellowship. In December of 1916 and into January of 1917, several of these men met in Eureka Springs, Arkansas, to form "The General Assembly of Apostolic Assemblies." D. C. O. Opperman was elected the first chairman. About the same time, G. T. Haywood of Indianapolis furnished the leadership for a group known as "The Pentecostal Assemblies of the World." Numerous small groups emerged over the years. In 1945, a merger occurred within the ranks of the oneness community forming a sizable organization now called the "United Pentecostal Church." This group has apparently not adopted the Wesleyan doctrine of sanctification. Great emphasis is placed upon being filled with the Holy Ghost, with the evidence of speaking with other tongues, and upon baptism in Jesus' name. Some would go so far as to identify the tongues' experience with salvation.[26]

It appears that the oneness movement is a split from the Keswick-oriented Assemblies of God, rather than being in the Wesleyan tradition.

More Recent Keswick Pentecostal Bodies

One of the spectacular charismatic figures in the burgeoning years of the pentecostal movement was Aimee Semple McPherson. Originally she grew up amid Wesleyan influences in Canada, but once launched upon her pentecostal career, she, like the typical Alliance people who turned pentecostal, dropped all vestiges of the Wesleyan tradition, speaking only of a Baptism in the Spirit as an enduement for service. For three years, from 1919 to 1922, Mrs. McPherson held credentials with the Assemblies of God, but eventually withdrew to form her own evangelistic association, the International Church of the Foursquare Gospel, with headquarters in a suburb of Los Angeles. The origins of the Foursquare Gospel seem traceable through the Assemblies of God and at least as far back as A. B. Simpson.[27]

A pentecostal revival in Des Moines, Iowa, in 1927, with Mrs. McPherson the featured attraction, resulted in the establishment of a Foursquare church in that city. Shortly, however, a split developed, growing out of the adverse publicity given Mrs. McPherson regarding her kidnapping incident and the charges of immorality that were levelled against her as a result of it. So many "Gospel Lighthouses" left the Foursquare movement at that time, that steps were taken to centralize control and ownership of local properties in the name of Angelus Temple in Los Angeles. Not only did a portion of the Des Moines church choose to leave the fold at that time, but throughout Iowa and Minnesota other ministers and churches followed suit. In 1932, thirty-two ministers in these states formed a new denomination called "The Open Bible Evangelistic Association." Three years later, a group with similar views, with offices in Eugene, Oregon, known as the "Bible Standard Churches," merged with the Des Moines group, forming the "Open Bible Standard" denomination. In the articles of faith of this group is a clear statement advocating progressive sanctification. There is very little discernible doctrinal disagreement between this body and the parent group, the International Church of the Foursquare Gospel, or the Assemblies of God from which the Foursquare sprang.[28] All of these groups are dispensational and premillennial.

It seems apparent, then, that the influences which began in the very early years of the pentecostal revival through the streams of the Keswick-type of holiness teaching and fundamentalism, did affect the eventual shape of a significant part of the pentecostal movement.

Conclusion

Indeed, we owe much to the great holiness revival of the late nineteenth century. It was the cradle in which the pentecostal revival was rocked. That other influences than the Wesleyan theology informed and shaped at least part of the pentecostal movement ought to give us a bigger picture of our God. It is instructive for all of us to learn that not only is there a theological diversity in today's charismatic movement, but that in the early traditional pentecostal revival, there was a similar richness of theological variety, as well. May God give us the humility to learn that the Spirit blows where He listeth!

NOTES

1. Frank C. Masserano, "A Study of Worship Forms in the Assemblies of God Denomination" (Th.M. thesis, Princeton Seminary, 1966), pp. 31–34.
2. *Ibid.*, p. 53.
3. See Frank Boyd, *Ages and Dispensations* (Springfield, Mo.: Gospel Publishing House, 1949).
4. Bruce Shelley, *Evangelicalism in America* (Grand Rapids, Mich.: Eerdmans, 1967), p. 62.
5. See Steven Barabas, *So Great Salvation* (Westwood, N.J.: Revell, n.d.).
6. Timothy L. Smith, *Called Unto Holiness* (Kansas City, Mo.: Nazarene Publishing House, 1962), p. 25.
7. Donald Gee, *The Pentecostal Movement*, enlarged ed. (London: Elim Publishing Company, 1949), p. 5.
8. See Gordon Lindsay, *The Life of John Alexander Dowie* (n.p.: Voice of Healing Publishing Company, 1951).
9. See A. E. Thompson, *The Life of A. B. Simpson* (New York: Christian Alliance Publishing Company, 1920).
10. See George P. Pardington, *The Crisis of the Deeper Life* (Harrisburg, Pa.: Christian Publications, n.d.).
11. Thompson, *op. cit.*, p. 258.
12. A. J. Gordon, *The Ministry of the Spirit* (Philadelphia: Judson Press, 1894), p. 74.
13. A. W. Tozer, *Wingspread* (Harrisburg, Pa.: Christian Publications, 1943), pp. 133–4.

14. W. I. Evans, *This River Must Flow* (Springfield, Mo.: Gospel Publishing House, 1954), see chapter 11.
15. Personal interview with an eyewitness, the author's mother, Mrs. W. E. Menzies.
16. "The Pentecostal Testimony," June, 1911, quoted in Carl Brumback, *Suddenly From Heaven—A History of the Assemblies of God* (Springfield, Mo.: Gospel Publishing House, 1961), p. 99.
17. Frank Bartleman, *Another Wave Rolls On*, ed. and rev. (Northridge, Calif.: Voice Publications, 1962), p. 112.
18. Charles Parham, *The Everlasting Gospel* (n.p., 1911; reprinted by Robert L. Parham, 1942), p. 137.
19. Frank J. Ewart, *The Phenomenon of Pentecost* (St. Louis: Pentecostal Publishing House, 1947), p. 105.
20. *A Historical Account of the Apostolic Faith* (Portland, Oreg.: Apostolic Faith Mission, 1965).
21. *Word and Witness*, December 20, 1913, p. 1.
22. Sarah E. Parham, *The Life of Charles F. Parham* (Joplin, Mo.: Tri-State Printing Company, 1930), p. 177.
23. See the minutes, General Council of the Assemblies of God, 1914.
24. General Council minutes, 1915, p. 5.
25. See General Council minutes, 1916.
26. See Arthur L. Clanton, *United We Stand: A History of Oneness Organizations* (Hazelwood, Mo.: Pentecostal Publishing House, 1970).
27. See Aimee Semple McPherson, *This Is That* (Los Angeles: Echo Park Evangelistic Association, 1923) for her early autobiography. A doctrinal statement is available in Aimee Semple McPherson, *The Foursquare Gospel* (Los Angeles: Echo Park Evangelistic Association, 1946).
28. Gotfred S. Bruland, "The Origin and Development of the Open Bible Church in Iowa" (M.A. thesis, Drake University, 1945).

The Anti-Pentecostal Argument

HORACE S. WARD

Horace S. Ward, Jr., is the son and namesake of a pioneer pentecostal missionary to South America. Born in Garanhuns, Brazil, Ward was raised in the Pentecostal Church of Christ, a small pentecostal group centered in Ohio. In 1966, he joined the Church of God (Cleveland, Tennessee) and has since made remarkable contributions to the educational system of his church. He was a member of the original ad hoc *committee that laid the early foundations for the Society for Pentecostal Studies which came to birth in 1970. Since 1971, he has served as president of West Coast Bible College in Fresno, California.*

While serving as a pastor and teacher at Ambassador Bible College in London, Ohio, Ward pursued his graduate studies at Ohio State University in Columbus, Ohio. In 1969 he received his Ph.D. degree in counseling with a minor in developmental psychology.

In the following paper, Ward points the reader to the vast anti-pentecostal literature that has appeared since 1906. The shifting grounds of criticism from the early charges of demon possession to the present-day serious exegetical and theological evaluations are dealt with in the chapter.

99

OTHER papers in this series have examined various strains of development within the modern pentecostal movement since the beginning of this century. It has been my purpose to peer through the barricades in order to observe the lines of opposition which have faced this revival movement. It comes as no surprise that the pentecostal revival with its emphasis on glossolalia has not always met with approval.

News of the pentecostal outpouring was hailed by many devout Christians around the world who quickly became recipients of the pentecostal experience. Almost as quickly, hostility was aroused. John T. Nichol reported:

> Within a short time, however, the Pentecostal revival became the object of scurrilous attacks. It was denounced as "anti-Christian," as "sensual and devilish," and as "the last vomit of Satan." Its adherents were taunted and derided from the pulpit as well as in the religious and secular press. Some leaders were actually subjected to violence. Those ministers and missionaries from the old-line denominations who embraced the doctrine of the Holy Spirit baptism were removed from their pulpits or dismissed by their mission boards.[1]

Without citing specifics, Donald Gee affirmed, "The pioneers of the Pentecostal movement paid a great price for their experience." [2] The severity of the opposition caused some to turn back.

In Oklahoma, early pentecostals were pelted with stones and eggs while the straw beneath them was seasoned with red pepper for their discomfort in worship. Their places of worship were vandalized. They were jailed and at times were threatened with hanging.[3]

Charles Conn discovered that "bullying threats and sneering insults" were the limit of persecution against the group in Cherokee County while they were preaching only sanctification. It was upon the introduction of glossolalia that severe persecution began.

Homes were burned, arson was attempted on the church building, and a section was later destroyed with dynamite. Finally a mob including several ministers and lay religious leaders tore the church building apart and set the logs afire. Homes were continually subjected to vandalism and to visits by terrorists. Conn reported:

> The children in the homes had the chore each morning of clearing away the stones from their yards and porches, sweeping up the broken glass and debris in preparation for the next bombardment.[4]

The Reverend Frank Bartleman, an early participant in the Azusa Street revival recalled:

> There was much persecution, especially from the press. They wrote us up shamefully, but this only drew the crowds. Some gave the work six months to live.[5]

He further asserted:

> Every movement of the Spirit of God must also run the gauntlet of the devil's forces. The dragon stands before the bearing mother ready to swallow up her child and so with the present Pentecostal work in its beginning.[6]

"The Work of the Devil"

The initial wave of opposition resulted from the opinion that pentecostals were the tools of Satan and were engaging in religious excesses at the behest of demon spirits.

In his diaries, Bartleman expressed concern for the excesses which gave rise to such criticism. "Persecution is strong. Already the police have been appealed to to break up the meetings. The work has been hindered much also by fanatical spirits of which this city has far too many." [7] He further reported, "The enemy did much counterfeiting." [8]

In defense of the infant movement, he wrote:

> Every natural birth is surrounded by circumstances not entirely pleasant. God's perfect work is wrought in human imperfection. We are creatures of the "fall." Then why expect a perfect manifestation in this case? We are coming "back to God." [9]

Other voices were not equally understanding and sympathetic toward the failings of the infant movement. Alexander Mackie tipped his hand by titling his compendium on pentecostalism, *The Gift of Tongues: A Study in Pathological Aspects of Christianity*. He stated in his introduction:

> It ought to be a matter of common knowledge that historically such religious experiences are practically always associated with anti-moral conduct and more particularly with transgressions of accepted moral standards in the *vita sexualis*.[10]

Mackie rejected the notion that glossolalia in the Acts of the Apostles was actually a work of God. To him it was proof that the Church "still must wage the struggle against pagan ideas and pagan practices within its own doors." [11] Giving his attention exclusively to reports from those tongues movements which preceded the twentieth-century outpouring, he came to this conclusion: "Christendom has waited long and patiently to see whether this thing—the gift of tongues—is of God. It is of sickness, of poverty, of fatigue, of disease, of crime. It is not of God." [12]

There were many who accepted the inerrancy of the Scriptures and who believed in the validity of that which occurred in the New Testament Church, who, on the other hand, totally rejected the divine origin of glossolalia in the pentecostal movement. Alma White, leader of the "Pillar of Fire" movement titled her anti-pentecostal polemic, *Demons and Tongues*. Her attitude could have been anticipated from an autobiography published in 1902, even before the pentecostal outpouring became widely known. A holiness pastor for whom she was scheduled to preach suggested that she might use the term "infilling of the Holy Spirit" as a suitable replacement for the term, "sanctification," but she recoiled in horror. She wrote, "It did not take much spiritual discernment to see the cloven hoof of the devil in this argument." [13] If she could see the devil at work in this change of terminology which was so widely accepted in the holiness movement, then it is not difficult to understand her reaction to the pentecostal revival after it had claimed both her husband and one of her churches.

Louis Bauman, a pastor in southern California, suffered losses from his congregation to the pentecostal movement and felt compelled to shed scriptural light on tongues. He wrote, "Probably the most widely spread of all satanic phenomena today is the demonic imitation of the apostolic gift of tongues." [14] After identifying it with a history of witchcraft, paganism, and heresy, he asserted:

> The first miracle that Satan ever wrought was to cause the serpent to speak in a tongue. It would appear he is still working his same, original miracle.[15]

Bauman reported numerous narratives concerning moral break-downs, broken homes, indecency, free love, and other lurid conduct which was attributed to the tongues movement.

Examples of high Christian character among pentecostal people met with this analysis by the Reverend Mr. Bauman:

> It may be pointed out that some exceedingly fine people are exercising the gift of tongues in our day. That matters not, for the "good man" argument never proves anything. The Apostle Paul long ago warned us that there would be "false apostles, deceitful workers, transforming themselves into the apostles of Christ." [16]

Christian character proved nothing, but moral breakdown was relevant evidence, according to this thinking.

Bauman listed ten scriptural principles related to the true gift of tongues and identified what he considered to be three common errors of the tongues movement. By these he felt that he was proving the demonic origin of the modern pentecostal movement.

Neo-pentecostalism spurred the reprinting of a polemic by H. J. Stolee which had originally appeared almost three decades earlier. Stolee determined that:

> This movement is subtle because it is satanic. That is the verdict of scriptures. It is verified by the horrid trail of schism, immorality and insanity that everywhere has marked its inroads into the church.[17]

To secure sufficient evidence against pentecostals, he freely included lurid accounts of pagan practices even among Eskimos and Africans who had no connection with pentecostalism.

One new feature in his polemic was a more positive response to the sincerity of some pentecostals. He wrote:

> Before closing this chapter, we want to add, in justice to true believers that are found in Pentecostal denominations, that the fundamental doctrines of the Bible are taught in most of their churches. They who are on conservative ground are not always responsible for the frenzy of their radical brethren. Still, the very fact that even the more conservative of Pentecostal folk do stress the desirability of ecstatic experiences is exactly what attracts many "seekers" from every communion and causes thousands to suffer shipwreck concerning the faith.[18]

Later he added:

> Many sincere people are entangled in this form of religious delusion. That must grieve us the most deeply. Not only are the carnal minded blinded thereby, but such who seek for peace of heart are misled and the pious are bewildered. It is difficult to discern the spirit of such a religious movement because the counterfeit is so amazingly like the genuine. Men who become Pentecostals are not agnostics, nor materialists; usually they are religious folks. They yearn for spiritual experiences and then because of neglect on the one hand, and aggressiveness on the other, they soon are spiritually adrift. Such persons must be taught, not taunted. They must be directed, not denounced. We need especially to be "speaking the truth in love" when we attempt to help those who are caught by the wiles of error.[19]

An interesting explanation was given for the fact that Paul commanded the Corinthians to "forbid not the speaking with tongues." According to Stolee, Paul was using psychology very effectively. Paul was not defending tongues, but avoiding the curiosity and interest which usually come from outright prohibition.

Harry A. Ironside, an early critic, associated pentecostalism with the holiness movement, to the credit of neither. He believed that there were pious Christians in the holiness movement, and he expressed the hope that he had written out of charity and without malice when he concluded:

And now I begin to see what a string of derelicts this holiness teaching left in its train. I could count scores of persons who had gone into utter infidelity because of it. . . . Many more (and I knew several such intimately) lapsed into insanity after floundering in the morass of this emotional religion for years—and people said that studying the Bible had driven them crazy.[20]

He believed that the tongues movement was proof that "superstition and fanaticism and the grossest character find a hotbed among holiness advocates." [21] He further asserted:

In the last few years hundreds of holiness meetings all over the world have been literally turned into pandemoniums where exhibitions worthy of a madhouse or of a collection of howling dervishes are held night after night. No wonder a heavy toll of lunacy and infidelity is the frequent result.[22]

He conceded that "many holiness teachers repudiate all connections with these fanatics," but insisted that the holiness doctrine was the "direct cause of the disgusting fruits I have been enumerating." [23]

Ironside was credited by Stolee as the source of a report concerning a service in Portland, Oregon, where a seeker "writhing and foaming as in an epileptic fit" received assistance from an altar worker who cried "receive ye the Holy Ghost" and then putting his mouth over the nose of the seeker, "blew powerfully into the nostrils." The report was further enlivened by an assertion that "seven persons (were) sent to insane asylums from that mission" and that a bald-headed girl had lost her hair as the result of brain fever contracted "through the unnatural excitement." [24]

It is reasonable to suppose that such narratives were significantly exaggerated, due to the antipathy of the reporters. It can also be shown that such outlandish behavior was not approved by the responsible leaders of the pentecostal revival. Nevertheless, fanaticism and ungodly spirits were evidenced in pentecostal meetings. Bartleman wrote:

Outside persecution never hurt the work. We had the most to fear from the workings of evil spirits within. Even spiritualists and hypnotists came to investigate, and to try their influence, and then all the religious sore-heads and crooks and cranks came seeking a place to work. We had the most to fear from these. But this is always the danger to every new work. They have no place elsewhere. This condition cast a fear over many which was hard to overcome. It hindered the spirit much. Many were afraid to seek God, for fear the devil might get them.[25]

All this was in sharp contrast to the worship which was truly characteristic of the pentecostal revival. Bartleman described in detail the reverence which prevailed in the sanctuary and in the tarrying room. He credited the success of the services to the leadership of the Holy Spirit, the spiritual sensitivity and responsiveness of the saints, and the maturity of the leadership who had been prepared for their roles by their proven experience in the holiness movement. His remarks are relevant to our day as he warns against the imitation of spiritual gifts and against any human means which might be used to simulate the spiritual gifts.

"Too Much of a Good Thing"

The second wave of opposition was characterized by a rational polemic based on doctrine rather than on rabid emotionalism. Broad areas of theological agreement were recognized, and opposition began to focus on the relevant issues relating to spiritual gifts, especially glossolalia.

The holiness movement was the seedbed of the pentecostal revival. To many, sanctification and Holy Spirit Baptism were synonymous. Many of their churches, including those now associated with the Church of the Nazarene, called themselves pentecostal.

Leading exponents of holiness repeatedly called for a pentecostal revival which would be characterized by the gifts of the Spirit. Joseph H. Smith, a leading holiness spokesman, taught a pneumatology which was generally in agreement with that of the pentecostal movement.[26]

A. B. Simpson and the churches associated with the Christian and Missionary Alliance were apparently sympathetic with the pentecostal revival, even accepting tongues as one evidence of the Holy Spirit Baptism. Bartleman reported numerous invitations to Christian and Missionary Alliance churches with opposition to his ministry evidenced in only a few of them.[27]

Violent opposition was keenly focused on glossolalia as the necessary and universal evidence for the Holy Spirit Baptism. Those who accepted tongues as one legitimate sign could consider pentecostals simply as overzealous or mildly fanatical. Those who rejected tongues altogether found it necessary to deny their divine origin and to attribute them to emotionalism, insanity, or possibly to demons.

More rational opposition also developed outside the holiness tradition. Before the turn of the century, C. I. Scofield had identified the Holy Spirit Baptism as being different from and subsequent to the indwelling of the Holy Spirit, and had held that spiritual gifts were special enduements for distinctive service. He wrote: "No Christian should be willing to perform the slightest act in the service of Christ until he is definitely filled with the Holy Spirit." [28]

The most acceptable non-pentecostal treatise on pentecostal doctrine was offered by R. A. Torrey. He viewed the Baptism of the Holy Spirit as:

1. A definite experience of which one may know whether he has received it or not.[29]
2. A work of the Holy Spirit distinct from and additional to his regenerating work.[30]
3. A work of the Holy Spirit always connected with and primarily for the purpose of testimony and service.[31]

Unlike representatives of the holiness movement, Torrey did not believe that it was a primary purpose of the Holy Spirit Baptism to make us holy or to make us happy.

Of special encouragement to pentecostals was an experience described by Torrey in which he felt such ecstatic joy that he uncontrollably shouted praises to the Lord, although he did not at that time speak in other tongues. One might wonder whether less resistance on his part might not have resulted in an actual case of tongues speaking.[32] The greatest divergence from the pentecostal doctrine was his insistence that any of the spiritual gifts might be a manifestation of the Holy Spirit Baptism and that Christians should not insist on or expect only tongues. He wrote: "It is the Holy Spirit Himself who decides what the particular gift or manifestation shall be in any given instance." [33]

Although Torrey must be credited with a scriptural rationale for pentecostal theology, it must also be reported that he denounced pentecostal excesses in language equal to that of many who were grouped among the rabid opponents of pentecostalism.

The most thorough opposition based on doctrinal differences is found among those strongly committed to dispensationalism. John Walvoord effectively expounded this particular view. The Baptism of the Holy Spirit was defined as referring exclusively to that act which unites a believer to the Body of Christ. It occurred at the time of regeneration and was never to be repeated.[34]

Walvoord regarded the infilling of the Holy Spirit as an experience distinct from his indwelling and gave considerable attention to the need for, the benefits of, and the conditions prerequisite to the Holy Spirit infilling. Beneficial results were to be found in the character, devotion, and service of the filled believer.[35]

The most significant difference between dispensational theology and pentecostal doctrine is to be found in the dispensational view that tongues ceased at the end of the apostolic age. Walvoord wrote: "With the completion of the New Testament and its almost universal acceptance by those true to God, the need for further unusual display of miraculous works ceased." [36]

He then went to the New Testament listings of spiritual gifts and arbitrarily determined that in each list some are permanent and others are temporary and have ceased.

> Certain gifts are clearly the possession of the church today as exhibited in their exercise in gifted men throughout the present

dispensation. . . . In contrast to these . . . stand other spiritual gifts known by the early Christians which seem to have passed from the scene with the apostolic period.[37]

He insisted that spiritual gifts are real and supernatural in their origin. To claim otherwise would be to deny the Scriptures. On the other hand, he stated:

> There are good reasons to believe that most, if not all the phenomena which are advanced as proof of modern speaking in tongues, is either psychological or demonic activity. A most convincing argument is the history of the tongues movement with its excesses and its obvious evil characteristics. Some earnest Christians, however, are numbered among those claiming to speak in tongues.[38]

Walvoord's attack on pentecostalism was incidental to his major purpose of developing a dispensational theology of the Holy Spirit. More recently, Robert Gromacki gave his full attention to the development of a dispensational polemic against the modern tongues movement. His major concern is neo-pentecostalism since it can no longer be ignored as a view which appeals only to the poor and ignorant. Four objections are raised to neo-pentecostalism:

> First, it is the penetration and the presence of old Pentecostalism within the churches of historic protestantism.[39]

> Second, the modern tongues movement is an essential part of the ecumenical atmosphere.[40]

> Third, the modern tongues movement reflects a confusion and ignorance of Biblical doctrine.[41]

> Fourth, the modern tongues movement is based upon experience, not doctrine.[42]

It is his contention that signs were important only to the Jews and that:

> Speaking in tongues was the sign of the initial introduction of the Holy Spirit's ministry to four different classes of people (Jews, Samaritans, Gentiles, Disciples of John the Baptist). It occurred then and only then for that particular purpose. These occurrences were

never intended to become a pattern for the reception of the Spirit by subsequent believers.[43]

Spiritual gifts, even the least of the gifts, are recognized by Gromacki to be of divine origin and to be "important to the function of the body of Christ." [44] Pentecostalism, however, cannot hold claim to these spiritual gifts because it has its basis in "Arminian, holiness theology," and, therefore, cannot hold claim to "historical continuity of the phenomena of tongues from the Biblical era to the present situation." [45] He further concludes, "The inward (love) and the outward regulations of the gift of tongues are not practiced by the tongues movement." [46]

He insists that biblical tongues were always known languages, as on the day of Pentecost, but that linguistic research has not recognized the sounds of modern glossolalia. Therefore, modern tongues are not recognizable languages and cannot be of God.[47]

His biblical exegesis and this additional empirical data lead him to say, "We conclude by quoting Paul, who said: 'Tongues shall cease.' (I Corinthians 13:8) They have." [48]

"Glossolalia—Eccentric but Harmless"

A new phase has now developed in the anti-pentecostal argument. At times it is difficult to even recognize that the literature is inimical to pentecostalism. The new attitude may result from a reduced virulence in pentecostalism, or a new respectability gained by neo-pentecostalism, or a general attitude of tolerance toward all eccentric ideologies. Hopefully, it has resulted from a more accurate knowledge and more genuine understanding of pentecostalism which now exists among non-pentecostals. The new phase of criticism includes those who have attempted a biblical analysis of glossolalia and those who are concerned with its psychological concomitants.

The most accurate representation of pentecostal doctrine is presented by Frederick Dale Bruner in his *Theology of the Holy*

Spirit.[49] The portion of his book which presents the tenets of pentecostalism could serve as a textbook for a study in pentecostal thought. He demonstrates a sincere appreciation for the accomplishments of the pentecostal movement and concedes a modicum of balance to exist in the content of pentecostal preaching. He even suggests that the historic church and the pentecostals need each other.

The core of his objection to pentecostalism is its divergence from Calvinism. He believes that any spiritual experience subsequent to regeneration must of necessity demean regeneration by suggesting its inadequacy. To him, the expectation of a subsequent work by the Holy Spirit implies a low opinion of what Christ has done. To impose any conditions for reception of a divine gift is to invalidate the New Testament emphasis on grace and faith. Glossolalia as an evidence is made unnecessary by water baptism since baptism symbolizes the éntire regenerative work effected by the Holy Spirit. He says, "Baptism is really the evidence of the Holy Spirit for it evidences the effective work of the gospel and the effected faith of the hearer and both are due, as we have seen, to the Spirit." [50]

Anthony A. Hoekema also presents himself as being kindly disposed toward pentecostals. "I should like to make clear at the outset that I am very grateful for what God is accomplishing through Christians of Pentecostal persuasion, particularly on the mission fields of the world." [51] He, too, however, finds it difficult to accept an experience subsequent to regeneration because the New Testament does not indicate a spiritual elite who are somehow superior to the remainder of the church because of an experience which is not common to the entire church.

He finds a significant distinction between tongues in the Book of Acts and those at Corinth, the former being signs validating and confirming the outpouring of the Holy Spirit, but the latter edifying the individual always and the congregation if interpretation followed. He interprets the purpose of Paul in I Corinthians 14 as devaluating tongues, and concludes that the spiritual blessings experienced by pentecostals do not result from glossolalia, but from their dedication and prayer. He believes pentecostals have contributed to the rest of the Church by emphasizing a constant fullness of the Spirit, concern for emotional needs, spontaneity in worship, prayer and constant dependence on God, importance of readiness to witness, and the value of small groups for Bible study.[52]

Donald W. Burdick believes that glossolalia in Corinthians as well as that in Acts is primarily evidential in purpose. He further believes that all glossolalia must be in the form of known languages as described in Acts 2. In this manner, glossolalia will always have an evangelistic effect and will be a sign to the unbeliever. The regulations which Paul established in I Corinthians 14 are seen as guarantees that this evidential and evangelistic ministry will be accomplished. Along with other dispensationalists, Burdick carefully separates the gifts of the Spirit into two categories:

> Those which are miraculous in an objective sense, and thus, evidential; and those which are miraculous only in a subjective sense (Word of Wisdom, Word of Knowledge, Faith, Discerning of Spirits, I Corinthians 12:8–10). At the end of the Apostolic age the former category of gifts gradually ceased to be the order of the day.[53]

Unlike many of the other polemicists, he sees no need of demeaning any spiritual gift, since they are all of divine origin and were given a proper function in the New Testament church. He simply insists that they have ceased, believing that all scriptural glossolalia must be known languages and that linguistic research has not identified modern glossolalia among the known languages. He, therefore, believes that tongues have ceased. He concludes:

> There is reason to believe that present day glossolalia is an abnormal psychological occurrence. Specific items in the explanation of the phenomenon may vary from case to case but the general explanation is the same for all instances.[54]

He thinks that it is acceptable for individuals with psychological problems to turn to Christ for help, and he believes that there are psychological benefits of glossolalia, but that there are dangers as well, and that it would be preferable not to speak in tongues.

Watson Mills views his responsibility as effecting a rapprochement between pentecostals and non-pentecostals.[55] Unlike Burdick, he views glossolalia as an unknown language which is not understandable except in the case of Acts 2 where the Scriptures clearly state otherwise. He appeals to non-pentecostals for tolerant acceptance of glossolalia as a spiritual expression, but he appeals to pentecostals for a less dogmatic stance concerning the initial evidence of the Spirit's indwelling.[56]

Efforts to examine pentecostalism in academic disciplines other than theology have been rather inconclusive. Application of linguistic principles to glossolalia has generally failed to identify the phenomenon with known languages. Glossolalia is not held by most theologians to be only an utterance in known languages, probably invalidating the negative conclusions from this type of research. The field of linguistics may find some interest in a volume recently authored by Ralph Harris in which he documents seventy-five cases of glossolalia in languages recognized by hearers but unknown to speakers.[57]

Morton Kelsey interprets glossolalia as an expression coming from the deep unconscious. Applying Jungian theory, he concludes that the phenomenon is psychologically beneficial to the participant.[58]

John Kildahl used various psychological tests to study the personality characteristics and psychological adjustment of individuals engaging in glossolalia. He discovered them to be somewhat submissive and dependent, but better adjusted than non-glossolalists. He further discovered that the better adjustment was a permanent characteristic.[59]

Wayne Oates views glossolalia as a childish expression which has become necessary due to the "conspiracy of silence about personal religion." He believes that it releases tension and is of some psychological benefit.[60]

William W. Wood engaged in a sociological and psychological study of pentecostal believers in a small southeastern community and concluded that psychological needs were being met through the pentecostal experience.[61]

An historical analysis of glossolalia led Glenn Hinson to the following indefinite conclusion: "If tongues and other phenomenal spiritual gifts have not hurt the church, neither have they helped particularly in the accomplishment of the church's mission." [62]

Although these studies have led to several favorable conclusions concerning glossolalia, they have attempted to treat the pentecostal experience as a human phenomenon, stripping it of its supernatural character. This is a dangerous attack at a vital point, for if the experience is totally human or psychic, it is not of God.

Personal Reflections

Criticism is beneficial if it drives one to the truth. Whether the language is hostile or honeyed, it should lead us to search the Scriptures and to examine ourselves. Nothing in this study is intended to deter any pentecostal from persistent care for sound doctrine, Christocentrism, love, humility, unity, orderliness, and mutual edification. It is noteworthy that these concerns were keenly felt in the pentecostal movement prior to the exhortations of its critics, and they receive continuing emphasis among pentecostals today.

The issues commonly raised in anti-pentecostal literature require a response in greater depth than this study allows. The thoughts which follow are sketchy, and do not purport to be adequately theological, exegetical, or apologetic. They are simply the personal reflections of one committed pentecostal.

1. *Evidential Glossolalia.* It is conceded by all evangelical critics cited in this paper that the purpose of tongues in the Acts of the Apostles was to evidence and confirm the reception of the Holy Spirit by at least three or four classes of believers. This confirmation was important to the recipient, bringing him to a full recognition that he had received "power from on high" and that he

was authorized both to cease tarrying in Jerusalem and to become active in service to Christ (Luke 24:49). The early church considered glossolalia to be the evidence of Holy Spirit Baptism according to the record concerning the outpouring in the house of Cornelius (Acts 10:46).

The need of the recipients for a sign does not abrogate the principle of grace. The issue at hand is not salvation but service and the token which signaled the preparedness of waiting laborers. It is evident that the glossolalists in Acts were prime beneficiaries of the evidence, for it signaled the end of their tarrying and the beginning of their power-endued testimony.

2. *Universal Evidence.* The most controversial issue concerning evidential glossolalia is whether the recipients described in Acts were symbols or patterns. Non-pentecostals generally believe that these cases were representatives of certain classes of people, such as Jews, Samaritans, Gentiles, and disciples of John, and that the glossolalic evidence was necessary only for the first recipients within each category. If these were representatives of all the distinct classes of men, would they not prove both the promise and the pattern to be for all? If their experience symbolized the gift of the Holy Spirit to all classes of men, then did it not also demonstrate that glossolalic evidence would accompany the gift among all classes of men?

Do these incidents provide a scriptural pattern by which we can recognize the Baptism of the Holy Spirit? Christ served the Lord's Supper only one time, but Paul recognized His manner as the pattern to be followed universally by the Church. One example is sufficient when God sets it. Are three or four examples then not sufficient? Only representative incidents were recorded in scriptural narratives. John himself confessed that much was left unwritten, but that enough was written for faith. For example, it is not recorded that Paul spoke in tongues at the time of his Baptism, but later he claimed to speak "more than ye all." When did he begin?

It is said that we are arguing from silence when we claim that tongues could logically be assumed in those New Testament cases where they are not specifically reported. Who is arguing from silence? Where is there one occasion where it is specifically stated that they received the Holy Spirit Baptism and did not speak with tongues? In the inspired record, surely a ratio of four to zero sounds more like thunder than like silence.

In these last days when the forces of evil are girding themselves for the final conflagration, dare the Christian warrior venture forth with less assurance of his spiritual preparedness than was required during the apostolic age?

3. *Cessation of Tongues.* The dispensationalist argument that tongues ceased with the apostolic era is based on historical as well as exegetical reasoning. The apparent failure of apostolic succession and the long list of allegedly heretical glossolalic forbears are marshaled as evidence that tongues have ceased.

On the other hand, contemporary opponents of the modern pentecostal revival have produced many venomous volumes of bigoted and inaccurate narratives which demonstrate that even sincere ministers and modern "church fathers" are not always unimpeachable witnesses concerning spiritual phenomena they have not experienced. Their testimony is not sufficient to call a requiem for a New Testament gift.

Many cases of glossolalia have been recorded throughout Church history, and it is the testimony of the Patriarch of Constantinople that in the Eastern Orthodox churches tongues never ceased.[63] Millions of devout Christians around the world are living testimonies to the fact that tongues have not yet ceased.

The most telling failure of the dispensationalists is in their dealing with the scriptural record itself. It has been necessary for them to arbitrarily divide the several lists of spiritual gifts in order to identify those which have ceased and those which continue. Even in I Corinthians 13, where Paul predicts cessation, they are willing to spare prophecy and knowledge, but not tongues. The reason given by Walvoord for his arbitrary selection was the fact that certain gifts are not observed as functioning today.[64] This sounds strangely like preferring experience over Scripture in a doctrinal matter.

Those who believe in the cessation of miraculous gifts assume that miracles always were produced to confirm the message. The truth needs no validation beyond its own truthfulness (Matt. 5:37).

The signs which Christ produced were the result of His compassion, not the result of the Jewish passion for a sign. In fact, He refused to produce signs for the Jews when they asked for one (Matt. 12:39; 16:4).

Signs were held to be inferior to the preached word (I Cor. 1:22–23). The rich man in hell was denied a sign for his brothers because they had Moses and the prophets. The Old Testament Scriptures were not all validated by miracles, for many cases can be found where books were authored by prophets who produced no miracles, and where miracle-working prophets wrote no inspired books.

Surely those who deny the genuineness of pentecostal manifestations, citing the ease with which demons and men counterfeit them, cannot believe that God selects such an inconclusive means to confirm the authenticity of the apostolic ministry? Yet the anti-pentecostal literature attempts to limit the supernatural gifts to such a purpose.

The miracles and gifts came because of divine compassion for human needs. The eternal compassion and the continuing need suggest that miracles also will continue until they are no longer needed, "when that which is perfect is come"—when I shall "know even as also I am known" (I Cor. 13:8–12).

4. *Inferior Gifts.* It is surely presumptuous for fallible man to call a gift of the Holy Spirit inferior, unless he does it as Paul, under inspiration, to identify its reduced value when it is improperly used.

The total context of Paul's comparison is a lengthy discussion of spiritual gifts as they operate in the corporate church. The private and devotional value of tongues is only briefly mentioned, since the thrust of his exhortation relates to the public ministry of the church and its members. In this context, private tongues and personal edification is inferior, but Paul emphatically declares an exception to this inferior state *if the tongue is interpreted.*

Is it *always* undesirable to speak "unto God"? (I Cor. 14:2). Do I *never* need to be edified? (I Cor. 14:4). If I pray only "with the understanding," will I ever fathom the mysteries of which Paul spoke? Must my spirit be always restrained from ecstatically praising "the wonderful works of God" (Acts 2:11) or from offering "unutterable" supplications for unrecognized needs "according to the will of God"? (Rom. 8:26–27).

The gift, which comes from the Holy Spirit, which personally edifies, which Paul practiced, which communicates with God, which must not be prohibited—the gift itself is the divine reply. It says: "In the right place—at the right time—for the right reason—in the right manner—speak." Whether it be through omission, or heresy, or exaggeration, or ridicule, or fright, to forbid is to disobey. In praises beyond words and in intercession beyond human understanding, let us speak.

Conclusion

The temperate tone of modern criticism should not be accepted as a vindication of pentecostalism. In many cases the writer has taken away with one hand everything he has conceded with the other hand. The anti-Pentecostal argument still consists mainly of the following points: (1) the evidential purposes of glossolalia in the Book of Acts are no longer valid; (2) glossolalia was a temporary gift; (3) glossolalia was an inferior gift; (4) glossolalia can be explained as a psychological and human phenomenon.

It is clear that the language and violence of the early argument has been subdued, but that the skepticism remains. Theological objections are virtually unchanged, but a new dimension of secular inquiry into a spiritual phenomenon has been inaugurated.

The viability of pentecostalism is demonstrated by its continuing growth. This attests to its evangelistic mission and to its capacity for meeting real human needs. Since its theology, its mission, its power, and its fruitfulness are in harmony with Scripture, pentecostalism can rightfully demand an honest examination of the proposition that it is a modern expression of the New Testament experience.

NOTES

1. John Thomas Nichol, *Pentecostalism* (New York: Harper and Row, 1966), p. 70.
2. Donald Gee, *The Pentecostal Movement: Including the Story of the War Years (1940–47)* (London: Elim Publishing Company, 1949), p. 45.
3. Joseph E. Campbell, *The Pentecostal Holiness Church, 1898–1948* (Franklin Springs, Ga.: Advocate Press, 1951), p. 206.
4. Charles W. Conn, *Like a Mighty Army Moves the Church of God, 1886–1955* (Cleveland, Tenn.: Church of God Publishing House, 1955), p. 35.
5. Frank Bartleman, *How Pentecost Came to Los Angeles* (Los Angeles: F. Bartleman, 1925), p. 54.
6. *Ibid.,* p. 45.
7. *Ibid.,* p. 63.
8. *Ibid.,* p. 45.
9. *Ibid.*
10. Alexander Mackie, *The Gift of Tongues: A Study in Pathological Aspects of Christianity* (New York: George H. Doran, 1921), p. vii.
11. *Ibid.,* p. 25.
12. *Ibid.,* p. 275.
13. Alma White, *Looking Back from Beulah* (Zarephath, N.J.: Pillar of Fire, 1902), p. 301. See also, Alma White, *Demons and Tongues*, 4th ed. (Zarephath, N. J.: Pillar of Fire, 1949), pp. 43, 56, 82.
14. Louis S. Bauman, *The Modern Tongues Movement Examined and Judged in the Light of the Scriptures and in the Light of Its Fruits* (Long Beach, Calif., 1941), p. 1.
15. *Ibid.*
16. *Ibid.*
17. H. L. Stolee, *Speaking in Tongues* (Minneapolis: Augsburg, 1963: original copyright 1936, under title of *Pentecostalism*), p. 112.
18. *Ibid.,* p. 71.
19. *Ibid.,* p. 112.
20. H. A. Ironside, *Holiness: The False and the True* (New York: Loizeaux Bros., 1955), pp. 38–39.
21. *Ibid.,* p. 38.

22. *Ibid.,* pp. 38–39.
23. *Ibid.,* p. 39.
24. Stolee, *op. cit.,* p. 65.
25. Bartleman, *op cit.,* p. 49.
26. Joseph H. Smith, *Things of the Spirit* (Chicago: Chicago Evangelistic Institute, 1940).
27. Bartleman, *op. cit.,* pp. 104–105.
28. G. I. Scofield, *Plain Papers on the Doctrine of the Holy Spirit* (Grand Rapids, Mich.: Baker Book House, 1899), p. 73.
29. R. A. Torrey, *The Holy Spirit* (New York: Revell, 1927), p. 109.
30. *Ibid.,* p. 112.
31. *Ibid.,* p. 117.
32. *Ibid.,* p. 199.
33. *Ibid.,* pp. 127–28.
34. John F. Walvoord, *The Holy Spirit* (Wheaton, Ill.: Van Kampen Press, 1954), p. 139.
35. *Ibid.,* pp. 189–224.
36. *Ibid.,* p. 174.
37. *Ibid.,* p. 168.
38. *Ibid.,* p. 186.
39. Robert G. Gromacki, *The Modern Tongues Movement* (Philadelphia: Presbyterian and Reformed Publishing Co., 1967), p. 141.
40. *Ibid.*
41. *Ibid.,* p. 142.
42. *Ibid.*
43. *Ibid.,* p. 140.
44. *Ibid.,* p. 111.
45. *Ibid.,* p. 140.
46. *Ibid.,* p. 141.
47. *Ibid.,* p. 107.
48. *Ibid.,* p. 143.
49. Frederick Dale Bruner, *A Theology of the Holy Spirit* (Grand Rapids, Mich.: Eerdmans, 1970).
50. *Ibid.,* p. 205.
51. Anthony A. Hoekema, *What About Tongue-Speaking?* (Grand Rapids, Mich.: Eerdmans, 1966), p. 5.
52. *Ibid.,* p. 136.
53. Donald W. Burdick, *Tongues: To Speak or Not to Speak* (Chicago: Moody Press, 1969), p. 39.
54. *Ibid.,* p. 75.
55. Watson E. Mills, *Understanding Speaking in Tongues* (Grand Rapids, Mich.: Eerdmans, 1972), p. 8.
56. *Ibid.,* p. 67.
57. Ralph W. Harris, *Spoken by the Spirit* (Springfield. Mo.: Gospel Publishing House, 1973).

58. Morton T. Kelsey, *Tongue Speaking: An Experiment in Spiritual Experience* (Garden City, N.Y.: Doubleday, 1964).
59. John P. Kildahl, *The Psychology of Speaking With Tongues* (New York: Harper and Row, 1972).
60. Wayne E. Oates, "A Socio-Psychological Study of Glossolalia," in Frank Stagg, E. Glenn Hinson, and Wayne E. Oates, *Glossolalia: Tongue Speaking in Biblical, Historical, and Psychological Perspective* (Nashville, Tenn.: Abingdon, 1967), p. 82.
61. William W. Wood, *Culture and Personality Aspects of the Pentecostal Holiness Religion* (The Hague: Mouton & Co., Publishers, 1965).
62. E. Glenn Hinson, "A Brief History of Glossolalia," in Stagg, *op. cit.*, p. 74.
63. Kelsey, *op. cit.*, p. 7.
64. Walvoord, *op. cit.*, p. 168.

Black Origins of the Pentecostal Movement

LEONARD LOVETT

Leonard Lovett is especially well qualified to write about black pentecostalism. An ordained minister in the largest black pentecostal denomination, the Church of God in Christ, Lovett has distinguished himself in the field of education. From 1970 to 1974 he served as pioneer dean of the C. H. Mason Theological Seminary in Atlanta, Georgia, official seminary for his church. For several years, this institution has been the only accredited theological seminary in the pentecostal world. At present, Lovett pastors the Pentecostal Memorial Church of God in Christ of Atlanta and is working on a Ph.D. in ethics and church history at the Candler Graduate School of Theology, Emory University.

The role of blacks in the beginnings of pentecostalism in the United States is a much-neglected and often misunderstood phase of the story. In recent years, however, much research has been done on this aspect of pentecostal history, bringing a better understanding of the significant contributions of blacks to the origins and ethos of the movement.

In the following selection, Lovett calls attention to the crucial importance of William J. Seymour and the Azusa

123

Street revival in the spread of pentecostalism. In particular, one should note his views on the "latter rain," the holiness movement, the "interracial theory," the "liberation theology" of young black pentecostals, and the influence of African "spirit possession" on those black pentecostal pioneers who were born as slaves in the American South.

A review of the literature of the pentecostal movement reveals four points of view concerning its origins and founding. One suggests that it began during the turn of the century under the leadership of Charles Fox Parham. Another emphasizes Parham and the Topeka Bible School events in 1901, and W. J. Seymour in the Los Angeles Azusa Street revival of 1906. Still another point of view sees an Afro-American origin under the leadership of W. J. Seymour in Los Angeles in 1906. A fourth strand suggests that it came suddenly from heaven to a converted livery stable in the ghetto and was initiated exclusively by the Holy Spirit.

I propose, in the following pages, to present a black perspective on the historical background of pentecostalism, to ruminate a bit about the black personalities who figured so importantly in the early days of the movement, and to offer a counter proposal regarding the proper interpretation of the past that, I hope, will cast some prophetic light on the future.

The pentecostal "latter rain" theory* of history has its locus in Joel's prophecy of the age of the Spirit (2:23–25). A departure from the traditional interpretations of Church history, it is based on an analogy to the two main rainfalls that occurred annually in Palestine. The first was called the early or former rain which fell in the autumn to prepare the ground for sowing for the winter harvest. After this, there would be an occasional light shower until the latter rain fell. The latter rain was heavier than the early rain.

The period from the first through the fourth centuries of Church history is designated the *Early Showers*. The pneumatic line moves from the descent of the Spirit of Acts through the fourth century, affecting such post-apostolic personalities as Montanus, Irenaeus,

---

* The "latter rain" interpretation of Church history has been used by several pentecostal writers to show the impact of the phenomenon on Christian history.

Clement, Polycarp, Tertullian, and Chrysostom in a charismatic way. The second period, from the fifth through the sixteenth centuries is designated the *Long Drought*. During this period, Pentecost all but disappeared except for occasional occurrences among such groups as the twelfth century Waldenses and Albigenses and such personalities as Francis of Assisi, Francis Xavier, and Dominic.

The third period, from the seventeenth through the nineteenth centuries, is designated the *Later Showers*. During this period, there were noteworthy outbursts of glossolalia. The phenomenon occurred among the Huguenots of France. The Ranters, who flourished in Britain during the Commonwealth era (1648–60), likewise experienced glossolalia. So did the early Quakers. A particularly remarkable pentecostal effusion occurred in England during the nineteenth century under the leadership of a Scottish Presbyterian pastor named Edward Irving. Mother Ann Lee, founder of the Shakers, who were heirs of Wesleyan and Quaker tenets, demonstrated pentecostal tendencies.

The fourth period, from about 1900, is designated the *Latter Rain*. Pentecostals believe that Pentecost all but disappeared from the Church for upward of 1500 years during the second and third period with only occasional showers. For half a century prior to 1900, many restless Christians had been praying for the promised Latter Rain. Between 1830 and 1905, isolated revivals of the Spirit brought promise of it. The Latter Rain did not break suddenly upon the world in one massive downpour, but began in scattered showers falling here and there before the real, torrential storm broke. Among the early raindrops of the Latter Rain expectation were the Welsh revival from 1904 to 1906, and the efforts of Charles Parham and other holiness adherents in the United States. It was at Azusa Street, however, the watershed of pentecostal history, where the Latter Rain poured.

There is obviously great danger in formulating some single theory of history and forcing the facts to fit the thesis. Adherents of the theory that twentieth century pentecostalism represents the

Latter Rain of the Spirit's activity in history must use caution and be open to the eclectic approach which emphasizes diversified causes to explain events. Belief in the Latter Rain theory presupposes a "faith" stance. I share and embrace such a stance unashamedly.

Perspective may be defined as a sense of proportion in viewing and judging things in their proper relationship. Previous studies on pentecostalism have not viewed black pentecostalism in its proper historical context because of a failure to appreciate the full spectrum of the heritage of blacks who were numbered among the early pentecostals.

To appreciate this assertion, we must first examine the broad background of pentecostalism. Nineteenth-century Methodism, the parent of the American holiness movement, is the most important historical religious tradition involved.

From the point of view of the history of doctrine, several influences should be acknowledged: (1) The holiness movement developed largely from adherents to Wesley's doctrine of sanctification who felt that the general stream of his followers had declined. (2) Pentecostalism with its emphasis on an instantaneous Baptism in the Holy Spirit, an event subsequent to conversion, took its cue from the Methodist-holiness quest for an instantaneous experience of sanctification, a "second blessing," or a "second work of grace" after justification. (3) Contemporary pentecostalism developed from the extreme left wing of the holiness movement among adherents who took seriously Wesley's doctrine of perfection. (4) Most of the leading black pentecostal leaders, while Baptist denominationally, followed the Wesleyan brand of sanctification.

Origin of the Holiness Movement

Under the influence of Jeremy Taylor, William Law, and Thomas a Kempis, Wesley had been driven to strive after "purity of intention," the core of his later doctrine. Wesley's *Plain Account of Christian Perfection* is now recognized as the doctrinal foundation of the holiness movement. For Wesley, sanctification, considered as a whole, is a process of development which begins at the very moment a person is justified.[1] Perfection is the completion of sanctification begun at regeneration. Perfection for Wesley meant one thing, purity of motive.

> It is nothing more nor less than that habitual disposition of the soul which, in sacred writings, is termed holiness; and which directly implies, the being cleansed from sin, "from all filthiness both of flesh and spirit," and by consequences, the being endued with those virtues which were also in Christ Jesus; the being so "renewed in the spirit of our mind," as to be 'perfect as our Father in heaven is perfect. . . .' Perfection in the sense of infallibility does not exist on the face of the earth.[2]

Charles Finney, born one year after Wesley's death, is referred to as the institutionalizer of revivalism, and is considered by some to be the second most important influence on early classical pentecostal belief. Bruner states that it was Finney's revival methodology that was the shaping influence on Methodist theology in the holiness churches, and formed the major historical bridge between Wesleyanism and modern pentecostalism.[3]

Methodologically, American revivalism has been the most important formative influence on the modern pentecostal movement. It was Sweet who stated that "revivalism . . . in a real sense may be characterized as an Americanization of Christianity, for in it Christianity was shaped to meet America's needs." [4] Indeed, it was especially through the preaching of Charles Finney and Dwight Moody toward the end of the nineteenth century that revival methodology became an important influence in American Christianity and the American churches. In the milieu of interconfessional revivals and holiness camp meetings, the modern pentecostal movement was formed.

McLoughlin refers to the holiness movement as the second wing of Protestantism and points out the similarity between the religious tenets of holiness believers and those of all pietistic movements since the Reformation. "These tenets consisted of an extremely literalistic reliance upon the Bible, a puritanical morality, pessimistic or escapist outlook on world history, and a perfectionist view of the meaning of salvation." [5] Older denominations were tempted to refer to holiness believers as "holy rollers," "come-outers," or "radical fringe" groups.

The Classical Pentecostal View

Between 1880 and 1907, the Methodists split into holiness and anti-holiness factions, because of a controversy over Wesley's doctrine of sanctification. The pentecostal movement began during the height of the turmoil. Several revivals accompanied by glossolalia occurred during the turn of the twentieth century almost simultaneously in the south and western sectors of the United States.

It was during this period that the Reverend Charles Fox Parham, a native of Muscatine, Iowa, started his ministerial career as a supply pastor in the Methodist Episcopal church in Kansas, and first isolated glossolalia as the evidence of the Baptism of the Holy Ghost, thereby laying the doctrinal foundations of the movement more than anyone else. It was at Bethel Bible College, Topeka, Kansas, January 1, 1901, under the leadership of Parham that the Baptism of the Spirit fell first upon a Miss Agnes N. Ozman, who spoke in tongues. Parham's Baptism came on January 3 along with that of several students, and under the influence of this new zeal, they sought to evangelize Missouri and Texas.

The classical[6] or old-line pentecostal interpretation of the origin of the modern pentecostal movement emphasizes the linkage of the Baptism in the Holy Spirit with the evidence of glossolalia. J. Roswell Flower, former General Secretary of the Assemblies of God, a major exponent of the classical view, says in reference to the pentecostal experience of Agnes Ozman:

This decision to seek for a Holy Spirit baptism with the expectation of speaking in tongues was a momentous one. It made the pentecostal movement of the twentieth century.[7]

It appears that Flowers' point of view prompted historian John Nichol to infer that this event was significant, not because Miss Ozman had spoken in tongues, for there had been sporadic outbursts of glossolalia throughout the history of the Church, but "that for the first time the concept of being baptized or filled with the Holy Spirit was linked to an outward sign—speaking in tongues."[8]

Unfortunately, Nichols is lured on by Klaud Kendrick's recommendation that a narrative of modern pentecostalism should begin with Charles Fox Parham,[9] and he hails him as the father of contemporary pentecostalism, a distinction not given to him by the leaders of the larger pentecostal groups. Vinson Synan, who has written one of the best accounts of the pentecostal movement, explains this disparity when he asserts that "most pentecostal writers acknowledge Parham's place as the formulator of the pentecostal doctrine," but that "none call him the father of the movement because of later questions about his personal ethics."[10] Donald Gelpi, a Jesuit priest, who theologizes about pentecostalism in his historical survey, *Pentecostalism: A Theological Viewpoint*, uncritically refers to Parham as the leader of American pentecostalism and reminds us that Parham preached a pentecostalized Wesleyanism.[11]

A study of several classical pentecostal writers on the issue of the founding of the contemporary pentecostal movement reveals for the most part a denominational bias and an apparent omission of the role of blacks. Conn, in his superbly written account of the Church of God, escapes the charge of denominational bias regarding the founding of the movement by clearly stating in his introduction that *Like a Mighty Army* is not a history of the pentecostal movement as a whole but of the Church of God, which is the oldest of the pentecostal groups.

Unlike Conn, some classical pentecostal historians fail to come to grips with their denominations' pre-twentieth century classification as holiness churches and write as though they were pentecostal from their inception. Furthermore, to convene a meeting where individuals received the Baptism of the Holy Spirit was not unprecedented, as the historical evidence has shown. However, the almost totally unplanned efforts of W. J. Seymour, a descendant of African slaves shipped to America, were unprecedented. The spiritual dynamism generated from that simple black mission in Los Angeles caused Frank Bartleman to emphatically state that "the color line was washed away in the blood." It is unfortunate that the blatant omission of Seymour by some classical pentecostal historians is so obvious and becomes a form of judgment on our ethnic and racial pride. That Seymour was an important figure in the twentieth-century outpouring is established in the following account from an eyewitness.

Let the Redeemed of the Lord Say So—Mack E. Jonas Interview

The following interview between the late Bishop Mack E. Jonas (1886–1973) and the author took place on October 3, 1971, in Cleveland, Ohio. Bishop Jonas was one of the first blacks to receive the Baptism of the Holy Ghost in the now renowned Azusa Street revival of 1906, the fountainhead of the contemporary pentecostal movement.

L.L.   Bishop Jonas, about how old were you when you received the Baptism of the Holy Ghost?

B.J.   I was about twenty years old.

L.L.   What kind of work were you doing at that time?

B.J.   I was working with the Pacific Creaming Co.

L.L.   How did you hear about the revival?

B.J.   A lady on Peters Street asked me had I been to the revival. I told her I didn't know about the revival going on. She told me it was happening on Azusa Street and asked me to come down. I had never been down, but when I did go, it was on a Sunday evening, I think it was . . . yes, it was on a Sunday evening. I sat back and listened to them testify. I had never been in a meeting like that before, so I went back on Wednesday. I sat back again and heard them testify and went back to my room and didn't go back anymore until that Friday night, and that Friday night was the twentieth of April, 1906. I went to the altar that night.

L.L. The Lord baptized you with the Holy Ghost?

B.J. No, not that night. I didn't get the Baptism of the Holy Ghost until the twenty-ninth of June, the same year, 1906.

L.L. Who was leading the prayer services?

B.J. An old gentleman by the name of Hiram Smith.

L.L. Was he leading the prayer services when you received the Baptism of the Holy Ghost?

B.J. Yes, he was.

L.L. I see. Was Brother Seymour on hand at that time?

B.J. He was there every night—every night.

L.L. And Hiram Smith?

B.J. He's what you might call a devotional leader. But Brother Seymour had started services.

L.L. What about the services held on Bonnie Brae Street?

B.J. Well, that was before I found the mission. I never did go to it on Bonnie Brae Street, but that's where a cottage meeting was held at Brother Asbury's house. There Sister Janie Moore received the Baptism of the Holy Ghost. She was the first one to receive the Baptism of the Holy Ghost on April 9, 1906, on Bonnie Brae Street.

L.L. Do you remember meeting Brother Seymour personally and talking with him?

B.J. No, I never met him before I got saved.

L.L. But after you were saved, did you talk with him?

B.J. Oh yes, after we met and went to church. He kept very much to himself and was very prayerful, a very quiet man.

L.L. Did you know Brother Charles Fox Parham?

B.J.   Yes, but I didn't meet him until he came to Los Angeles, late in the year of 1906.

L.L.   Specifically what did you hear about him?

B.J.   Well, I heard about the meeting, I heard he was the first one preaching the light of the Baptism of the Holy Ghost. I think he had a Bible School in Topeka, Kansas. And from there, he went to Houston, I believe it was, yes, Houston, and had a revival there in a tent meeting. I heard that the white and colored was meeting together, but he kind of separated the white on one side and colored on another side. That was before Brother Seymour went to Los Angeles.

L.L.   Why do you think he separated the blacks and whites?

B.J.   Well, it was in the south, and people didn't believe in white and colored mixing, and going to the altar, bowing together in prayer like that.

L.L.   Do you believe that affected Brother Parham's ministry? Do you believe that it kept him from being as effective as he would have been?

B.J.   Well, I was in the city, but Elder Seymour left Dallas, I think.

L.L.   Houston, I believe.

B.J.   And went to Los Angeles. In Los Angeles he had his meeting, everybody went to the altar together. White and colored, no discrimination seemed to be among them. I heard Brother Parham preach about twice. He came to Azusa Street and he preached. He and a bunch of other missionaries were traveling together, but anyway, he didn't stay in Los Angeles long.

In 1907 I left Los Angeles. Of course I was there in 1907 when Bishop Mason came out. [Bishop Charles Harrison Mason founded The Church of God in Christ.]

L.L.   Oh, you remember Bishop Mason coming to Los Angeles?

B.J.   Yes sir, I shook hands with him right on the grounds.

L.L.   He was sanctified when he arrived, wasn't he?

B.J.   Oh, yes, both of them, he and Elder D. J. Young. Three of them came together, he, Elder D. J. Young and Elder John Jeter.

L.L.   Based on your observation of the leadership in the Azusa Street revival, who would you say should rightly be called the father of the pentecostal movement?

B.J.   Seymour! Seymour!

L.L.   Seymour?

B.J.   Yes sir, he's the one that started that work.

L.L.   I see, I see. There is a school of thought that says Brother Parham should be called the father of the pentecostal movement, because four students received the Baptism of the Holy Ghost in his school, and Brother Seymour was one of them, and they say he should be rightly called the father of it. But based on your observation, what really happened? Did Brother Seymour lead the Azusa Street meeting?

B.J.   Yes, he was the one. He had met Brother Parham and probably worked under him before he came to Los Angeles. Seemed like this discrimination was separating, keeping the white and colored from worshiping together. That's when he left, was it Dallas? Was it Houston? Houston! And went to Los Angeles. He, Elder Warren, and Sister Farrow. They were his workers. Elder Seymour, Elder Warren, and Sister Farrow and, of course, the people fought them there, holiness people, white and colored. He was having meetings from place to place, sometimes at Bonnie Brae where the Holy Ghost first fell until they got a place on Azusa Street, where they opened an old Methodist church that had been damaged with fire.

L.L.   Do you remember when Brother Seymour received the Baptism of the Holy Ghost?

B.J.   No sir I do not. That was one of his fights he had to undergo while he was there. This man was preaching something, and he hadn't gotten it himself, but he kept preaching. He hadn't spoken in tongues even when I received it, but he was preaching it to white and colored both. Now I was the first colored man who got saved in the Azusa Street meeting.

L.L.   Is that so?

B.J.   Yes sir, I was the first one. People weren't gathering in when I went there in April, the fire hadn't spreaded—at least the people weren't coming in large numbers. The night I first went there, just a few were in there having services, and I sat and listened. They called people to come and be prayed for healing; they would go up—some say they were healed—but I had never seen nothing like that before. That was the first time I was ever in a holiness service.

On the basis of this eyewitness account and additional research, the writer doubts whether Parham assumed any kind of leadership role in the revival or was asked by William J. Seymour to help curb certain excesses. It is also doubtful that Parham's revival meetings were interracial in nature. Seymour, the one-eyed, unattractive apostle of Pentecost from Houston, defied the racist mentality of his time and opened the revival to everyone, a factor of supreme importance in explaining the success of the revival. Parham later ceased attending the Azusa Street meetings because of their "disgusting similarity to Southern darkey camp meetings." [12] In later years, Parham became a great supporter of the Ku Klux Klan.

Interracial Origins of Pentecostal Movement

John Hardon writes that two names stand out in pentecostal history: Charles Fox Parham and William J. Seymour. "Parham was white and Seymour a Negro, which partly explains the interracial character of most pentecostal churches." He further mentions that Parham's disciple, Seymour, carried the pentecostal message to California and attracted large crowds in the now famous Azusa Street revival. In three years, Azusa attracted the curious and fervent from all parts of America and even from overseas. [13]

Vinson Synan builds the best case for the interracial origins of the modern pentecostal movement. He admits the controversial nature of his position and, in a rather guarded manner, says that Parham and Seymour share roughly equal positions as founders of modern pentecostalism: Parham laid the doctrinal foundation of the movement, while Seymour served as the catalytic agent for its popularization. "The early Pentecostal Movement," says Synan, "could be classed as neither 'Negro' nor 'White,' but as interracial." [14] Interestingly, Synan refers to bishop R. L. Fidler of the Church of God in Christ as a Negro pentecostal who is pro-Seymour. Fidler, however, is a white man.

Synan concedes that Seymour was, in fact, the key figure in the Azusa Street meeting, a fact he claims is extremely important to pentecostals of all races. "While all pentecostals acknowledge their debt to Seymour, few are willing to recognize him as the founder of the movement." Synan further alleges that Negro pentecostals refer to Seymour as the "apostle and pioneer" of the movement and often attempt to demonstrate that the pentecostal movement began as a Negro phenomenon, later accepted by whites.[15]

The problem with Synan's and Hardon's interracial theories is that both fail to make the clear-cut critical distinction between the early interracial stages of the movement and the actual founding. Whites came to an already black Azusa Street revival. It may be safer to say that the Azusa Street revival was conducted on the basis of complete racial equality. But the question is not about interracial fellowship (though the sincerity of whites who claim to be in true fellowship with blacks can be challenged because they have refused to defy mores and prejudices by serving under black leaders), but rather about who was used by God to initiate a simple prayer service in a converted livery stable at 312 Azusa Street in 1906. The exponents of the interracial view are so eager to make their point that they fail to see that Parham's efforts, at best, were a continuation of sporadic light showers, while Seymour's Azusa Street revival was the torrential downpour that created a major worldwide flood. Even Synan admits:

The Azusa Street Revival is commonly regarded as the beginning of the modern pentecostal movement. Although many persons had spoken in tongues in the United States in the years preceding 1906, this meeting brought this belief to the attention of the world and served as the catalyst for the formation of scores of Pentecostal denominations. Directly or indirectly, practically all of the Pentecostal groups in existence can trace their lineage to the Azusa Mission.[16]

John Wycliffe was to the Protestant Reformation what Parham was to contemporary pentecostalism. Wycliffe was the dawn star of Protestantism, but Martin Luther was its catalyst. Seymour was to contemporary pentecostalism what Luther was to the Reformation, a major catalyst.

Black Origins of the Contemporary Pentecostal Movement: From a Stable to the World

In most discussions of early American revivalism, historians omit the active role of blacks, mentioning rather the impact of the revival on the institution of slavery. By the same token, it is far easier not to deal with the fact that "the tradition of violent possession (which is the same as 'spirit-possession') associated with the earliest camp meetings is far more African than European, and hence there is reason to hold that, in part at least, it was inspired in the whites by their contact with Negroes." [17] Herskovits describes the phenomenon of "spirit possession" as a "type of highly emotionalized religious and ecstatic experience commonly designated by such terms as 'filled with the Holy Ghost,' 'lost in the Spirit,' 'speaking in tongues and rolling.' " [18] Spirit possession by a deity is the outstanding manifestation of West African religion and is by no means undisciplined. "In the region of Africa from which the slaves were principally drawn, the outstanding aspect of religion is its intimate relation to the daily round." As a cultural anthropologist, Herskovits believes the slaves were not completely stripped of their culture upon their arrival in America. A number of "Africanisms" survived the brutal attempt to emasculate slaves. As

with the black spirituals, the "Africanisms" such as spirit possession, the dance, and shout songs are related to the functional
character of West African religion.[19]

It may be categorically stated that black pentecostalism emerged
out of the context of the brokenness of black existence. Interestingly, William J. Seymour, W. E. Fuller, first overseer of the black
wing of the Fire-Baptized Holiness Church of the Americas, C. H.
Mason, founder of the Church of God in Christ, and G. T.
Haywood of the Pentecostal Assemblies of the World, were the
sons of emancipated slaves. Their holistic view of religion had its
roots in African religion.

One cannot meaningfully discuss the origins of contemporary
pentecostalism unless the role of blacks is clearly defined and
acknowledged. Earlier historical accounts make little or no reference to William J. Seymour. But it was Seymour who opted to
respond to an invitation to preach at the Nazarene Church on
Santa Fe Street. His commitment to the belief that speaking in
tongues was the initial evidence of receiving the Holy Spirit
resulted in a padlocked church. It was with the determination of his
African forebears that he responded to the challenge of a bolted
door, and from a converted livery stable in the ghetto on Azusa
Street in Los Angeles in 1906, he transformed that bolted door into
an international gateway for the pentecostal movement. Without
instruments, choir, collections, advertising, or Madison Avenue
techniques—without any organized church support—people from
some thirty-five nations heard the message of Pentecost during this
three-year revival and returned to spread the news in their own
lands.

Not only did blacks initiate the Azusa Street meeting which is
now recognized as a "watershed" in pentecostal history, but for
many years they maintained interracial ties during a crucial period
in the history of American race relations. During the interracial
period of the movement between 1906 and 1924, many white
ministers from pentecostal fellowships, including the Assemblies of
God, were ordained by the late Bishop Charles H. Mason, founder

of the largest black pentecostal group, the Church of God in Christ.

"God chose what is foolish in the world to shame the wise" (I Cor. 1:27 RSV). When whites could not "Europeanize" pentecostalism (Parham led the way by speaking in derogatory terms of certain excesses at the Azusa meeting) and purge it of its "Africanisms," they separated and formed their own denominations. Thus white pentecostals conceded to the pressures of a racist society.

Black pentecostalism is what it is, for the most part, because of its own unique experience in America. Attempts to objectively evaluate black pentecostalism have been hampered by preconceived notions about such things as illiteracy, religious fanaticism, unrestrained emotionalism, and exhibitionism. Historically, some of these notions are justifiable, but they should not prevent a fair hearing. Black pentecostals would contend that their encounter with the Spirit defies theological interpretation at points because of its suprarational and supernatural character. Objective evaluations of black pentecostalism collapse before a dimension of spiritual effusion that cannot be prestructured, preplanned, preprogrammed or regulated.

The history of fragmentation and divisiveness among black pentecostals on such matters as the nature and function of charismatic gifts and Baptism has been a problem in objectively evaluating the movement. The paucity of historical material has also hampered objective evaluation. There are over ten "Churches of God," and tracing their history can be problematic. Or consider two entirely different denominations, the Free Church of God in Christ with headquarters in Enid, Oklahoma, founded in 1915 by J. H. Morris, which merged with the Church of God in Christ in 1921 (by 1925 it departed and adopted the name, Free Church of God in Jesus Christ), and the Church of God in Christ founded in 1895 by Charles H. Mason, with headquarters in Memphis, Tennessee.

Black pentecostals exalt personal encounter with the Spirit when they testify, "I went to a meeting one night, my heart was not right but the Lord followed me," or "I sing because I'm happy, I sing because I'm free." Some of the younger black pentecostals have now come to believe that even the serious task of liberation, which means freedom from personal hang-ups as well as from the bondage of the oppressor, cannot be fully accomplished until witnesses are endued with power from on high. Young black pentecostals such as James Forbes, Bennie Goodwin, and Ithiel Clemmons are at home with such themes as "saved, sanctified, baptized with the Holy Ghost for liberation." They point to such texts as, "God anointed Jesus of Nazareth with the Holy Ghost and with power; who went about doing good, and healing all that were oppressed of the devil; for God was with him" (Acts 10:38); "The Spirit of the Lord is upon me" (Luke 4:18); and "And Jesus returned in the power of the Spirit into Galilee" (Luke 4:14).

Black pentecostalism affirms with dogmatic insistence that liberation is always the consequence of the presence of the Spirit. Authentic liberation can never occur apart from genuine pentecostal encounter, and likewise, authentic pentecostal encounter does not occur without liberation. No man can genuinely experience the fullness of the Spirit and remain a bona fide racist. This was demonstrated during the early pentecostal movement and is evident in some phases of the neo-charismatic movement.

In the early days of the pentecostal outpouring, we learn of G. B. Cashwell, a white man and a seeker after the Baptism of the Holy Spirit. He experienced revulsion, however, when in the providence of God it was a group of blacks who first laid hands on him. Only later did he receive the gift when in deep repentance he sought out William Seymour and several other blacks to pray for him. The conviction of the Holy Spirit broke his racial pride and unlocked a floodgate of blessing.

There is a power in the world that can bridge racial, denominational, national, cultural, and class barriers. It is not too late for the nation to respond. If America hears, she can be saved; if not, she will be destroyed from within.

NOTES

1. Thomas Jackson, ed., *The Works of John Wesley* (Grand Rapids, Mich.: Zondervan, 1959), XI, 442.
2. *Ibid.,* p. 394.
3. Frederick Dale Bruner, *A Theology of the Holy Spirit* (Grand Rapids, Mich.: Eerdmans, 1970), p. 37.
4. William Warren Sweet, *Revivalism in America: Its Origins, Growth and Decline* (New York: Charles Scribner's Sons, 1945), p. 11.
5. William G. McLoughlin, Jr., *Modern Revivalism: Charles Grandison Finney to Billy Graham* (New York: Ronald, 1959), p. 466.
6. "Classical pentecostals" refers to the early pentecostals whose public image entailed many elements such as emotionalism, fanaticism, theological and biblical fundamentalism, and an apocalyptic eschatology. However, there are areas of classical pentecostalism where such negative elements were not typical.
7. J. Roswell Flower, "Birth of the Pentecostal Movement," *The Pentecostal Evangel,* November 26, 1950, p. 3.
8. John Thomas Nichol, *Pentecostalism* (New York: Harper and Row, 1966), p. 7.
9. Klaud Kendrick, *The Promise Fulfilled: A History of the Modern Pentecostal Movement* (Springfield, Mo.: Gospel Publishing House, 1961), p. 36.
10. Vinson Synan, *The Holiness–Pentecostal Movement in the United States* (Grand Rapids, Mich.: Eerdmans, 1971), p. 99.
11. Donald L. Gelpi, *Pentecostalism: A Theological Viewpoint* (Paramus, N.J.: Paulist Press, 1971), p. 31.
12. Synan, *op. cit.,* p. 180.
13. John A. Hardon, *The Protestant Churches of America* (Westminster, Md.: Newman Press, 1957), p. 170.
14. Synan, *op. cit.,* p. 168.
15. *Ibid.*
16. *Ibid.,* p. 114.
17. Melville J. Herskovits, *The Myth of the Negro Past* (New York: Harper and Brothers, 1941), p. 231.
18. *Ibid.,* p. 211.
19. *Ibid.,* pp. 214–15.

Aspects of the Origins of Oneness Pentecostalism

DAVID REED

David Reed serves as the rector of St. Paul's Episcopal Church in Shelton, Connecticut. He is a Ph.D. candidate in theology at Boston University where his dissertation topic is, "The History and Theology of Oneness Pentecostalism."

Although Reed is an ordained Episcopal clergyman, his birth and background were in the oneness pentecostal tradition. His family was prominent in the United Pentecostal Church in eastern Canada. Now a trinitarian, Reed writes with considerable understanding about the movement which he now calls "evangelical unitarian pentecostalism."

The "Jesus' name" or "oneness" movement is one of the perplexing developments in the early days of the pentecostal revival in the United States. The following article sheds light on the theology of the early oneness leaders. A major theme is Reed's attempt to place the oneness pentecostals in the evangelical mainstream of American church history.

IN the history of our world, many new movements have been born in the womb of expectancy. The worldwide pentecostal camp meeting set in Los Angeles in April, 1913, was no exception. It had been advertised for months, and the crowds were overwhelming. A well-known and powerful evangelist, Mrs. Woodworth-Etter, was the leading preacher for the month-long revival. Hundreds were receiving the Baptism in the Spirit and being healed. As Frank Ewart reports, the preachers "had no need to come all the way from their own churches to get in a revival, for they had revivals at their home churches." [1]

Anticipation was heightened by the fact that this meeting was probably the high-water mark in the early pentecostal revival. Adherents were increasing at a phenomenal rate. And within a year, plans would be made to consolidate and organize the efforts of these pioneers.

What finally occurred during the revival that had historical import was recorded by one who was present, Frank Ewart.[2] With hearts now prepared, the mood of expectancy was heightened by a sermon from Jeremiah 31:22 assuring the listeners that God was going to perform a "new thing" in their midst.

The moment came at a baptismal service during which a Canadian evangelist, R. E. McAlister, in an exhortation, pointed out that the apostles baptized not in the triune formula but in the name of the Lord Jesus Christ.

The congregation was visibly startled, and McAlister was straightway informed that a Dr. Sykes of heretical reputation so baptized. Notwithstanding McAlister's immediate effort to qualify his statement publicly, it was too late.

Many were provoked to thought, and one, John G. Scheppe, was inspired to study and prayer throughout the night. In the early hours of the morning, he ran through the camp, shouting that the

145

Lord had shown him the truth on baptism in the name of Jesus Christ. Many listened, and not long hence, many believed.

While Scheppe left no account of his revelation, and his name appears again only in the clergy lists of the early non-trinitarian organizations, the one to reap the future benefit of McAlister's catalytic observation was Ewart. He reports that he spent many hours with McAlister after the revival; and following a year of study on the subject of baptism, he preached his "first public sermon on Acts 2:38, on April 15, 1914." [3]

Just how much of the doctrine Ewart gleaned from McAlister and Scheppe is difficult to determine. We do know that, after the camp, McAlister shared with Ewart the following insight:

> Lord, Jesus, Christ, being the counterpart of Father, Son, and Holy Ghost, . . . made Jesus' words in Matt. 28:19, one of those parabolic statements of truth, which was interpreted in Acts 2:38 and other scriptures. [4]

Scheppe's revelation at the camp seems also to have concentrated on the name of Jesus. [5] Harry Morse, a later oneness leader who was present and heard Scheppe expound his views, recalls that he listened attentively to "Brother Scheppe's new ideas on water baptism and the oneness of the Godhead." [6] This may indicate some rudimentary beginnings of the oneness doctrine of God, but it is more probable that the revelation dealt with the name of Jesus as carrying the full power and authority of the Godhead. This would be in line with McAlister's insight and also Ewart's admission that it was not until later that he personally received the "full revelation" of the radical oneness of God in Jesus Christ:

> It was long after this preacher [McAlister] had left the city of Los Angeles, where I had a pastorate, before the revelation of the absolute Deity of our Lord Jesus Christ, burst upon me. I saw that as all the fullness of the Godhead dwelt in Jesus, bodily; therefore, baptism, as the Apostles administered it, in the Name of the Lord Jesus Christ, was the one and only fulfillment of Matt. 28:19. [7]

In other words, the oneness revelation was initially and primarily a discovery of the name of God as used in Christian baptism.

It was only after Ewart had preached his first sermon on the new message that the baptismal formula received its full theological justification in a unitarian concept of God. The link between the two was developed by harmonizing Matthew 28:19 and Acts 2:38, whereby the name "Jesus" was interpreted to be the singularly revealed name of the Father, Son, and Holy Spirit. From this point onward, the movement spread rapidly within the pentecostal ranks.

That this new revelation eventually claimed nearly one-fifth of all American pentecostals warrants calling the 1913 camp meeting an historic event. The adherents were first known as "Jesus only," which finally gave way about 1930 to "Jesus' name" and "oneness," and more recently to "Christian monotheists." [8]

Oneness Theological Origins

The main teaching as it emerged centers on the name of Jesus as the dispensational revelation of the name of God. The primary clue is found in Matthew's use of the singular form of the word "name" with reference to Father, Son, and Holy Spirit. Excluding the charge of poor grammar on Matthew's part, oneness teachers contend that the only plausible explanation is that the apostles knew something that has been lost to most of the Christian church since apostolic times; namely, that Jesus was speaking of his own name. And this was confirmed, they contended, when they observed in Acts that the apostles indeed obeyed Christ's command and baptized in the name of the "Lord Jesus" or "Jesus Christ."

It was probably this attempt to harmonize the two passages, along with an analysis of them, that more than anything else contributed to the eventual denial of the doctrine of the Trinity. Matthew 28:19 is the one passage in Scripture that embodies the triune formula which was later applied to the doctrine of God. When the oneness leaders pointed out the conflict between the apostolic and later church practices on baptism, it is no surprise that the conflict extended to the doctrine of the Trinity itself.

The only explanation of the Trinity with which these protestors were likely to be familiar was the one common within certain segments of Protestantism, which interprets the "three persons" as three distinct intelligences and conscious wills, yet one God.[9] But their impatience with what seemed in this to be incipient tritheism was only a secondary reaction. More crucial was the conviction that the trinitarian doctrine actually seemed to minimize the full revelation of God in Christ. If only one person in the Godhead became incarnate, they believed the mathematical conclusion conflicted with Paul's clear teaching that, "In him [Christ] dwelleth all the fulness of the Godhead bodily" (Col. 2:9).

On such a trinitarian scheme, Jesus was neither the *full* revelation of the Deity nor the revelation of the *full* Deity. Ewart reacted against this very situation when he wrote that he received the revelation of "the absolute Deity of the Lord Jesus Christ." [10]

Andrew D. Urshan, another early oneness preacher and writer, shared the same suspicion of the subordination of Christ in the trinitarian doctrine:

> In these days of ours, not only are thousands of so-called Christians denying the absolute Deity of our Lord, But those who believe it are trying to preach Him feebly as God the Son, and by so doing they think they have gone to the limit of exalting "The Lord of Glory." [11]

The truth about God and Christ for oneness pentecostals is rooted in the Old Testament doctrine of God and the oft-ignored doctrine of the name of God. Any plurality in the nature of God is straightway rejected on the grounds of the radical monotheism of the Old Testament (e.g., Deut. 6:4, Isa. 43:10). And the two concepts of nature and name are linked together by the ancient notion that a person and his name are inseparable. The name serves to reveal the person. Indeed, all the power that a person possesses can be taken up in and demonstrated through His name.

Thus God was known to His covenant people through the revealing of His name. His nature was so bound up with His name that the revealed name of God, YHWH, was as sacred as Yahweh

Himself, worthy of adoration and pregnant with divine power. God's giving of His name was, in fact, an act of giving Himself, because it was only through His name that He was known.

As with other Christians, oneness pentecostals interpret the messianic prophecies in terms of Jesus and transfer to Him the prerogatives and characteristics of God Himself. In fact, they frequently use the same arguments as Trinitarians to prove the full deity of Jesus, but do so to discredit what they believe to be the trinitarian doctrine of a divine but subordinate Son. Their dual insistence on the radical unity of God and the related doctrine of His name gives them a distinctive hermeneutical approach to the Son of Mary: He is not the incarnation of the second person of the trinity but the *full* revelation of the *one* God of Israel, whose finally revealed name for this dispensation is *Jesus*.

The traditional interpretation of the name "Jesus" is that it refers to the human person, and the various Christological titles, such as "Christ," "Lord," and "Son of God," direct us to His deity. Oneness exegetes, on the other hand, interpret the name "Jesus" as a divine appellation. Just as Yahweh was the divine name of God in the Old Testament, so Jesus is His divine name in the New.

This name was divinely given to Joseph by the angel: "And she shall bring forth a son, and thou shalt call his name JESUS: for he shall save his people from their sins" (Matt. 1:21). And Peter witnessed to the fact that salvation resided only in that name: "Neither is there salvation in any other: for there is none other name under heaven given among men, whereby we must be saved" (Acts 4:12). Jesus himself declared: "I am come in my Father's name" (John 5:43). And to prove that where the Father's name is there is the Father, they refer to the messianic prophecy in Isaiah 9:6: "His name shall be called Wonderful, Counsellor, The mighty God, *The everlasting Father* . . ." (italics mine). It is not the Eternal Son then who becomes incarnate in Mary but the Father Himself. The Son is the human body that was begotten in Mary, but His deity is that of the Father. The Son is the "face of God," [12] the "express image" (Heb. 1:3) of the Father, the visible manifestation of the invisible God. In other words, our knowledge and experience of God is a radically Christocentric one: only in the human face of the Son and in His name can one see the Father. Not that the Father and the Holy Spirit are absorbed in the Son, but He who was in the human Son is the one divine Person who is elsewhere called Father and Holy Spirit.

Oneness teachers, therefore, reject the accusation by some trinitarians that they deny the Father, insisting they reject only the idea that He is a "separate and distinct person" [13] from the Son. Since God is a transcendent and omnipresent Spirit, it is impossible to confine Him to a human body. Yet all that God is, is seen in Jesus Christ. A. D. Urshan summarizes this view:

> He [Jesus] was on earth yet at the same time He was in heaven. He was in heaven, yet He was on earth. So our Lord, as eternal God, the Spirit, is everywhere invisible; but, as God manifested in the flesh, He was on earth bodily. Not two Gods, but one Omnipotent God, who is the Son according to His blessed humanity, but God the Almighty, according to His absolute Deity. [14]

In response to the trinitarian charge, G. T. Haywood, one of the outstanding black pentecostal leaders and an early convert to oneness, wrote:

> There is no one who knows the word of God, and has been baptized in Jesus' name, that denies the Father and the Son. They acknowledge the Father and the Son in Christ Jesus. . . . The Fatherhood of God is found only in the Son, who was God manifested in the flesh. [15]

Much of the confusion was due to a misunderstanding in terminology. When oneness teachers asserted that the whole Godhead was in Jesus Christ, they were referring to Jesus, in His person and name, as revealer of the whole Godhead. Ewart stated it this way: "In the Apostles' doctrine, Jesus was the visible manifestation of the invisible God, both in name and nature." [16]

It should be pointed out that the oneness leaders did not actually deny some form of the trinitarian scheme, and in fact did express their doctrine of God in the terminology of the Father, Son, and

Holy Spirit. For instance, the *Articles of Faith* of the United Pentecostal Church state:

> We believe in the one everliving, eternal God: infinite in power, Holy in nature, attributes and purpose; and possessing absolute, indivisible deity. This one true God has revealed Himself as Father, through His Son, in redemption; and as the Holy Spirit, by emanation.[17]

Nathaniel A. Urshan, son of A. D. Urshan, defined the triune reality in a similar way:

> We do not believe in three separate personalities in the Godhead, but we believe in three offices which are filled by one person. Those offices are the office of the Father, the office of the Son and the office of the Holy Spirit.[18]

Other alternatives to the "three separate and distinct persons" were three "aspects," "forms," and "manifestations" of the one God.[19]

The decisive point of conflict between the two doctrines was the question of the nature of this divine threefoldness. Words such as "offices," "aspects," and "manifestations" suggested at best a functional trinity, whereas the words "hypostases" and "persons" sprang from a distinctly ontological one. While the one acknowledged only a trinity of revelation, the other grounded it in the very being of God.

While most oneness exponents maintain a strong unitarian view of God's being apart from His revelation, there is the occasional acknowledgment that a distinction exists within the Godhead. Thus Urshan admitted in 1919:

> I personally cannot refrain from believing that there is a plurality in God's mysterious Being, and that this plurality is shown as a three-ness, not three separate, distinct Beings or Persons, but a mysterious, inexplicable, incomprehensible three-ness.[20]

Elsewhere he likened this threeness to the elements of heat, light, and power.[21]

More recently, a similar opinion was expressed by Kenneth Reeves:

> The size of God being what it is, and the multi-intelligence that He possesses . . . indicate that there is a vast internal communication within God. The intercession of the Spirit within believers indicates some form of communication.[22]

With neither man did the crucial distinction between time and eternity become problematical. They proceeded to speak of God solely in terms of His redemptive activity. The theological consequences of limiting the Trinity to time and history never arose. And it was precisely this limitation that was the crucial one in defining the oneness view as unitarian.

The problem of distinction was further compounded by the lack of clarity in Scripture itself. There is extremely little speculation on the nature of God apart from His redemptive work. And although the New Testament writers began the task, it remained a delicate process of transferring the triune revelation back into the very being of God.

The distinctive oneness doctrine concerning God and Christ, as it centered in the person and name of Jesus, reached its full expression in the sacrament of water baptism in the name of the Lord Jesus Christ. Perhaps more than anything else, it was the issue of rebaptism that heaped on the early oneness disciples the contempt of their trinitarian counterparts. And it is still today the primary issue for oneness people. There is certain latitude permitted concerning the doctrine of the Godhead, but one proves his ultimate allegiance to Christ only when he takes on His name in baptism.

The theology of baptism varied within the oneness ranks. But they all agreed that full obedience to the Gospel called for baptism according to Acts 2:38. This singular act, they said, brought the promise of power through the invocation of the name. One must be buried in that name in order to receive the power it bears. Ewart rather boldly suggested that the Church had been deprived of this power since the end of the apostolic age because the name was missing. But,

> When we received a revelation of the true meaning of the commission, in Matt. 28:19, it instantly brought our practices and precepts in line

with those of the Apostles, and miracles again attended the use of the name.[23]

A second "benefit," if you like, of bearing the name was persecution.[24] Scattered through oneness literature is the theme that the one who takes on the name of Jesus should expect maltreatment even as Jesus Himself.

With their particular view of baptism, oneness pentecostals have been harshly accused of "baptismal regeneration and unevangelical ritualism." [25] Many teach that according to Acts 2:38 and other baptismal passages the primary purpose of baptism is to remit one's sins and make him a child of the Kingdom. Since there is salvation in no other name, and one appropriates that name definitively in baptism, then the rite of baptism is in some way salvific.

Although the distinction may be only semantic, oneness teachers have protested this identification with baptismal regeneration, pointing out that the efficacy is not in the water but in the name. Ewart wrote that "the theory of Baptismal regeneration . . . is absolutely without scriptural backing." [26] And Urshan elaborated on the importance of the name by showing that its distinction from water is that of essence from mode. While water is the "true mode of baptism," [27] the "essence of baptism is in the Name of Jesus and not in the water, and the Name of Jesus is the saving Name of God our Saviour." [28]

To this baptism in the name of Jesus Christ was added the promise of the Baptism in the Holy Spirit, thus forming a "water-Spirit baptism" couplet. The "water-Spirit birth" couplet in John 3:5 (i.e., "born of water and of the Spirit") was then harmonized with the baptism couplet in Acts. The result is a rather sectarian doctrine of the new birth that has influenced many oneness people to regard their trinitarian brethren as little more than "God's chosen exceptions."

Oneness Origins in American Revivalism

Having now summarized the distinctive theology of the oneness movement in its most representative forms, we are ready to return to the historical question of origins.

Unlike many religious movements, the oneness movement began within and has remained an integral part of the modern pentecostal phenomenon in America. Except for its distinctive doctrines of God, Christ, and baptism, its beliefs are essentially the same as those of its counterpart, the Assemblies of God.[29]

In the broadest sense, pentecostal origins are rooted deeply within the American religious spirit. This tradition adopted the qualities of independence, pragmatism, and concern for the common man, which resulted in an openness to new and innovative insights and experience.

The particular expression of American religion inherited by pentecostalism was the great revivalistic tradition of the late nineteenth century. Geographically, pentecostalism follows the same pattern of concentration as its predecessors; namely, through the south, middle west, and Pacific coast.[30]

This pietistic form of revivalism placed great emphasis on what William Warren Sweet calls "the religion of the heart, rather than a religion of the head." [31] It is this same spirit that gave birth to the oneness revelation. Scheppe, Ewart, and others were motivated not by cold logic but by a heartfelt devotion to Christ and the Bible. Commenting on the new revelation, Ewart observed: "Mere intellect cannot open the treasury of the Name of God. God speaks to the heart. If the heart is dead, the Name is sealed." [32]

The burning passion of revivalism was the salvation of souls. The cross of Christ and its power to transform the life of a sinner is preached with unwavering devotion. And, characteristically, one cannot overlook among oneness pentecostals this same passion for practical results. It is apparent in the persistent appeal to the power of God manifested when the name of Jesus is proclaimed.

Another characteristic of revivalism is its subjective and practical use of the Bible. That the Bible is the "only religion of Protestants" is given manifold evidence in the writings and sermons of its preachers. But, as H. Richard Niebuhr points out, "Gospel experience alone could convince of gospel truth." [33] Objective truth was of little value unless it produced subjective experience.

Oneness pentecostals have been accused of appealing to extra-biblical revelation for their doctrine.[34] But it is obvious that the leaders themselves intended only to apply the same principle as their predecessors; namely, that the source of the doctrine is the Bible itself, confirmed practically in the community by the power that accompanies it.

This concern for practicality deeply affected the attitude of the revivalists toward doctrine. While distinctive doctrines came out of such movements as millenarianism, fundamentalism and the holiness movement, there was little interest in the doctrine of the Trinity, and the orientation was predominantly Christocentric. An excellent illustration appears in a sermon preached by Henry Ward Beecher in the 1850s, attacking the liberals of his day:

> Could Theodore Parker worship my God?—Christ Jesus is his name. All there is of God to me is bound up in that name. A dim and shadowy effluence rises from Christ, and that I am taught to call Father. A yet more tenuous and invisible film of thought arises, and that is the Holy Spirit. But neither are to me aught tangible, restful, accessible. . . . But Christ stands my *manifest* God. All I know is of him and in him.[35]

This tendency, with its application in the conversion experience, remained in revivalism. William McLoughlin points to this singular theme as it was adapted by Billy Sunday:

> Sunday succeeded in reducing the systematic theology which Finney had taken five hundred pages to elaborate, into a single sentence of ten words: "With Christ you are saved; without him you are lost." [36]

Although they professed to believe in the Trinity, one cannot help but feel that they simply borrowed an orthodox formulation and used it pragmatically to support their strong belief in the deity

of Christ and His work on the cross. Their anti-creedal bias and
impatience with speculative thinking shielded them from a clear
understanding of the theological issues that brought about the
Nicene and Chalcedonian formulations. The following comment
by the revivalist, Sam P. Jones, is applicable to many within his
tradition:

> If I had a creed I would sell it to a museum. . . . It was over creed that
> men fought, and not over Christ. Orthodoxies are what has ruined this
> world.[37]

Although strong on biblical teaching, earliest pentecostalism
shared the same suspicion of creeds and man-made doctrines,
perhaps in part because they in particular had been on the
receiving end of doctrinal heresy-hunters. Had it not been for the
oneness controversy, it is probable that the pentecostal movement
would have been satisfied with a brief statement of the one God,
eternally existent in three persons: Father, Son, and Holy Spirit.

The prayers and gospel songs of revivalism likewise reflected a
truncated Christocentric view. McLoughlin points out that Sunday
would frequently open his prayer with, " 'Now Jesus, you
know . . .' or 'Well, Jesus, isn't this a fine bunch here tonight?' "[38]
Perhaps an extreme example, it serves to point out the fact that the
highly structured trinitarian liturgical collects and prayers of
orthodoxy are conspicuously absent.

A cursory glance at the gospel songs that were born in the
frontier camp meeting will show their non-doctrinal content and
Jesus-centered piety. The adoration historically accorded "God the
Father Almighty, Maker of Heaven and Earth" is now transferred
to "Jesus, Lover of My Soul." H. Richard Niebuhr calls this
phenomenon in itself a form of Christo-unitarianism or "practical
monotheism of the Son."[39] Referring to the Christocentric hymns,
he says:

> Such expressions are not indeed necessarily exclusive of devotion to
> the Father and the Spirit, but practically the whole thought about
> God is concentrated here in the thought about the Son; he is the sole
> object of worship and all the functions of deity are ascribed to him.[40]

Finally, the Christocentrism of the millenarian movement of the last century helped pave the way for oneness pentecostalism. Although firmly trinitarian in its theology, the overriding concern was the eschatological hope of Christ's second coming and our living forever under His reign.

This shift in revivalistic piety from orthodox creeds and speculation on the Trinity to a full-orbed Christocentrism in worship, thought, and practice was undoubtedly a major factor in the appearance of the oneness movement.

Oneness Origins in Early Pentecostalism

When this phenomenon finally did appear in 1913, it must have looked like a radical innovation to many fellow pentecostals. But there were elements within the early revival itself that were conducive to the emergence of such a movement.

First, all early pentecostals depended heavily upon the guidance of the Holy Spirit. Not intending to add revelation to Scripture or go beyond it, they believed in the subjective confirmation of biblical truth. While trinitarian pentecostals occasionally charge their oneness brethren for claiming a subjective revelation,[41] it must be remembered that it was the same principle of interpretation that established the "initial evidence" teaching in pentecostalism just a few years earlier. In December of 1900, Charles Parham had been teaching at Bethel Bible College on the Baptism in the Holy Spirit and had reached an impasse concerning the proper evidence of the experience. He departed for three days, leaving his students to study the Bible thoroughly on the subject and on his return report their findings. To his amazement, the unanimous decision was that speaking in tongues was the initial physical evidence of the Baptism.[42] For Parham, then, the common mind of the student body was sufficient sign for divine confirmation of the doctrine.

Secondly, the early pentecostal revival was fertile soil for the proliferation of many new ideas. The confusion that resulted

apparently forced the first steps toward organization. Howard
Goss' classic statement on the state of affairs is enlightening:

> A preacher, who did not dig up some new slant on a Scripture, or get
> some new revelation to his own heart ever so often . . . was
> considered slow, stupid, unspiritual.[43]

Consequently, whatever future damage it might have caused, the
initial revelation at the 1913 camp meeting was probably not in
itself a radical departure from the spirit of early Pentecostalism.

Third, and most important, is the fact that the early pentecostals
expended their energies in an intensive study of one book in the
New Testament above all others, the Acts of the Apostles. And it is
precisely here that we find the apostolic pattern of baptism in the
name of Jesus Christ and a high preponderance of the expression,
"in Jesus' name."

In sum, the fact that the oneness revelation swept through the
pentecostal movement like wildfire so that at one point it threatened to engulf it, is ample confirmation for the idea that the early
revival was charged with a belief in divine confirmation to the soul,
a spirit of expectancy, and a body of devotionally laden themes
from the apostolic Church. Without these ingredients, the new
revelation may have been considerably less spectacular.

Oneness Doctrinal Roots

We must finally turn to the distinctively doctrinal roots of the
oneness movement, dealing respectively with baptism in Jesus'
name, the name of God in Jesus Christ, and the oneness of the
Godhead.

The practice of baptism in the name of Jesus Christ is no new
phenomenon in the history of the Church. Martin Luther encountered a dispute over the formula in his day.[44] G. T. Stokes referred
to certain Plymouth Brethren and other sects in Great Britain who
used the exclusive formula of Acts 2:38.[45] And there are still
occasional reports of individuals and groups that are trinitarian in

doctrine but practice baptism in the name of Jesus Christ.[46] Carl Brumback confirms that, "Some had used the shorter formula for years, so its use was no drastic innovation." [47]

We know that Charles Parham became concerned over the right formula as early as 1902 and switched to the Acts pattern temporarily.[48] As with the "initial evidence" doctrine, he received the divine confirmation when he and his students were, "waiting upon God that we might know the scriptural teaching on water baptism." [49] Howard Goss was converted in 1903 under Parham's ministry and confirms that he was baptized in Jesus' name.[50]

Andrew Urshan was convinced of the propriety of the apostolic formula as early as 1910 and immediately began to baptize his converts in Jesus' name.[51] But it was not until 1919 that he officially affiliated with the oneness movement.

Thus there was sufficient precedent, even among pentecostals, for the use of the apostolic formula. What was new after Ewart's year of study was the insistence on *re-baptism* supported by a strong doctrinal base in the name. Were it not for this, perhaps a spirit of liberality might have prevailed sufficient to prevent a schism.

There seems to have been a revival of interest in the name of God in Jesus Christ during the latter part of the nineteenth century and continuing into the twentieth. It may, in fact, have been during this period that the prayer ending "in Jesus' name" became common. Finney, during an instruction on prayer, stated:

> If you intend prayer to be effectual, you must offer it in the name of Christ. You cannot come to God in your own name. . . . But you can come in a Name that is always acceptable. . . . Now Jesus Christ gives you the use of His name.[52]

Also, R. A. Torrey admonished, "We should pray in the Name of Jesus Christ." [53]

A number of works were written during this time that show a growing interest in a theology of the name. In *Is God a Trinity?* (1876), John Miller, a "high-Calvinist" Presbyterian minister, suggested that the singular "name" in Matthew 28:19 can make sense only if applied, as did the apostles, to the Lord Jesus Christ:

Why does it say "name"? . . . Our blessed Lord was God and man. As "Lord," he was the Greek for Jehovah; as "Jesus" he was Jehovah a Saviour; as Christ, he was an Anointed Man.[54]

This non-trinitarian treatise survived through a third edition in 1922.

A work by R. D. Weeks, *Jehovah-Jesus*, also published in 1876, was later rediscovered and edited by a oneness leader, C. Haskell Yadon. Although not representative of most oneness teaching on the Godhead, it is anti-trinitarian and teaches that the *one* Jehovah is fully revealed as Jesus Christ. This belief is substantiated, among other ways, by reference to the two names:

JESUS signifies JEHOVAH SAVIOR: and the reason assigned for giving him this name, shows that it was significant of divinity; no other than God can save from SIN. This latter term is applied to God and to Christ indiscriminately and repeatedly in this sense.[55]

Andrew Urshan sought out many writers who had taught on the name of God in Christ. He frequently published extracts of their writings along with his own. One, J. Monroe Gibson, stated in his book, *Christianity According to Christ* (1888):

The name of God is that by which He has made Himself known to us, specially in the course of revelation; above all, the two great names of "Jehovah" in the Old Testament and "Jesus" in the New.[56]

Urshan quoted similar passages on the name of Jesus from other sources such as *Sunday School Times*, the *Sunday School Illustrator*, and what appears to have been a Yahwist magazine at the turn of the century, *Eusebia*.[57] He also mentioned lectures on the name of God by F. L. Chapell,[58] who was a professor at Gordon Bible College and disciple of the prominent millenarian leader, A. J. Gordon.[59]

Essex W. Kenyon's, *The Wonderful Name of Jesus* (1927), is an excellent example by a leading fundamentalist of a comprehensive treatment of the name of Jesus. Kenyon taught that it is through this name the power of the person and work of Jesus is made present in the Church today: "All He was, all He did, all He is and all that He ever will be is in that Name now." [60]

As if to culminate an era, a lay scholar by the name of William Phillips Hall was commissioned by Arno C. Gaebelein to do an intensive study on the name of God in Scripture. After years of study, he published in 1929, *Remarkable Biblical Discovery, Or "The Name" of God According to the Scriptures.* Ewart read it with fascination, and oneness people continue to refer to it. But unlike the oneness emphasis on the name of Jesus, Hall discovered that the power and authority needed in the Church and for the salvation of men is enshrined in the name "Lord":

> Not only should they believe in Him as Lord, but they should confess His Name Lord, as the Name of God, the Name of all that God is, in prayer for salvation.[61]

From this, Hall concluded that it is essential to be baptized in the name of the Lord Jesus Christ. Ewart reported the effects of this discovery:

> It is a matter of fact that thousands of people, after reading Mr. Hall's book, . . . were baptized into the Name of Jesus the Christ, and not a few ministers among them.[62]

A partial answer to why such a "name" movement appeared at this period in history may lie in the critical condition of the Church. Suffering from external erosion by the new science and internal sterility by skepticism, the Church was seeking ways to regain her authority and spirituality. Since one of the critical debates in the fundamentalist-modernist battle was over the virgin birth and deity of Jesus, certain students of the Bible claimed to discover the defense they needed in the scriptural teaching on the sacred name.

First, an analysis of the name of the Lord Jesus Christ yielded a cogent biblical argument for His full deity. In his foreword, Hall remarked that had his discovery not been lost to the Church, "it appears that there never would have been any doubt whatever among Christians of the Deity of the Lord Jesus Christ." [63]

Secondly, a study of the name of Jesus reveals the power available when it is invoked. The supernatural power manifested in the apostolic Church can be present today. Oneness literature abounds in such assurances of divine power. And in a personal letter to Ewart, Hall expressed this hope:

> I believe and trust that through the reception and application of the truth of the Name of God, as set forth in my book, the pure faith and power of the early church may be restored to us in this end time.[64]

And as I mentioned above, Kenyon interpreted the name of Jesus as the means legally given the Church to make present the full reality and power of the absent Lord.

Thus by means of a "theology of the name," the American evangelical church attempted to renew in its day the authority of Christ by reestablishing His full deity and power. And to this movement, oneness pentecostalism has made its contribution.

Finally, let us look at the doctrinal roots of the oneness view of God. Embedded deeply within the broad anti-trinitarian tradition, these pentecostals were first known by the name "Jesus only." It was soon dropped for doctrinal reasons, since it suggested, as some trinitarians still insist,[65] a denial of the Father (i.e., a form of Patripassianism). This accusation was vigorously repudiated by their leading exponents as early as the twenties.[66] The designations "Jesus name" and "oneness" are satisfactory for common identification but lack the sense of historical "linkage." The title "Christian monotheism" is too limiting as it judges the historic Christian Church by negation as tritheistic. On such an assumption, trinitarians are, by definition at least, not even Christian.

Since these designations fail theologically and historically to describe the movement, I shall offer the title, "evangelical unitarian pentecostalism." I believe this title describes the movement in terms of the broader evangelical unitarian stream that has always existed in Christendom.

The oneness movement is unitarian in the sense that it is one of the many anti-trinitarian protests within the history of the Church. A. L. Clanton, a oneness editor, denies any similarity between the oneness pentecostals and unitarians, except in their common rejection of the doctrine of the trinity.[67] I agree that much of popular opinion associates unitarianism with the liberal movement in New England. But, as H. Richard Niebuhr points out, there are really three forms of unitarianism, each focusing on one of the persons of the trinity.[68] While there are those "unitarians of the Son" or of Jesus who do deny the deity of Christ, many do not. These place a great emphasis on revelation instead of reason, and on redemption through the shed blood of Christ. They affirm both His deity and His humanity. To this category, I give the appellation "evangelical." And it is to this segment of "evangelical unitarians" that the oneness pentecostals belong.

Even within the unitarianism of New England, there was in the mid-nineteenth century an evangelical revival which Timothy Smith rightly calls, "Evangelical Unitarianism." [69] Quoting Frederic Dan Huntington, pastor of South Church in Boston, Smith records:

> A large group of Unitarians believed the essence of Christianity to be a "special, supernatural redemption from sin, in Christ Jesus" the "eternally begotten Son of God," the "ever-living present head of the Church and personal intercessor for his disciples." [70]

On these evangelical themes of redemption, there is great similarity with what Clanton describes as fundamental beliefs of oneness pentecostals:

> Oneness Pentecostals believe in the Virgin Birth of Jesus, and that He was therefore divine. He was God manifest in the flesh. They further believe that without the shedding of blood there could have been no redemption.[71]

An excellent illustration of evangelical unitarianism in the last century stemming from other than the New England tradition is the book by John Miller mentioned earlier, *Is God a Trinity?*[72]

Miller denied being a Socinian, Arian, Pelagian, or Arminian. A
Presbyterian minister in Princeton, New Jersey, he confessed to be
"high Calvinist in all the realities of my creed." [73] In place of the
"Platonic trinity," he set forth a view of God that "puts the
WHOLE GODHEAD in Christ" [74] and recommended the apostolic baptismal formula, "in the Name of the Lord Jesus Christ." [75]
Within his Christo-unitarian proposal, he held the evangelical
doctrines of incarnation, redemption, mediation, intercession,
regeneration, justification, adoption, sanctification, the final judgment, and the glorification of the redeemed. [76]

Regarding God, "no hypostatic difference separates off the
Father from the Son; but the One God is Emmanuel, God with
us." [77] Not the second hypostasis of the Trinity but Jehovah
Himself became incarnate in the human Son of Mary. Consequently, the only appropriate name of Jehovah is LORD JESUS
CHRIST, "the One Glorious Name (sing.), enthroned as Father,
enshrined as the Son, and engrafted as the Holy Ghost." [78] In sum,
in all its major points, Miller's doctrine was almost a duplicate of
the doctrinal position of the later oneness pentecostals.

Although there may be theological deficiencies in the evangelical
unitarian scheme, it should be pointed out that there appears to be
nothing *substantially* different from trinitarianism that would
endanger the Gospel. They share with trinitarians a basic commitment to Scripture and revelation as over against the liberal
unitarians, on the one hand, who assert reason over biblical
revelation, and the sectarian unitarians, on the other, who posit a
revelation equal and additional to Scripture. That oneness pentecostals, therefore, be regarded as "hopeless heretics" is an obvious
overreaction in light of the evangelical tradition to which they
belong.

Thus oneness pentecostalism can be interpreted as being neither
a totally new innovation nor merely the reoccurrence of an ancient
heresy. But both aspects are present in a religious phenomenon that
has blended together devotional and doctrinal themes already
inherent within its own revivalistic and pentecostal traditions.

Unfortunately for the pentecostal movement, it was the unique and the heretical combined with the zealotry of the early oneness protagonists' that, combined with trinitarian pressure, within months brought about their final alienation from the pentecostal fellowship. The year of 1915 was a stormy one, full of conversions and counter-conversions, charges and countercharges, conferences and clashes.

The final showdown came in October, 1916, at the Fourth General Council of the Assemblies of God held in St. Louis. When the dust had finally settled, over one-fourth of the ministerial and assembly membership was missing.

Amidst rumors of their demise, the new movement reappeared within a year in organizational form.[79] Its growth to one-half million members in over twenty organizations in the United States can still be traced to the appeal it had in 1913.

NOTES

1. Frank J. Ewart, *The Phenomenon of Pentecost* (St. Louis: Pentecostal Publishing House, 1947), p. 76.
2. *Ibid.*
3. *Ibid.*, p. 51.
4. *Ibid.*, p. 77.
5. Carl Brumback, *Suddenly From Heaven—A History of the Assemblies of God* (Springfield, Mo.: Gospel Publishing House, 1961), p. 191.
6. Quoted in Arthur L. Clanton, *United We Stand: A History of Oneness Organizations* (St. Louis: Pentecostal Publishing House, 1970), p. 16.
7. Frank J. Ewart, *The Name and the Book* (Chicago: Daniel Ryerson, 1936), p. 40.
8. Kenneth V. Reeves, *The Godhead* (2306 Grand Avenue, Granite City, Ill.: The author, 1971), p. 6.
9. R. A. Torrey, *What the Bible Teaches* (New York: Revell, 1898), p. 20.
10. Ewart, *Name*, p. 40.
11. Andrew D. Urshan, *The Almighty God in The Lord Jesus Christ* (1121 S. Mott St., Los Angeles: The author, 1919), p. 10.
12. *Ibid.*, p. 81.
13. This was Urshan's favorite expression to describe the doctrine of the Trinity.
14. Urshan, "The Divinity of Jesus Christ, Or the Absolute Deity of the

Son of God According to the Old and New Testament," *The Pentecostal Witness*, 3 (April 1, 1927), 2.

15. G. T. Haywood, "Dangers of Denying the Father," *The Pentecostal Outlook*, 1 (April, 1932), 3.

16. Ewart, *Name*, p. 118.

17. *What We Believe and Teach—Articles of Faith of the United Pentecostal Church* (St. Louis: Pentecostal Publishing House, n.d.), p. 3.

18. Nathaniel A. Urshan, *Consider Him—David's Son and David's Lord* (Indianapolis: The author, n.d.), p. 12.

19. See Reeves, *op. cit.*, pp. 18, 29.

20. A. D. Urshan, *Almighty God*, p. 77.

21. Andrew D. Urshan, "The Blessed Trinity of God Revealed in Nature and Demonstrated or Personified in Jesus Christ Our Lord," *The Pentecostal Witness*, 3 (July 1, 1927), 2–3.

22. Reeves, *op. cit.*, p. 19.

23. Ewart, *Name*, p. 79.

24. See *ibid.*, chap. 6.

25. Brumback, *op. cit.*, p. 192.

26. Frank J. Ewart, "The Significance of Water Baptism," *The Apostolic Herald*, 16 (January, 1941), 12.

27. Andrew D. Urshan, *The Doctrine of the New Birth Or The Perfect Way to Eternal Life* (Cochrane, Wis.: Witness of God, Publishers, 1921), p. 35.

28. Andrew D. Urshan, "Twenty-seven Questions and Answers on the New Birth," *The Pentecostal Outlook*, 12 (August 1943), 11.

29. For a summary of the nineteenth-century origins of American pentecostalism, see William Menzies, *Anointed To Serve: The Story of the Assemblies of God* (Springfield, Mo.: Gospel Publishing House, 1971), chap. 1.

30. James H. Nichols, *History of Christianity; 1650–1950* (New York: Ronald Press, 1956), p. 273.

31. William Warren Sweet, *Revivalism in America: Its Origin, Growth and Decline* (New York: Scribner's, 1944), p. 25.

32. Ewart, *Name*, p. 85.

33. H. Richard Niebuhr, *The Kingdom of God In America*, Harper Torchbooks (New York: Harper & Row, 1959), p. 108.

34. Brumback, *op. cit.*, p. 202.

35. Quoted in Thomas J. Sawyer, *Who Is Our God? The Son or the Father? A Review of Rev. Henry Ward Beecher* (New York: Thatcher & Hutchinson, 1859), p. 3.

36. William G. McLoughlin, Jr., *Billy Sunday Was His Real Name* (Chicago: University of Chicago Press, 1955), p. 123.

37. Mrs. Sam P. Jones, *The Life and Sayings of Sam P. Jones* (Atlanta, Ga.: Franklin-Turner Co. Publishers, 1907), pp. 461–62.

38. McLoughlin, *op. cit.*, p. 177.

39. Niebuhr, "The Doctrine of the Trinity and the Unity of the Church," *Theology Today*, 3 (October 1946), 371–84.
40. *Ibid.*
41. E.g., Brumback, *op. cit.*, p. 193.
42. Parham's account in Brumback, *op. cit.*, pp. 22–23.
43. Howard A. Goss, *The Winds of God—The Story of the Early Pentecostal Days (1901–1914)* (New York: Comet Press Books, 1958), p. 155.
44. John Dillenberger, ed., *Martin Luther*, Anchor Books (Garden City, N.Y.: Doubleday, 1961), p. 297.
45. G. T. Stokes, *The Acts of the Apostles, vol. 1*, vol. 17 of *The Expositor's Bible*, ed. W. Robertson Nicoll (New York: A. C. Armstrong and Son, 1903), p. 140.
46. E.g., Dr. Aberhart, former Premier of Alberta, Canada, whose radio ministry and Prophetic Bible Institute were well-known during the thirties and forties. Personal letter from Cyril Hutchinson, President of Berean Bible College, January 8, 1974.
47. Brumback, *op. cit.*, p. 192.
48. Account in Fred J. Foster, *"Think It Not Strange"—A History of the Oneness Movement* (St. Louis: Pentecostal Publishing House, 1965), pp. 70–71.
49. Quoted in *ibid.*, p. 71.
50. Foster, *op. cit.*
51. Andrew D. Urshan, *The Life Story of Andrew Bar David Urshan: An Autobiography* (Stockton, Calif.: W. A. B. C. Press, 1967), p. 141.
52. William H. Harding, ed., *Finney's Life and Lectures* (Grand Rapids, Mich.: Zondervan, 1943), pp. 79–80.
53. Torrey, *op. cit.*, p. 445.
54. John Miller, *Is God A Trinity?* 3rd ed. (Princeton, N.J.: The author, 1922), p. 128.
55. C. Haskell Yadon, *Jehovah-Jesus: The Supreme God—Son of God, Son of Man* (304 5th Ave. East, Twin Falls, Idaho: The author, 1952), pp. 29–30.
56. Quoted in A. Urshan, *Almighty God*, p. 38.
57. That it is Yahwist is deduced from the fact that it consistently uses the Hebrew form "Yah-sous" when referring to Jesus.
58. Andrew D. Urshan, "The Name of God," *The Pentecostal Outlook*, 9 (January 1940), 4.
59. Ernest R. Sandeen, *The Roots of Fundamentalism—British and American Millenarianism–1800-1930* (Chicago: University of Chicago Press, 1970), p. 164.
60. Essex W. Kenyon, *The Wonderful Name of Jesus* (Los Angeles: West Coast Publishing Co., 1927), p. 42.
61. William Phillips Hall, *Remarkable Biblical Discovery Or "The Name" of God According to the Scriptures*, abridged (St. Louis: Pentecostal Publishing House, 1951), p. 23.

62. Ewart, *Name*, p. 139.
63. Hall, *op. cit.*, p. 7.
64. Quoted in Ewart, *Name*, p. 138.
65. See Carl Brumback, *God in Three Persons—A Trinitarian Answer to the Oneness or "Jesus Only" Doctrine Concerning the Godhead and Water Baptism* (Cleveland, Tenn.: Pathway Press, 1959), p. 48.
66. See Haywood, *op. cit.*, and *The Victim of the Flaming Sword* (Indianapolis: Christ Temple Book Store, n.d.), p. 51.
67. Arthur L. Clanton, "We Are Not Unitarians," *The Pentecostal Herald*, 42 (March 1967), 5.
68. Niebuhr, "Doctrine of Trinity," p. 372.
69. Timothy L. Smith, *Revivalism and Social Reform in Mid-Nineteenth-Century America* (New York: Abingdon, 1957), Ch. 6.
70. *Ibid.*, p. 95.
71. Clanton, *op. cit.*, p. 5.
72. Miller, *op. cit.*, first edition in 1876.
73. *Ibid*, p. 16.
74. *Ibid.*
75. *Ibid.*, p. 128.
76. *Ibid.*, p. 132.
77. *Ibid.*, p. 39.
78. *Ibid.*, p. 129.
79. The name of the organization that emerged from the schism with the Assemblies of God was the General Assembly of Apostolic Assemblies, being formed in January, 1917. One year later it merged with the Pentecostal Assemblies of the World, a small fellowship which, although dating back to 1907, actually became consciously oneness only after the emergence of the General Assembly of the Apostolic Assemblies. Prior to that it had been trinitarian.

The Hidden Roots of the Charismatic Renewal in the Catholic Church

EDWARD O'CONNOR, C.S.C.

Edward O'Connor, C.S.C., was born in Denver, Colorado, and grew up in Pittsburgh, Pennsylvania. In 1940 he entered the Congregation of the Holy Cross and in 1948 was ordained as a priest in the Roman Catholic church in Washington, D.C. He received the S.T.D. degree in theology from the Angelicum University in Rome in 1960. He has been a member of the Department of Theology at the University of Notre Dame, South Bend, Indiana, since 1952.

The author of several books on biblical themes, O'Connor is best known for his 1971 book, The Pentecostal Movement in the Catholic Church *(Ave Maria Press) which received the National Catholic Book Award for that year.*

O'Connor has been involved in the Catholic Charismatic Renewal group at Notre Dame since its inception in March, 1967. His influence in the Catholic Charismatic Service Committee has helped to coordinate the renewal among Catholics.

The following chapter sheds new light on the long process of preparation in the Catholic Church which ultimately bore fruit in the unexpected appearance of the

Catholic pentecostal movement. The crucial contributions of popes Leo XIII, John XXIII and Paul VI, as well as Elena Guerra and Cardinal Suenens, are especially important and moving.

IT is only a little over seven years since the first charismatic prayer meetings were held under Catholic auspices in the spring of 1967. In that time, the renewal has spread among Catholics all across the United States, into Canada, South America, Europe, Africa, and the far East. It is flourishing as far away as Australia and New Zealand, and in Rome itself there are several established groups of charismatic Catholics. No one has yet made a serious effort to determine the numbers of people involved, but the most conservative estimate would be that there are between 50,000 and 100,000.[1] This suggests that the soil was ready and waiting for the seed that fell on it. The present paper seeks to indicate the chief forces by which this renewal was being prepared for in advance, without anyone perhaps suspecting it.

Leo XIII and Elena Guerra

The most obvious and perhaps the most important preparation for the charismatic renewal within the Catholic Church was the encyclical letter, *On the Holy Spirit*, published by Pope Leo XIII in 1897.[2] In it, the Pope bemoaned the fact that the Holy Spirit was little known and appreciated,[3] and summoned people to renew their devotion to Him. This letter gave a routine summary, precise and authoritative but not otherwise remarkable, of Catholic teaching about the Holy Spirit. It spoke in a general way of the gifts of the Spirit, but said nothing specific about the charismata. Nevertheless, the simple fact of its appearance was important.[4] It was a sign from the highest authority in the Church drawing attention to the actual importance of this article of Christian faith. Millions of people either read the encyclical, or were touched by it indirectly through sermons, books, etc. A considerable number of valuable studies on the role of the Holy Spirit were stimulated in large part by this papal action.

It is natural to wonder what prompted Leo to publish this encyclical, which his more famous writings on the social order, on the restoration of Thomism, and on the divisions among Christians had hardly led us to expect. It seems, in fact, to have been one of the more charismatic acts in the career of this remarkable Pope. It resulted from the suggestion of an obscure Italian woman, Elena Guerra (1835–1914),[5] who had gathered a group of women into a sisterhood devoted to the Christian education of girls. The characteristic feature of Elena's spirituality was an indomitable and all-encompassing devotion to the Holy Spirit. It grieved her that most people thought so little of the Holy Spirit. Inspired by a practice she had learned as a child in her parish church, she used to recommend that the ten days between the yearly feasts of Ascension and Pentecost be spent in prayer and preparation for the gifts of the Spirit, in imitation of the Apostles in the Cenacle.* Eventually she had the audacity to write to Pope Leo, urging him to recommend this practice. To the amazement of many people who had tried to dissuade her, the Pope responded promptly by a letter officially endorsing her idea of a "new Cenacle." [6] Although the Pope had not met her, he told his counselors that if she had any other such inspirations for the welfare of the Church, they should be communicated to him.

With this encouragement, Elena wrote again, urging the Pope to establish this practice throughout the Church as a "permanent and universal Cenacle." This he did six months later, by the Encyclical *On the Holy Spirit*, which prescribed that every Catholic church should prepare for the feast of Pentecost by a novena of prayer.[7]

Moehler, Scheeben and the Theology of Charismata

While this action of the Pope seems to have been essentially a

---

* Upper Room.

charismatic and prophetic one, and not the result of any preceding theological or doctrinal currents, it did nevertheless harmonize with some theological developments taking place, especially in Germany. The three points relevant to us are: Moehler's ideas on the place of the Holy Spirit in the Church; Scheeben's theories on the work of the Spirit in individual sanctification; and the gradual rediscovery by historians of the role of charismata in the early Church.

Johann Adam Moehler's book, *Unity in the Church*, published in 1825, opened a new epoch in Catholic ecclesiology. It presented the Church as an organic community of life, derived from the Holy Spirit and expressed in mutual love.[8] The essence of Catholicism, Moehler declared, is man's participation in the divine life which the Holy Spirit imparts to him; and from this derives the rationale for its unity in doctrine and government.

These views were by no means original; Moehler's very thesis is that they represent the mind of the Fathers of the Church. Nevertheless, they came as a fresh new breath in the Catholic theology of that time, which, in its preoccupation with defending ecclesiastical authority against the encroachment of secular powers, the hostility of developing nationalism, the mockery of anti-clericalism, and the theologies of the Reformation, had become dominated by a juridical tone and an authoritarian outlook.

A few decades later, Matthias Scheeben (1835–88) drew the attention of theologians to the work of the Spirit in the individual Christian. His theology was above all an effort to make people aware of the heart of the mystery of grace: that the Father, Son, and Holy Spirit come to dwell in us. The habitual teaching of the schools, in its anti-Lutheran stress upon the intrinsic transformation of man produced by grace, had not sufficiently emphasized the divine presence. Also, traditional theology held that all three divine persons act as a unit in their dealing with creatures, and so are present and active in us in the same way. Scheeben felt that this did not do justice to the distinct role which Scripture seems to attribute to the Holy Spirit. Reviving and revising a theory ventured by Petau (1583–1652) two centuries earlier, he held that the Holy Spirit takes possession of us in a special way not shared by the Father and Son, as a kind of life-principle or "quasi-formal cause," divinizing us and uniting us with the Father and Son.[9]

This theory touched off one of the most animated debates in modern Catholic theology, which continued until the Second Vatican Council (1962–65) drew the attention of theologians to other problems. It led to a new theory of the divine indwelling, formulated by the Jesuit de la Taille in the slogan, "created actuation by uncreated act." [10] It likewise provoked a more assiduous study of the classical doctrine of the indwelling, which made it clear that the teaching of St. Thomas on this point, when grasped in its purity and richness, was far more dynamic and vital than had been realized.[11] But the significance of this debate did not lie so much in the theories proposed, which despite their formidable technical language were sometimes superficial and confused, but in its motive and effects. It was motivated ultimately by an acute dissatisfaction with theories which seemed, rightly or wrongly, not to account adequately for the personal, life-giving, joy-filling presence of the indwelling Spirit. And it had the effect of drawing attention to this truth which is the taproot of Christian spirituality.

The third current of theology that needs to be cited here may be described as a revalorization of the charismatic.[12] Whereas Luther, Calvin, and most of the Reformers rejected miracles, visions, and the like as no longer having any role to play in the life of the Church, Catholic theology and piety have always acknowledged a place for them. Nevertheless, in reaction against false mysticism, spiritual masters tended to stress the exceptional character of these graces, and to warn against the danger of believing them lightly or valuing them too highly. As a result, the notion of charism, while never denied or rejected, was largely neglected by Catholic theologians during the past few centuries.

This situation has recently changed, however, due largely to historical studies initially stimulated by the Lutheran historian, Augustus Neander.[13] In studying the origin of ecclesiastical office, he drew attention to the fact that charismatic figures had played a remarkably prominent role in the primitive Church. This point was taken up and pursued by scholars[14] who, for the most part, had no desire to promote the supernatural or the charismatic. They were often motivated rather by a certain animosity toward the institutional Church. Defenders of the institution, on the other hand, were compelled by such studies to acknowledge that besides the official leadership of the Church, there was also an important place for charismatics. Thus, the notion of charismatic which was scarcely mentioned in the standard theological manuals of the nineteenth century gradually recovered a place of respect.

As early as 1918, the French Dominican Clérissac maintained that most of the charismata, and prophecy in particular, were permanent endowments of the Church.[15] During the 1930s, several German theologians seeking to close the gulf between a desiccated academic theology and the actual spiritual life of the Christian people affirmed that theology is not merely a scientific discipline but also a *charism*, a grace-gift of the Holy Spirit for the building up of the Church.[16] During the 1940s and 1950s, due especially to Yves Congar, O.P., in France, and Karl Rahner, S.J., in Germany, it became a theological commonplace that the charismatic is an ordinary and essential factor in the life of the Church.

The Liturgical, Biblical Lay and Ecumenical Movements

The writings thus far considered helped to intensify an awareness of the Holy Spirit's action, but did not create a new climate in popular spirituality. Moehler's insistence on the role of the Holy Spirit in the Church, Scheeben's theory about the presence of the Spirit in the individual soul, and the thesis that the charismata still have a function in Christianity today, were the work of professional theologians who had direct influence only on small circles of their fellow theologians. Pope Leo's Encyclical had a much broader influence, but gradually it, too, fell largely into oblivion.

Other developments, however, although not specifically concerned with the Holy Spirit, had much to do with making the Catholic populace at large more conscious of Him. The liturgical movement, the biblical movement, the ecumenical movement, and what might be called the movement for rehabilitation of the laity, converged to bring about a lively new consciousness of the mystery of the Church.[17] This, perhaps the most significant development in the Catholic mentality during the first half of the twentieth century, tended to foster a greater awareness of the role of the Holy Spirit. Moreover, in various ways, these four movements prepared people directly for some of the particular fruits that were to arise out of the charismatic renewal.

Of the four, the liturgical movement is the oldest and has probably had the most powerful impact. In its first phase, it was concerned primarily with arousing a deeper appreciation of the liturgy and bringing about a better celebration of it. As the movement progressed, and sought for more persuasive arguments, it engendered reflection on the very nature of the liturgy as the prayer of the Church as such. The liturgy was recognized as a mystery of Christ still active in the Church by His Spirit.

A second movement, which promises to be even more significant in its long-range influence, is that of the gradual rediscovery of the dignity and responsibility of the Christian layman. In the regimen of Christian life which became established during the Middle Ages and remained set until the end of the eighteenth century, laymen had a relatively passive place in the Church. Ecclesiastical activity was regarded as the clergy's domain. But when the political and social upheavals of the eighteenth century effectively banished Christian influence from public life, both political and literary, a number of remarkable laymen emerged as effective spokesmen for the Church: in France, Chateaubriand, de Maistre, Veuillot,

Montalembert, Ozanam . . . ; in Germany, Goerres; in Great Britain, O'Connell; in the United States, Orestes Brownson.[18] The twentieth century saw a gradual recognition, initiated largely by Pope Pius X (1903–14),[19] that the lay apostolate is not only a surrogate for the work of priests when the latter are lacking or impeded from their proper function, but an integral component of the Church's action.

The theological foundation for this position is the participation of the laity in the priestly and prophetic ministry of Jesus Christ, which implies the anointing by the Holy Spirit which every Christian receives after the type of Christ Himself. The dignity and responsibility of the Christian layman were expressed thus by Vatican II:

> Since the supreme and eternal priest, Christ Jesus, wills to continue his witness and serve through the laity too, he vivifies them in his Spirit. . . . Besides intimately associating them with his life and mission, Christ also gives them a share in his priestly function of offering spiritual worship for the glory of God and the salvation of men. For this reason, the laity, dedicated to Christ and anointed by the Holy Spirit, are marvellously called and equipped to produce in themselves ever more abundant fruits of the Spirit.[20]

The third movement which we have to consider, the biblical movement, prepared for the charismatic renewal not so much by directing attention to the Holy Spirit, as by anticipating one of the most characteristic fruits of the renewal, the desire to read Scripture. In recent centuries, the Bible has been more reverenced than read by most Catholics. It was held in honor as the Word of God; but people were (not without reason!) apprehensive about the danger of heresy when Scripture is read by someone not adequately trained. Theologians and clergymen looked upon the Bible as the ultimate authority in their profession, but seldom read it simply as the word of the heavenly Father addressed to his children. Most laymen scarcely read it at all, but were content with the brief excerpts they heard each Sunday at Mass. There were of course beautiful exceptions, such as Thérèse of Lisieux or Elizabeth of the Blessed Trinity, but these were not typical.

It was the role of the biblical movement to restore Scripture to its due place in Catholic life and theology. It is important, however, to distinguish two levels on which it operated: that of scholarship, and that of religious experience. On the level of scholarship, the biblical movement brought about a great advance in scientific objectivity and competence: objectivity in reading the text for its inherent, native meaning, rather than with the preoccupation of settling arguments with which the text is not concerned; competence, in the mastery of the critical methods developed during the late nineteenth and early twentieth centuries.

During the first half of this century, Catholics, along with evangelical and fundamentalist Protestants, had many misgivings about these critical methods which were often used in a predominantly rationalist spirit that was corrosive of faith and made people insensitive to the authentically religious values of the Word of God. Church leaders motivated by essentially pastoral concerns sometimes failed to distinguish between intrinsic validity of methods which can teach us much about the human composition and motivation of the sacred Scriptures, and the prejudicial use to which they were put by those whose historic role it had been to invent and perfect them. (Today we tend to deal too harshly with the naïveté of these men who, despite their limitations, were maintaining the substantial truth of the Word of God.) But the passage of time clarified the issues, and the biblical movement brought about both a purification of the scientific and critical methods from the rationalism that had fostered them, and a recognition of their capacity to contribute powerfully toward a better understanding of the Word of God. Contact with sound exegesis has helped to safeguard Catholic charismatics from some of the distortions which a misguided literalism and fundamentalism have imposed on the pentecostal movement elsewhere.

However, it is not primarily at the level of scholarship that the biblical movement prepared for the charismatic renewal, but on the religious level. For the neglect of Scripture is not merely or even primarily an academic deficiency, but a privation of one of the main sources of nourishment for the Christian life. Moreover, the scientific study of Scripture does not *ipso facto* nourish spiritual growth. The exegete today, like the rabbi of Jesus' day, is prone to get entangled in his scholarship and fail to hear the real message of the Word of God.

Hence, the most significant effect of the biblical movement was to convince numbers of people, both clergy and laity, of the need to read Scripture regularly and prayerfully, not as an historical document, but as the living Word of the heavenly Father. The resulting familiar contact with the Gospel message helped many people to recognize the authenticity of the charismatic renewal.

However, it is hard to come to a lively personal appreciation of Scripture simply by dint of application. Many who tried failed; others persevered, but were reading the Bible out of a sense of duty, not because of an actual experience of its vitality. For such people, the effects of the biblical movement were simply to convince them about what Scripture *ought* to mean for them, even when in fact it did not. In their case, it has often been the charismatic renewal which effectively brought about the inner spiritual sense of and taste for Scripture that they had longed for.

The ecumenical movement is the most recent and least developed of the four movements we are describing, but its contribution to the charismatic renewal is the most obvious of all. Making its influence felt within the Catholic Church only a few years before the renewal, it made it possible for Catholics to be open to people of other denominations with much greater freedom than previously. This has been an important psychological factor in preparing people to accept such practices as spontaneous prayer, freer expression of religious emotion, glossolalia, and other practices usually associated with non-Catholic denominations.

There are other interesting relationships between the ecumenical and charismatic movements. Both originated in the Protestant world about the beginning of the present century. 1906 is the date of the Azusa Street revival in Los Angeles which turned pentecostalism into a world movement. 1910 is the date of the World Missionary Conference in Edinburgh, Scotland, which unleashed the modern ecumenical movement.

Neither of these movements received much welcome in the Catholic world for several decades. But during the 1950s, the ecumenical movement gradually won acceptance there, and the charismatic renewal followed a decade later. In the Protestant world, these two movements developed largely in a relationship of hostility to one another. Although exceptions are becoming more numerous in the present decade, most of the pentecostal denominations tend to regard ecumenism as the strategy of Satan, emasculating the Gospel. The ecumenists, on the other hand, generally have little patience for the enthusiasm and militant evangelism of the pentecostals, which at times seem to imperil the spirit of interdenominational understanding.

While some of these same tensions have occurred in the Catholic Church, on the whole, the charismatic renewal there has had a strongly ecumenical character from the outset. This is due partly to the historical fact that, in the beginning, it was often through Protestants that Catholics were introduced to the renewal. A deeper reason is the fact that one of the characteristic fruits of the pentecostal spirit is a loving readiness to accept all Christians as brothers and sisters in the Lord. Some would hold that the charismatic renewal holds out our greatest hope for an effective ecumenism in the future, that it is the Holy Spirit's own ecumenism. He brings the scattered children of God back into one in a way which men are unable to undertake: by pouring forth God's love in human hearts (Rom. 5:5).

The Mystical Body Consciousness

One of the notions that figured strongly in Adam Moehler's theology of the Church was that of the Body of Christ, the "Mystical Body," as it has traditionally been designated in Catholic thought, to distinguish it from the real or personal body in which Jesus lived His earthly life, and from the sacrament of His body, the Eucharist. However, this notion was not very congenial to the mentality of the nineteenth century, and for several decades only a thin stream of theologians and preachers made much use of it. Shortly after World War I, however, this mentality changed dramatically, due to a convergence of factors, not all of which are clear. Two of the more important, certainly, were the movements just described for the renewal of the liturgy and the lay apostolate, for which the doctrine of the Mystical Body provided an effective theological basis. Likewise, this doctrine responded to a deep hunger for spiritual growth and for human communion, that welled up in the aftermath of the war. At any rate, the idea of the Mystical Body seized hold of the Catholic consciousness with great power, and became probably the chief source of inspiration for spiritual and apostolic life, and the most intensely studied point of doctrine, during the 1930s and 1940s. Despite resistance and misgivings of many critics, sometimes provoked by the exaggerations of its proponents, the doctrine gained an irresistible hold, its highest authorization coming toward the end of the Second World War, with the publication of the encyclical, *Mystici Corporis*, by Pope Pius XII, in 1943.[21]

The Mystical Body movement, if it may be so called, or at any rate the spirituality of the Mystical Body, involves recognizing, on the one hand, that the Christian life is not an affair of isolated individuals, and on the other hand that the Church is not simply an assembly for public worship, but a vital communion of the faithful with one another in Christ. And it is the Holy Spirit, seen as the soul of the Body of Christ, who is the fundamental explanation of this mysterious communion, and the source of all its spiritual energy. Thus, in his encyclical, Pius XII says:

> Christ is in us through his Spirit, whom he gives to us, and through whom he acts within us in such a way that all divine activity of the Holy Spirit within our souls must also be attributed to Christ. . . .
> This communication of the Spirit of Christ is the channel through which those gifts, powers and extraordinary graces, found supera-

bundantly in the head as in their source, flow into all the members of the Church.[22]

Another implication of the Mystical Body concept, of no small importance, is that each member of the Church thereby comes to be seen as part of an organic whole, having his own proper charism and function, meant to be integrated with those of the other members of this body. Pius XII touched lightly but definitely on this point when he declared:

> To the members [the Holy Spirit] is present and assists them in proportion to the various tasks and offices and the greater or less grade of spiritual health which they enjoy. . . . It is he who, while personally present and divinely active in all the members, also acts in the inferior members through the ministry of the higher members.[23]

Thus this doctrine which was the mainstay of Catholic spirituality during the mid-twentieth century drew attention to the Holy Spirit as the proper source of the Church's vitality. No more appropriate preparation for the charismatic renewal could have been asked for; the spirituality of the Body of Christ almost compels a person to invoke the gifts of the Spirit.

There is a sign of this in a brief but nevertheless momentous reference to the charismata which occurs in the Encyclical. During the 1930s, reaction against an overly hierarchical conception of the Church had led some theologians, especially in Germany, to an excessive enthusiasm for its charismatic aspects. The Pope rejected both of these extremes, declaring:

> One must not think . . . that this ordered or 'organic' structure of the body of the Church contains only hierarchical elements and with them is complete; or, as an opposite opinion holds, that it is composed only of those who enjoy charismatic gifts—though members gifted with miraculous powers will never be lacking in the Church.[24]

This succinct affirmation of the limited but essential role of the charismata was to become the principal point of reference for all that would be said on this subject in connection with Vatican II.

Vatican II and the Recent Popes

Our final consideration has to do with the Second Vatican Council (1962–65) and the two popes who presided over it. John XXIII is widely regarded as one of the most charismatic figures of the twentieth century. He has been called, "a man completely docile to the Holy Spirit, a man who, completely free from himself, followed the path of the Holy Spirit." [25] There is no mistaking the touch of grace in the unpretentious simplicity with which he assumed his office, the rich, compassionate, and candid humanity with which he treated people, and the intrepid gaiety with which he undertook projects of immense magnitude and difficulty for the renewal of the Church. He emerged from the trappings and protocol of his office as a living person to touch the hearts of men everywhere, evoking and galvanizing their aspirations for a better world. This is all the more striking because he had been elected as an interim pope, an old man who was expected to do nothing except take care of the office in routine fashion until some more vigorous leader should emerge.

He conceived the Vatican Council, the principal work of his papacy, in pentecostal terms. Thus, he repeatedly alluded to the fact that the idea for it came, not as a fruit of reflection, but as a sudden inspiration when he was asking himself what he might do in favor of Church unity.[26] He compared the Council itself to a new Pentecost, in which the bishops of the world would gather around the successor of Peter, as once the apostles had gathered together with Peter, in the company of the Virgin Mary, to await the coming of the promised Paraclete.[27] He directed the whole Church to pray that the Holy Spirit would renew His wonders "in this our day as by a new Pentecost." [28] His last message to the assembled bishops predicted that when the Council had ended and its decrees been put into effect, "then will dawn that new Pentecost which is the object of our yearning." [29]

The Council itself proved to be a kind of experience and a discovery of the Holy Spirit by the assembled bishops. The first document to be taken up by the Council, the Constitution on the Liturgy, in its first draft contained almost no mention of the Holy Spirit.[30] When the bishops of Chile objected that this should not be so,[31] three references to Him were inserted into the Constitution (5 and 6).[32] From then on, however, things were different. The most important product of the Council, the constitution *On the Church*, gives a rich summary of the Holy Spirit's activity. The subsequent conciliar texts pursued the theme; altogether the Spirit is cited 258 times;[33] He is represented as the source of all true holiness and authentic activity, in the world and in the Church, for the clergy and for the laity, for light as well as for strength, for the community assembled in liturgy as well as for the individual in private prayer, for canonical and sacramental action as well as for spontaneous personal initiatives.

Several points in the Council doctrines have particular relevance to the charismatic renewal. Thus it is declared that, in addition to the grace of office conferred on the hierarchy, the Holy Spirit gives "special graces (charismatic gifts) to the faithful of every rank." Whether outstanding or commonplace, they are to be received with thanksgiving and used in the liberty of the Spirit, because they are useful for the upbuilding of the Church. On the other hand, the Council points out that this liberty of the Spirit is not meant to cover anarchic independence, because the gifts are to be used in communion with our brothers in the Church, and under the direction of the pastors, whose responsibility it is to pass judgment on the authenticity of the charismata, and to supervise their orderly exercise. The pastors themselves are twice cautioned "not to extinguish the Spirit" (I Thess. 5:12, 19–21).[34]

No previous Church document had ever spoken so expressly about the charismatic, and nothing prior to the Council would have led anyone to expect this statement, which was not even hinted at in the original draft of the Constitution on the Church. It appeared just in time to serve as the *Magna Charta* of the charismatic renewal, which was to get its start in the Catholic church within two years, although no one then could possibly have anticipated it.

The Council went on to make another point of almost equal importance. It declared that Christians of other denominations "are joined with us in the Holy Spirit, for to them also he gives his gifts and graces, and he is operative among them with his sanctifying power." [35] Since non-Catholic brethren have often been instrumental in leading Catholics to the Baptism in the Spirit, this text was crucial in reassuring the latter that such an experience is in no way prejudicial to their belief in the authenticity of the Catholic Church as the true fellowship in the Holy Spirit established by Jesus Christ, which the Council also affirms unambiguously.[36]

It was the Second Vatican Council that effectively brought to the attention of the whole Catholic populace the recognition of the charismatic which had been growing among the theologians. In the second draft of the *Constitution on the Church*, there was a reference to the value of the charismata which the Holy Spirit confers on the faithful.

> It is not only through the sacraments and Church ministries that the same Holy Spirit sanctifies and leads the people of God and enriches it with virtues. Allotting his gifts "to everyone according as he will" (I Cor. 12:11), he distributes special graces among the faithful of every rank. By these gifts he makes them fit and ready to undertake the various tasks or offices advantageous for the renewal and upbuilding of the Church, according to the words of the Apostle: "The manifestation of the Spirit is given to everyone for profit" (I Cor. 12:7). These charismatic gifts, whether they be the most outstanding or the more simple and widely diffused, are to be received with thanksgiving and consolation for they are exeedingly suitable and useful for the needs of the Church.

When this paragraph came up for discussion, Cardinal Ruffini of Palermo protested sharply against it:

> It plainly implies that in our age many of the faithful are endowed with many charismatic gifts; but this is plainly contradicted by history and by daily experience. For the charisms . . . were abundant at the beginning of the Church; but after that they gradually decreased and have almost completely ceased. . . . Contrary to the opinion of many of our separated brethren, who speak freely of the ministry of

charismatics in the Church, they are extremely rare and quite exceptional.[37]

Several days later (Oct. 23, 1963), Cardinal Suenens from Belgium replied:

> This document says very little about the charisms of the faithful; this can suggest the impression that we are dealing here with a phenomenon that is merely peripheral and accidental in the life of the Church. But it is now time to bring out more explicitly and thoroughly the vital importance of these charisms for the building up of the Mystical Body. We must at all costs avoid giving the impression that the hierarchical structure of the Church is an administrative apparatus with no intimate connection with the charismatic gifts of the Holy Spirit which are diffused throughout the Church.
>
> . . . To St. Paul, the Church of Christ does not appear as some administrative organization, but as a living, organic ensemble of gifts, charisms and services. The Holy Sprit is given to all Christians, and to each one in particular; and He in turn gives to each and every one gifts and charisms "which differ according to the grace bestowed upon us" (Rom. 12:6).[38]

This view prevailed, and the text was retained in the final, official version of the Constitution (section 12).

Pope John had already invited the Council to "read the signs of the times." This means nothing less than discerning the significance of the movement of history as God sees it, and it presupposes the intervention of the Holy Spirit in the secular world. Vatican II responded to his summons particularly by the Constitution, *The Church in the World Today*, which declared:

> The Church believes itself led by the Spirit of God, who fills the earth; motivated by this faith, it endeavors to read the signs of the times: the signs of God's presence and purpose in the events, needs and desires of our age.[39]

Further on, it adds that "God's Spirit, who providentially directs the unfolding of time, is not absent from the development of the social order." [40]

Finally, the closing paragraph of the Decree, *Ecumenism*, is worth noting. It urges both Catholics and non-Catholics to do what they can for the restoration of Church unity, "without prejudice to the future impulses of the Holy Spirit." [41] While it would be an exaggeration (and in fact a contradiction) to represent this statement as an anticipation of the charismatic renewal, we must not minimize the startlingly prophetic character of this clause in which the Council admonishes us that the Holy Spirit may take initiatives which surpass all our expectations; and that our human undertakings in favor of Church unity (and renewal) must always be kept open and subordinate to His.

Pope John died soon after the First Session of the Council which he had conceived and summoned; it was Pope Paul VI who had to preside over the completion of the Council and the implementation of its decrees. He has been so incessant in summoning the Church to attend to the hidden action of the Holy Spirit he may well deserve the name, *Pope of the Holy Spirit.* Space does not permit a summary of his teachings; only a few high points can be pointed out. He speaks repeatedly of the charismatic, both to stress its importance and to insist that it must not be separated from the institutional aspect of the Church. On the feast of Pentecost (May 23, 1973), in announcing the opening of a "Holy Year" or Jubilee Year, dedicated to renewal and reconciliation, he declared:

> All of us need to place ourselves windward of the mysterious, but now, in a certain way identifiable breath of the Holy Spirit. It is a fact not without significance that it is just on the blessed day of Pentecost that the Holy Year unfurls its sails in the individual local churches, so that a new 'navigation,' that is a new movement, really 'pneumatic,' that is charismatic, may drive believing humanity in one direction and in harmonious emulation towards the new goals of Christian history. [42]

In his most memorable statement on the Holy Spirit, Pope Paul in effect recapitulates all the developments and movements we have been summarizing:

> We have asked ourselves on several occasions what are the greatest needs of the Church. . . . What need do we feel, first and last, for this blessed and beloved Church of ours?

We must say it, almost trembling and praying, because it is her mystery, and her life, you know: the Spirit, the Holy Spirit, the animator and sanctifier of the Church, her divine breath, the wind in her sails, her unifying principle, her inner source of light and strength, her support and consoler, her source of charisms and songs, her peace and her joy, her pledge and prelude to blessed and eternal life (cf. *Lumen Gentium*, n.5).

The Church needs her perennial Pentecost; she needs fire in the heart, words on the lips, prophecy in the glance. The Church needs to be the temple of the Holy Spirit (cf. I Cor. 3, 16–17; 6, 19; II Cor. 6, 16), that is, of complete purity and inner life. She needs to feel within her, in the silent emptiness of us modern men, all turned outwards because of the spell of exterior life, charming, fascinating, corrupting with delusions of false happiness, to feel, we say, rising from the depths of her inmost personality, almost a weeping, a poem, a prayer, a hymn, the praying voice of the Spirit, who, as St. Paul teaches us, takes our place and prays in us and for us "with sighs too deep for words," and who interprets the words that we by ourselves would not be able to address to God (cf. Rom. 8, 26–27). The Church needs to find again the eagerness, the taste, the certainty of her truth (cf. Jn. 16, 13), and to listen with inviolable silence and docile availability to the voice, or rather the conversation, speaking in the absorption of contemplation, of the Spirit who teaches "every truth" (ib.). And then the Church needs to feel flowing through all her human faculties the wave of love, that love which is called and which is poured into our hearts "by the Holy Spirit who has been given us" (Rom. 5, 5).

Living men, you young people, and you consecrated souls, you brothers in the priesthood, are you listening to us? This is what the Church needs. She needs the Holy Spirit. The Holy Spirit in us, in each of us, and in all of us together, in us who are the Church.[43]

NOTES

1. A careful estimate made in January, 1973, revealed that there were approximately 37,500 Catholics enrolled in American and Canadian prayer groups registered at the Communication Center in South Bend, with an average of almost exactly forty per group. There was not enough information available to make even a rough conjecture for the number in the rest of the world at that time, but it was undoubtedly much smaller.

By June of 1974, the Center had registered 2,185 "Catholic Charismatic prayer groups" in the world, of which 1,631 were in the U.S., 264 in Canada, and 290 in the rest of the world (forty-three of them in Great Britain). If we suppose that the average of forty per group can be maintained for this figure, that would indicate a figure approaching 100,000 for Catholics in those groups at that date.

Such hazardous calculations are not to be mistaken for statistics; but unfortunately no serious statistical estimate has yet been made. I know of no grounds whatsoever for the estimates of 200,000, 300,000 or even "half a million," which have been appearing in the newspapers for the past year or more.

2. *Divinum Illud Munus, Acta Sanctae Sedis,* 29 (896–97), 644–58. English translation, *On the Holy Ghost* (New York: America, 1944).

3. *Ibid.*, p. 16 of the English translation.

4. It appeared, incidentally, just four years before the outburst of the pentecostal movement in Topeka, Kansas (January 1, 1901).

5. Cf. V. Gaudet, "A Woman and the Pope," *New Covenant*, 3, no. 4 (October 1973), 4–6.

6. Brief of May 5, 1895. *Acta Sanctae Sedis,* 27 (1894–95), 645–47.

7. A full account of Elena Guerra's life and of her correspondence with the Pope is given by L. Cristiani, *Apôtre du Saint-Esprit* (Paris: Apostolat des editions, 1963).

8. Johann Adam Moehler, *Die Einheit in der Kirche* (Tübingen: Laupp, 1825; mod. ed. with notes, Cologne-Olten, 1957), section 20.

9. I have given only a rudimentary summary of this complex and confused theory, which allows also for the Father and Son to be united with us directly by other titles. Cf. *The Mysteries of Christianity,* #27ff., especially #30. English translation by Vollert (St. Louis: Herder, 1951). This book appeared originally in German in 1867 and was revised in 1887 and 1888, after the publication of the *Handbuch der Dogmatik* (1883–87); hence it gives, as Vollert points out, Scheeben's final statement of his theory.

10. M. de la Taille, "Actuation Créée par Acte Incréé," *Revue des Sciences Religieuses,* 18 (1928), 253–68. Cf. De Letter, "Created actuation by uncreated act," *Theological Studies* (1957), 61–92.

11. For example, A. Gardeil, *La Structure de l'Âme et l'Expérience Mystique* (Paris: Gabalda, 1927); R. Garrigou-Lagrange, *Christian Perfection and Contemplation* (St. Louis: Herder, 1937).

12. I have given a detailed survey of this development in "The New Theology of Charisms in the Church," *American Ecclesiastical Review,* 161, no. 3 (September 1969), 145–59.

13. Neander's *General History of the Christian Religion and Church* began to appear in Hamburg in 1825. English translation, London, 1853 and following.

14. This interest has not yet by any means abated. Some of the most

important contributions to it have been made in the past three decades. The most recent survey of the problem is, *Le Ministère et les Ministères selon le Nouveau Testament* (Paris: Seuil, 1974).

15. Humbert Clérissac, *Le Mystère de l'Eglise* (Paris: Cerf, 1918). Cf. 5th ed., presented by J. Maritain, p. 81ff.

16. The chief spokesmen for this "charismatic theology" were Anselm Stolz, O.S.B., Thaddeus Soiron, O.F.M., and G. Söhngen. A resume of their positions with precise bibliographical references can be found in John Aurricchio, S.S.P., *The Future of Theology*, (Staten Island: Alba House, 1970).

17. There were, of course, other factors also contributing to this result, which cannot be gone into here. Cf. E. Ménard, O.P., *L'Ecclésiologie Hier et Aujourd'hui* (Bruges, Paris: Desclée de Brouwer, 1966).

18. Cf. Yves Congar, *Lay People in the Church* (London: Bloomsbury, 1951), pp. 359–60.

19. Letter to Cardinal Bertram, Nov. 13, 1928. *Acta Apostolicae Sedis*, 20 (1928), 384–87. Cf. *Ubi Arcano Dei, Acta Apostolicae Sedis*, 14 (1922), 673–700.

20. *The Church*, 34. Cf. *The Apostolate of the Laity*, 7.

21. *Acta Apostolicae Sedis* 35 (1943), 193–248. Several English translations have appeared, using either the Latin title, *Mystici Corporis*, or the English, *The Mystical Body of Christ*. I am citing the National Catholic Welfare Conference edition of 1943. The paragraph numbering in other translations sometimes varies slightly, making references difficult.

22. Para. 76 of the NCWC translation.

23. *Ibid.*, para. 77 and 53.

24. *Ibid.*, para. 17.

25. Cardinal Léon-Joseph Suenens as reported in *The Catholic Messenger* (Davenport) May 7, 1964.

26. Cf. A. Wenger, *Vatican II, Première Session* (Paris: Centurion, 1963), 17–18; *Acta Apostolicae Sedis* 54 (1962) 788 (*The Pope Speaks* 8, 209); *Acta et Documenta Concilio Oecumenico Vaticano II Apparando* 1 (1960), 105 (*The Pope Speaks* 6,236). . . .

27. Apostolic Constitution *Humanae Salutis* (Dec. 25, 1961); Abbott, *Documents of Vatican II*, p. 709.

28. *Abbott*, p. 793.

29. Address at the close of the First Session, Dec. 8, 1962. *Osservatore Romano*, Dec. 10–11, 1962; *The Pope Speaks* 8 (1962–63), pp. 401–2.

30. There was, however, the citation of Eph. 2:21–22 in the prologue.

31. Cf. *Acta Synodalia Sacrosancti Concilii Oecumenici Vaticani II*, vol. 1, pars 1 (Rome: Vatican, 1970), pp. 609–10.

32. *Op. cit.* Pars 3, p. 117. Cf. *Vatican II, An Inter-Faith Appraisal*, ed. J. Miller (Notre Dame, 1966), p. 29.

33. Pope Paul pointed this out in an address of May 23, 1973; cf. *Osservatore Romano*, English ed., May 31, 1973.

34. *The Church*, 12; *The Apostolate of the Laity*, 3.
35. *The Church*, 15. Cf. *Ecumenism*, 3.
36. Cf. *The Church*, 8 and 13; *Ecumenism*, 2.
37. *Acta Synodalia. Sacrosancti Concilii Oecumenici Vaticani II*, vol. 2, pars 3, pp. 627, 630. Cf. the similar observations of Bishop Florit of Florence on October 23; *ibid.*, pp. 252–55.
38. *Ibid.*, 175–78. An English translation of this speech has been published in *Council Speeches of Vatican II*, ed. Y. Congar, H. Küng, and D. O'Hanlon (Paramus, N.J.: Paulist Press, 1964), pp. 29–34). A revised version of this speech was published by the Cardinal as an appendix to his pastoral letter for Pentecost, 1973, entitled *Redécouvrir le Saint-Esprit.*
39. *The Church in the World Today*, 11. Cf. 15.
40. *Ibid.*, 26. Cf. 38.
41. ". . . quin futuris Spiritus Sancti impulsionibus praeiudicetur," *Ecumenism*, 24. The Abbott translation reads, "without prejudicing the future inspiration of the Holy Spirit."
42. *L'Osservatore Romano* (English edition), May 31, 1973.
43. *L'Osservatore Romano* (English), Dec. 7, 1972. Cf. "The Holy Spirit and the Life of the Church," *The Pope Speaks*, v. 12, pp. 79–81.

Pentecostalism in the Context of American Piety and Practice

MARTIN MARTY

Martin E. Marty is professor of Modern Church History at the University of Chicago where he also served as Associate Dean of the Divinity School. A prolific writer, he has written many books and articles which have established him as one of the foremost observers and critics of the American religious scene. He also serves as Associate Editor of the Christian Century *and co-editor of* Church History.

In the following chapter, Marty focuses his attention on the rise of pentecostalism against the broad background of American piety. Of special interest is Marty's treatment of behavior and practice among American pentecostals.

The Rise and Spread of Pentecostalism

IF any twentieth-century spiritual movement in the United States deserved the designation, "a people's religion," it was pentecostalism. If any contemporary western people's religion has been observed or has expressed itself through marked behavioral patterns, it was also this pentecostalism. Though often largely sequestered from the view of middle-class and influential Americans from 1900 to 1960 and while not in range of the experience of most Americans even after that date, it was the fastest-growing Christian element.

Pentecostalism emerged and developed largely without well-known leaders; elites were late in developing; no impressive intellectual or theological framework held it together; its impact on the political life of the nation was small, secondary, and indirect.[1] Changes have occurred since 1960 as old-line pentecostalism became more adapted to the surrounding culture and when a new version which was often called the charismatic movement became visible. Much of both Spirit movements' life has remained a mystery to non-participants.

Many adherents date their origins literally from the turn of the century. At a New Year's Eve and New Year's Day religious meeting in Topeka, Kansas, on December 31, 1900, and January 1, 1901, a Miss Agnes Ozman received the gift of speaking in tongues. It was claimed that without knowledge of the languages, she spoke Chinese and, later, Bohemian. The *Kansas City World* immediately grasped that "these people have a faith almost incomprehensible at this day." [2] Her associates soon recognized that this was a new day in religion. They have subsequently been able to create almost intact worlds alongside those of more conventional piety and more familiar institutions.

Pentecostalism derived its name from Pentecost, the Jewish

195

festival reported on in the biblical book of Acts (chapter 2). On that occasion, which has been viewed by many as the true birthday of the Christian Church, Jesus' disciples were reported on as having spoken in other tongues "as the Spirit gave them utterance." The Spirit there referred to is the Holy Spirit to whom Christians bear witness, along with the Father and the Son, when they speak of God as the Holy Trinity. Pentecostalism has always concentrated on God as Spirit, having picked up with this language many metaphors of fire. In Acts 2 "tongues as of fire" rested on the disciples.[3] As would be expected in a Spirit movement, a premium has always been placed on uncontrollability, spontaneity, surprise. At the same time, the phenomena associated with these have often produced rather controlled, predictable social behavioral patterns.

These patterns were observable on a worldwide scale. Those who considered interest in pentecostalism to be motivated by a faddism born of ecstatic religious outbreaks in the 1960s and 1970s gradually became alerted to the durable and widespread character of this Christian force. Some of those trained to look at the world as a global village or as "spaceship earth," [4] came to recognize that pentecostalism would almost certainly become the major Christian form of expression in what were called the developing nations.

R. Buckminster Fuller trained his devotees to look at the globe as a tiny, graspable sphere, and to do their thinking about its future as if it were a comprehensible object the size of a basketball. If in the Fullerian imagination Christianity were to be pictured as a viscous substance, this faith could be seen to be flowing to the southern hemisphere, much as paint does in the Sherwin-Williams commercials: "We cover the earth." And that movement into the southern hemisphere was predominantly pentecostal. So pronounced was this direction that historian Walter Hollenweger had to caution "sophisticated people in Europe and America" against the idea that pentecostalism was "of importance only for the poor and for the Third World." [5]

Many Christian missionary scholars projected Africa as the focus of Christendom by the end of the century. The majority of the thousands of missionary-founded and autochthonous sects in that continent had decisive features in common with pentecostalism. They were often founded by charismatic leaders. They fused the language of the Spirit brought them by missionaries with native African ideas of religious spontaneity and emotion. Sub-Saharan missionaries of the conventional sort, both Roman Catholic and Protestant, went back home or often transformed their activities toward education, health care, and development. They left the rest of the field to pentecostals.[6]

In Latin America, an often dormant Roman Catholicism reposed in a generally secularized set of cultures while Protestantism either had never established itself or had languished. Largely Protestant but sometimes Catholic pentecostalism eventually came to dominate, and by 1970 was already the majority evangelical faith in Chile, Brazil, and the like. The future seemed to belong to the Spirit movements there just as it did in Indonesia. Hundreds of thousands of Indonesians were converted through pentecostalism to Christianity in the 1960s and 1970s. A global "trickle-up" effect into the northern hemisphere, whence pentecostalism orginated, also occurred. Spirit-filled faith prevailed in the Caribbean and was the largest form of Protestantism in Roman Catholic nations like France, Italy, Portugal. Already in 1960 the South African-born pentecostal leader David du Plessis could boast:

> At the turn of the century there was no Pentecostal Movement. Today, it consists of a community of more than ten million souls that can be found in almost every country under the sun.[7]

From Central and North America it moved toward domination in Mexico, while spreading from the mid-south and southwestern United States into much of the north. Whenever an observer suddenly had his eyes opened to the outbreak, he found himself becoming acquainted with a whole new religious map. Suddenly Topeka, Kansas, and Charles Fox Parham's Bethel Bible School, where Agnes Ozman received the gift of the Holy Spirit, became familiar names. Curiosity about a few late-nineteenth-century pre-pentecostal stirrings led him to North Carolina or Georgia. He could be sure that something had been consolidated when he looked back on the Azusa Street revival of William J. Seymour, a black evangelist, in 1906. There in Los Angeles, urban America first became aware that something new was underway. Cleveland, Tennessee, home of one of several groups called "The Church of God" would soon show up on his screen, as would Tulsa, which became a center, a Rome or Geneva, of pentecostal ventures in an urban time.[8]

The Later Charismatic Counterparts

If the observer was catholic enough to include neo-pentecostalism, he or she would soon be noticing Van Nuys, California. An Episcopal priest named Dennis Bennett there announced to his congregation in 1960 that he and some of them had received the gift of the Holy Spirit and were engaging in *glossolalia*, speaking in tongues. The mental map looked back to Clinton's Cafeteria in Los Angeles where in 1951 a group which served as a transition between old-line and new-style pentecostalisms was born. Under the tutelage of a dairyman named Demos Shakarian, it became the Full Gospel Business Men's Fellowship International (FGBMFI). From the Episcopalian suburbs in California through the Lutheran suburbs of Minneapolis to the often Presbyterian precincts in Yale and some other divinity schools, middle-class Protestants joined in. After 1968, the campuses of Duquesne and Notre Dame Universities and the University of Michigan at Ann Arbor became centers for a more sophisticated version. Along with the outbreaks in standard-brand Protestant churches, these have often come to be called and may well be permanently designated as the charismatic movement, after the *charismata* or gifts of the Holy Spirit.[9]

Pentecostals liked to look back to a famous *Life* magazine article by the then president of New York's prestigious Union Theological Seminary, Henry Pitney Van Dusen, as the time after which new publics became familiar with the practices and behavior of their kind. In that piece in 1958 he termed pentecostalism Christendom's "Third Force," alongside conventional Catholicism and Protestantism. Those who study the pentecostal map and are aware of the Spirit movements' claims found good warrant to begin to think of it as "first force" Christendom. It was forceful while the more staid counterparts foundered or remained static. Thus J. A. Synan, keynoting the Fifth Pentecostal World Conference in Toronto in 1958, reasoned: "They say Pentecost [alism] is the *third* great force in Christendom. But it is really the *first* great force. . . ." Partisans relished recall of mistaken prophecies like that of a noted Methodist professor in 1913: "The present day tongues movement is likely to run its course in a few months or a few years," and were ready to say that it was *non*-charismatic Christianity that was running its course. In the midst of these bold claims for the Spirit movements, the overwhelming secularity of the surrounding world was often overlooked.[10]

Pentecostal people also verged on recognizing that just as their "third force" might actually be a "first force," so their sociological position as marginal alongside mainline churches threatened or promised to be altered. From some points of view, they could discern enough continuity with American revival movements pre-1900 that they could see themselves as innovative revivers of characteristic American piety and behavioral patterns—forms which had been repressed or suppressed in later more genteel and accommodated Christianity. Perhaps *they* were becoming mainline, whether because of their statistical successes or their own increasing compromises with the surrounding culture.

Roman Catholics had more difficulty knowing how to connect with that early American piety because of its Protestant character. They did not always know what to do with historic pentecostalism after they had sent a card of thanks and offered friendly relations. Father Donald Gelpi, S.J., posed the question in 1971. Given "polar opposites of piety" between Protestant and Catholic styles, how could the two ever be brought together theologically? His answer was a question: "Doesn't it seem possible that there is a

relation of potential complementarity between Catholic and Pentecostal piety?" [11] He spoke for people who wanted to see Catholic
pentecostalism or the charismatic movement as emergent normative churchmanship.

The Map of Spirit Movements

Observers and historians often had difficulty grasping pentecostalism when it was still close to its first-generation period of
ferment and fertility. It had spawned a bewildering array of new
sects and denominations. Joseph Washington pointed in awe, for
instance, at the variety of names of black pentecostal churches.
(The movement was born racially integrated; it then divided but
later showed some signs of entente between blacks and whites.
Pentecostal churches were the third largest cluster among American blacks, after Baptist and Methodist in rank.) He made note of,
among others:

> The Fire-Baptized Holiness Church of God of the Americans, 1922,
> . . . Church of God in Christ, 1895, . . . Church of Christ, Holiness
> United States of America, 1894, . . . Triumph the Church and
> Kingdom of God in Christ, 1936, . . . The Sought Out Church of God
> in Christ and Spiritual House of Prayer, Incorporated, 1947, . . . The
> Latter House of the Lord for All People and the Church on the
> Mountain, Apostolic Faith, 1936, . . . Church of the Living God, the
> Pillar and Ground of Truth, 1925, . . . Apostolic Overcoming Holy
> Church of God, 1919, . . . the National David Spiritual Temple of
> Christ Church Union, 1932, . . . the House of God, the Holy Church
> of the Living God, the Pillar and Grounds of the Truth, House of
> Prayer for All People, 1914.[12]

If their white counterparts' names took up less space on
letterheads, when they became sufficiently established to have
letterheads, they were no fewer in number. Historian John Thomas
Nichol categorized scores of churches, including the large ones:
Church of God, Cleveland, Tennessee (272,276 members in 1972
recording); Church of God in Christ (425,000), Assemblies of God

(670,000), Pentecostal Church of God of America (115,000), and the United Pentecostal Church (150,000). By 1973, bibliographer David W. Faupel could list nine Pentecostal publishing houses in the United States along with dozens of periodicals; these could be consulted in at least seven sets of archives, as pentecostalism found a sense of history.[13]

As with the new map, so with a fresh array of founders and celebrities, as pentecostalism moved toward becoming an establishment. Historians came to be at home not only with names like Ozman, Parham, and Seymour, but also with those of ecumenical leaders such as David du Plessis, other historians such as Nichol and Vinson Synan or, in Europe, Nils Bloch-Hoell or Walter J. Hollenweger, who wrote a multivolume dissertation on this subject at Zurich. Celebrities abounded: David Wilkerson, who formed the pentecostal Teen Challenge shared an aura with singers Pat Boone and Johnny Cash; they joined an informal pantheon which has included the colorful Los Angeles evangelist Aimee Semple McPherson and the televised healer and university founder, Oral Roberts of Tulsa. The charismatic movement similarly produced, in addition to that of Dennis Bennett, the names and reputations of Kevin and Dorothy Ranaghan of Notre Dame, Father Donald Gelpi, and the like.

The story of these places, events, institutions, and people was late in coming to the attention of America's religious historians. The two best general histories in the early 1970s were Sydney E. Ahlstrom's 1158-page work, which devoted three pages each to black and white pentecostalism and a long footnote to the more recent charismatic movement, and Winthrop Hudson's revised edition of *Religion in America*, which allotted two pages to pentecostalists and four to charismatics; they were both more generous than most of their colleagues.[14]

The Assumptions of Scholarly Observers

When non-pentecostals began to analyze and chronicle the movements, their assumptions were regularly challenged. Here was a classic case of conflict between participants and observers, insiders and outsiders. Few Spirit-filled people would sit still for scholarly comment like that of anthropologist Felicitas Goodman, a friendly witness, who concluded concerning their prime behavioral expression, speaking in tongues, that

> glossolalia should be defined as a vocalization pattern, a speech automatism, that is produced on the substratum of hyperarousal dissociation, reflecting directly, in its segmental and suprasegmental structure, neurophysiologic processes present in this mental state.[15]

That was *not* how it felt, they would say. Most of them would like to recognize glossolalia and other gifts as simply unananlyzable intrusions of the supernatural into a world that natural-minded scholars would never comprehend and which they could only distort.

Increasingly, particularly with the founding of the Society for Pentecostal Studies and because of the presence of charismatic movements at major intellectual centers, they found that outsiders were not necessarily destructive and could be sympathetic. It came to dawn on some historians of religion that while they cherished and relished ecstatic movements in almost every religion ever known to humans, they tended to overlook or see as inauthentic the cognate versions on western religious soil. Some of them eventually overcame the prejudice and took the local and contemporary phenomenon more seriously than before.

Thanks to Morton Kelsey, a charismatic movement advocate who did not speak in tongues, a few learned to make use of C. J. Jung's concept of archetypes as an interpretive tool. Kelsey saw glossolalia as the intrusion of the unconscious just before personality integration.[16] More acceptable was William J. Samarin's linguistic approach. Samarin saw pentecostalism as a functioning feature of a complex behavioral movement, and played down psychological interpretations. Movement people shared his resistance to attempts which would classify their practice as irrational and neurotic or simply as the result of their original lower-class status with its deprivations.

Samarin found that recorded snatches of Pentecostal tongue-speaking were always "strings of syllables, made up of sounds taken from among all those that the speaker knows, put together more or less haphazardly but which nevertheless emerge as word-like and sentence-like units because of realistic, language-like rhythm and melody." So glossolalia was anomalous, not aberrant behavior. It represented extraordinary practice, but its practitioners were not necessarily abnormal people. Samarin argued that pentecostals claimed this activity was Holy Spirit inspired, because they had no other way to account for the drastic alterations in their outlooks as a result of it. Thus he could not himself grant supernatural status to the event but could see the pentecostal to be undergoing valid and authentic religious experience, a symbolization of God's immediate presence. People spoke in tongues because this was a behavior their peers expected of them and for which they set up circumstances. It was clear that, while not wholly acceptable, such a thoughtful attempt at understanding was coming to be regarded as bridge-building in character.[17]

While often classed by historians as a species of the genera ecstatic ("standing outside one's self") or enthusiastic ("being possessed by a God"), pentecostalism was not always ready to accept such categorization. In terms of Stanley Krippner's famous essay on twenty altered states of consciousness, pentecostals in action were people who moved from (#20) "normal," "everyday" styles, "characterized by logic, rationality, cause-and-effect thinking, goal-directedness, and the feeling that one is in control of one's mental activity" to what Krippner but not they called (#7) "states of rapture," characterized by "intense feeling and overpowering emotion, subjectively evaluated as pleasurable and positive in nature." These included "religious activities (e.g., conversion, 'evangelistic' meetings, 'speaking-in-tongues')," and the like. In other words, seen as part of a specific historical movement, tongue-speaking by the Holy Spirit was *sui generis* and deserved separate analysis.[18]

Historians who reached for terms like "ecstatic" and "enthusiastic" were often trying to join pentecostals in tracing continuities in their history. The apostle Paul claimed to have spoken in tongues, though theologically and from a communitarian angle he placed glossolalia low among the charismatic gifts. "Thank God, I am more gifted in ecstatic utterance than any of you, but in the congregation I would rather speak five intelligible words, for the benefit of others as well as myself, than thousands of words in the language of ecstasy" (I Cor. 14:19 NEB).[19] Did this gift simply die out with the apostles, to be restored only in the latter days of the twentieth century? Many pentecostals, on the soil of American Protestant primitivism, had no difficulty with such a restorationist approach. Others were more traditionalist and catholic in their outlook.

To those who sought antecedents and continuities, the second century Montanists belonged in the history. The early church historian Eusebius had said of Montanus' behavior:

> He became beside himself, and being suddenly in a sort of frenzy and ecstasy, he raved, and began to babble and utter strange things, prophesying in a manner contrary to the constant custom of the Church which had been handed down by tradition from the beginning.[20]

Not until the time of the Protestant Reformation were there new pneumatics on any reasonably large and visible scale. John Wesley in the eighteenth century was seen by many as "the spiritual and intellectual father of the modern holiness and pentecostal movements which have issued from Methodism within the last century,"[21] and particularly from Wesleyan holiness movements—not all of which turned explicitly pentecostal and some of which distanced themselves vigorously from groups which encouraged speaking in tongues. At the same time, a number of British movements of the nineteenth century, among them the Irvingite outburst after 1830, made their way to the United States. For the most part, efforts to make much of historical continuities between the first and the nineteenth century were rather fruitless, and historians were usually left to fend for themselves as they tried to make sense of a generally fresh Christian phenomenon in their own time.

Roman Catholic charismatics, however, had to make special efforts to find a past because of their sense of tradition and organic growth. Donald Gelpi traced the lineage directly and indirectly through such varied movements and moments as the subheads in his historical chapter would indicate: Montanism, Donatism, The Waldenses, The Cathari, The Anabaptists, Jansenism, Quietism, The Convulsionaries, Quakerism, The Camisards, The Moravians, Methodism, Revivalism, American Protestant Pentecostalism. "But that history can yield little more than an initial awareness of some of the issues which Catholic Pentecostalism raises," in part because not a single one of these enthusiastic movements was orthodox from a Roman Catholic point of view.

> Perhaps the most troubling question for most Catholics on their first confrontation with the Pentecostal experience is the following: Why did the charismatic phenomena which most characterize Pentecostal piety seemingly disappear from the Catholic community?

Gelpi found no satisfactory answer and instead moved on to the suggestion that instead of doing historical research, Catholics had to recognize their "serious obligation to reflect on the significance, purpose, and cultivation of these and other spiritual gifts in the light of more traditional and institutional forms of Catholic belief and worship." [22]

Pentecostalism: Belief without Theology

From what has been written to this point, it should be obvious that pentecostalism and charismatic movements made twentieth century contributions to the life of a "nation of behavers." They were in no sense theologically inventive, nor were they constituted on intellectual or cognitive foundations. True, they accented the Holy Spirit in the Trinity as most other Christians did not. They made more of charismatic gifts than most Christians did. But the overwhelming number of pentecostalists wanted to be seen as orthodox Christians, content to resort to very simple biblical and experiential language. They borrowed but tended to be bored by and sometimes opposed to intellectual formulation. Bibliographer David W. Faupel condensed it all into one line. "A Pentecostal Theology has never actually been written." [23] Most pentecostal teachers used theologies from other traditions. Their own efforts have been casual, sporadic, feeble, and neglected.

Roman Catholic humorist Kieran Quinn gave the representative non-pentecostals' view when he said that Catholic charismatics "do not trust scholarship, biblical or theological, and well they should not. Reason and scholarship have always been the nemesis of enthusiasm. Under rational inquiry pentecostalism falters." [24] Within the movement, there have been consistent and emphatic voices critical of intellectuality and theological formulation—or even social analysis. David Wilkerson spoke for the pentecostal masses when he complained that "often experts deplore and criticize those who speak with tongues and then protect themselves from being judged or criticized themselves by hiding behind research charts and special degrees." [25]

Even pentecostal and charismatic humor and lightheartedness reflects the dismissal of theological seriousness. Hans Jacob Frøen spoke to Lutheran charismatics about an acquaintance: "My friend by nature tends to be somewhat obstinate and set in his ideas. (He's another theologian, so you might expect him to be!)" [26] Such comments are playful and harmless but revelatory of the group's assumptions. Some would say pentecostalists were "typically American" in their lack of theological constitutiveness and preoccupation. They were an exaggerated example of what is common in America. They simply make more than others do of behavior on the basis of a few simple, profoundly held ideas about reality and the divine.

These beliefs converged on the concept of the Holy Spirit's work and the believers' acceptance of His gifts. Frederick Dale Bruner pointed to the distinctive basic belief behind the behavior patterns:

> If we wished to be unacademically schematic in making our point we would suggest that, in generally christocentric Protestantism, along-side of particularly chariscentric Lutheranism, theocentric Calvinism, ecclesiocentric Anglicanism, kardiocentric Anabaptism, and hagio-centric Methodism may be ranged the most recent significant arrival on the stage of Protestant church history—what may somewhat awkwardly be called pneumobaptistocentric Pentecostalism.[27]

Linguistic barbarisms aside, Bruner has successfully isolated the central feature for pentecostals and charismatics alike.

Institutional and Political Derivativeness

If pentecostalism was as sterile theologically as it was experientially or behaviorally, so, too, it had not been particularly innovative institutionally. If the familiar forms "church," "sect," and "denomination" had already taken complete shape on American soil before the twentieth century, it must be said that pentecostalism lived within this framework. In a gross generalization, it might be said that old-line pentecostalism (1900–) had always been in the process of moving from being sectarian to being churchly, while newer charismatic movements were always in the process of moving from being churchly toward becoming sectarian. But pentecostalism did "denominationalize" while charismatics largely remained in their churches. Churchliness, in this context, meant general inclusiveness, accommodation to culture, and taking responsibility for spheres of life not simply under ecclesiastical domain. For Ernest Troeltsch, the church type could, "to a certain extent, . . . afford to ignore the need for subjective holiness for the sake of objective treasures of grace and redemption."

Less behaviorally casual was the sect; in the case of the Spirit movements, the sect was concerned with "subjective holiness." It was behaviorally demarcated—in the case of pentecostalism this is the prime feature—and marked by an awareness of conversion and of a new personal relation in life. In the analysis of Howard Becker, Leopold von Wiese and, among historians, Sidney E. Mead, the denomination was an advanced state of the sect. While von Wiese and Becker saw that some enthusiasm departed in this stage, Mead saw it merely as an accommodation to the "voluntaryism" imposed by a society which legally separated civil and religious realms. Such a society needed neutral definitions of religious forces. But when they were separately constituted, as the pentecostal sects were and the charismatic movements had not been, they were denominations. Most important to note at this point, however, was that at whatever stage in transit one observed pentecostalisms, as denominations en route from sect to church or as movements from church toward sect, they cohered on practical and social behavioral lines. It was on those lines that they had been recognized and to which they had devoted most attention as a result of their beliefs and experiences.[28]

A third observation is also in order. Just as they were not theologically or institutionally inventive, so pentecostalists have also not made major contributions to the *polis,* to political life in the broadest sense. Outsiders instinctively ranked them toward the conservative side of the political spectrum. Certainly, they rarely attempted to take corporate stands on most social issues, and they dealt largely with the personal and ecclesiastical sides of their adherents' lives. In general, their political opinions paralleled those of the social classes and majorities in the locales from which they come. As a result, there have often been populist tinges to the expressions of individual pentecostals. But these movements generally lacked major significance in the political sphere when they were compared, for example, to the descendants of New England established Protestantism or later urban Roman Catholicism. Only rarely have specifically pentecostal self-defenses involved them in legal decisions, as in the case of fighting off proscriptions against handling poisonous snakes in religious ritual, as some more remote and extreme pentecostal groups have done and attempt still to do.

That leaves religious social behavior as the main observable, demarcating, and defining feature of pentecostal denominations and charismatic movements. Herein is much of their strength. In a pluralist, semi-secular and semi-religious culture, the conventional Catholic and Protestant churches have often seen most of their behavioral expressions eroding or becoming attenuated. Belonging to them gave many people an insufficient sense of identity and difference. Pentecostalism could manifest a behavioral distancing from ordinary, everyday religious and secular experience. There lay its charm and also its threat to the more behaviorally accommodated and less prescriptive groups.

Outsiders All Stress Social Behavior

One way to begin to prove this point is to take into account outsiders' perceptions. Almost all of them stressed pentecostals' social behavior. A few fundamentalists have consistently criticized pentecostals for departing from a theological accent on God's "propositional revelation" in the Scripture, as codified in the church's scholastic traditions. In the sacramental churches, the believers' first baptism receives more attention. Protestant traditionalists also make much of God's decisive act which justifies sinners. Pentecostalists give this less attention. Pentecostal belief centers in the experience of a "second blessing," a Baptism in the Holy Spirit which has to be added to water baptism. This is integral to all pentecostals' and charismatics' self-definition. Their enemies see the second Baptism as an explicit or at least implicit downgrading of the first baptism and of the justifying act which is supposed to be complete in itself.

"Almost universal to Pentecostal inventory is the centrality of the baptism in the Holy Spirit as the source of Pentecostal power," according to Frederick Dale Bruner. David du Plessis, from within the movement, said, "We dare to believe that the blessing [of the Baptism in the Holy Spirit] is as valid two thousand years after Pentecost as it was twenty years after the first outpouring of the Spirit." [29] For the neopentecostals, Dorothy Ranaghan underscored again that "the central experience which crystallizes and initiates this newness of life in faith is known as the baptism in the Holy Spirit," for "the reception of power." "The baptism in the Holy Spirit is a 'pentecostal experience' in the sense that it calls forth, it sends forth, an individual with a newness and empowering of the Spirit in the same way that the first apostles were sent forth." [30]

Critical of both movements was the conservative theologian Anthony A. Hoekema, who also said that "the central doctrine of Neo-Pentecostalism is its teaching on the baptism in the Holy Spirit. So basic is this teaching to the Neo-Pentecostal movement that if you take this doctrine away from it, what you have left is no longer Neo-Pentecostalism." He then asked whether in the basic scriptural text Paul agreed with neopentecostals that "Spirit-baptism is an experience distinct from conversion which should be sought by all Christians," and answers, "Nothing could be further from the truth." [31] On that point he spoke for all Christian non-pentecostals. There the line was drawn.

These theological cavils, important as they may be, were highly secondary to the most observable feature of pentecostal perception by others. From the beginning, pentecostals have been known for ecstatic and enthusiastic behavior, for social forms which encouraged and demanded emotionalism, for stimulating rousing and not always controllable rituals. Ask any "man on the street" about his vision of pentecostals from, say, 1900 until about 1960, and he would probably condense it all in one term: they are "holy rollers." They "speak in tongues." Almost never did such observers manifest any curiosity at all about the cognitive ordering of pentecostal life, or the expounding of pentecostal teaching. Knowledge of these was not necessary for those who were outside and intended to remain so, or who did not seriously entertain the idea of exposing themselves to charismatic circumstances. In the behavioral sense, of course, it may be said that pentecostalism was in continuity with so much else that seemed normative in American religion. Some might even be led to think of it as being simply "more typical" than most other movements.

The social historian is not concerned with the religious behavior of an isolated individual; it was pentecostalism's ability to generate predictable social expressions (in the name of spontaneity) that made it important. Bruner observed aptly, that:

> contrary to general expectation, highly individualistic Pentecostalism is remarkably corporate and congregational in its life. The Pentecostal church-meeting or assembly where the individual gifts are principally exercised is close to the center of the Pentecostal secret. Here the experiences of the many merge into the one and by this confluence the power of the Spirit is felt in multiplication.[32]

The pentecostalist is aware that his social patterns are scorned by many. Father Kilian McDonnell believed that on these terms, neither Protestant nor Catholic pentecostal and charismatic groups were properly judged; to the public their movement "conjures up images of emotionalism, fanaticism, religious mania, illiteracy, messianic postures, credulity, and panting after miracles"—all behavioral, not theological, preoccupations.[33] On the other hand, some non-pentecostalists like Southern Baptist Wayne Oates lauded individual members precisely because they were behaviorally so different, not shy or inarticulate about religion, ready to look non-respectable, fanatic, sick, and foolish.[34]

Behavior Rooted in Belief: The Demarcating Line

Tucked away in a sentence earlier we made reference to a theme that needs to be lifted out and dramatized at this point. To speak of social behavior here does not imply something external to the religious vision. On the contrary, it is seen to be derived from and then related back symbiotically to pentecostals' deepest religious experience and belief. But all of them insisted that the behavior *has* to be present, has to be somehow evidential, manifest, and visible. The reader of almost any pentecostal literature, from tracts and sermons through books and denominational reports, is confronted constantly by words having to do with the receipt of the second blessing accompanied by behaviorally complex signs and gifts. A catalog of some of these is valid and even necessary to make the point.

Linguistically, we are told that all this means that Baptism in the Holy Spirit is "a definite act"; there must be "initial evidence"; recipients seek an "objectively observable act," and an "evidential sign"; this Baptism offers "the empirical evidence of salvation"; the second blessing is "tangible"; glossolalia is "visible evidence"; Charles Fox Parham sought tongues speaking as "the only evidence" of this Baptism; there are to be "manifestations, powers, and services," an "externalization"; how believers act becomes all important in the holiness and charismatic traditions.[35] Here, as so often, Samarin handled the aspect best from a scholarly point of view:

> What is a validating experience for the individual, . . . is a demarcating one for the group; it symbolizes the group's difference from others. In this respect glossolalia serves the same function that any form of speech may have, like the in-group languages of students (slang) or secret societies. The latter, of course, also have communicative functions in the strict sense of the term. . . .
>
> Symbols can become frozen, but when a movement is new, they are especially significant. Thus, the demarcating function of glossolalia is more important for neo-Pentecostal groups than it is for the established ones which perpetuate themselves biologically (where children are born into Pentecostal homes) rather than sociologically. (However, where Pentecostalism is spreading rapidly, as in Brazil, we can expect glossolalia to retain its symbolic demarcating function, unless other symbols have superseded it.) In these groups, then, it is not enough for a newcomer to identify himself as a Christian. The members will want to know if he has had "the experience." One of the best answers is simply, "Yes, I have spoken in tongues." This marks solidarity with the group. Indeed, reliable reports indicate that some groups will not integrate a person unless he gives evidence of being a tongue speaker. The expression is not theirs, but this is their "requirement for membership."

Samarin says well that not all neo-pentecostals would recognize themselves this way, "yet it is unquestionably suggested by the way they talk about tongues and the way they treat the interested participant in their meetings." He underestimates the degree to which other behavioral elements in pentecostalism including some that are less visible and controversial than glossolalia serve for demarcation.

Glossolalia, Samarin continues, is symbolic externally but also internally. "That is, it helps the members to reaffirm their difference as often as they will." And, for a final recourse to his findings, just as glossolalia serves these external and internal symbolic roles, there is a third behavioral consequence: "It achieves a pragmatic purpose. As a manifestation of the divine, [it] contributes a sacred note to a meeting, something it does much less frequently and to a lesser degree in private experiences." It is a power that "electrifies the whole building." It contributes to the spontaneity of a meeting. Because this spontaneous search for the Spirit's expression ran across the spectrum from Appalachian sects to high Anglican and Catholic charismatic life, "this use of glossolalia clearly illustrates how speech not only helps realize the ethos or way of life of a society but also the ethos of a social occasion," in this case, the meetings of the groups.[36]

Sometimes the language of behavioral demarcation is extravagant and colorful. Frequently it will come to the point as graphically as does Werner Skibstedt, who when claiming that the pentecostal experience meant nothing less than "the rediscovery of Christianity" added that—and the emphasis is his—and *"the reception of the gift of the Holy Spirit in an extraordinary, yes, in an eye-catching way."*[37] In a world of conventional Christians who were accused of being afflicted with myopia, astigmatism, dyslexia, and blurred vision, the eye-catchingness of charismatic and pentecostal life was enchanting.

While the famed black religious leader Father Divine should not be classified with Christian pentecostalists, phenomenologically his movement, derived from reminiscences of Christianity in black

America, was in some ways a cognate to pentecostalism. Several of his neologisms can be taken over to describe something of this attractive evidential feature, this eye-catchingness. He said, "I visibilitate God!" "I tangibilitate! I materialize every assertion, for God is the materializer of all of His Earth's Creation!" When the Prophet (James F.) Jones visited Father Divine, he left with the words, "I know that the chassis of your divine mind has been lubricated with divine lubrimentality." [38] This was the extreme and obsessive (as well as linguistically delightful) end of the quest for evidentiality and tangibility, theologically distanced from but behaviorally akin to pentecostalism.

Speaking in Tongues as Central Feature

While speaking in tongues was not the only gift, it served best, as Samarin showed, for symbolic, pragmatic, and behavioral demarcation for group belonging and personal integration. According to Father Donald Gelpi, it became a "kind of *pons asinorum* of the Pentecostal movement. Non-Pentecostals find it strange and exotic, often to the point of repugnance, while pentecostals are all too often inclined to regard it as a *sine qua non* of spiritual living. Both positions leave one open to exaggeration and distortion." [39] From the beginning, this was the most frequently observed phenomenon. In 1906 the Los Angeles *Times* covered the Azusa Street outbreak with the headline, "Weird Babel of Tongues." Presciently, its reporter noted that "a new sect . . . is breaking loose." [40] An advocate, Don Basham, answered a question he posed himself: "Can I receive the baptism in the Holy Spirit without speaking in tongues?" His answer: "We must admit that the baptism in the Holy Spirit can be received without the manifestation of tongues, but we encourage no one to seek the baptism without expecting tongues. . . . SOMETHING IS MISSING IN YOUR SPIRITUAL LIFE IF YOU HAVE RECEIVED THE HOLY SPIRIT YET HAVE NOT SPOKEN IN TONGUES." [41]

When the newer charismatic movement began, its spokesmen

recognized the importance of this behavioral phenomenon. Dennis Bennett's stentorian phrasing shows how he regarded it: "The Holy Spirit did take my lips and tongue and form a new and powerful language. . . ."[42] Whether or not speaking in tongues were to be stimulated; whether it was to be accompanied by the laying on of hands; what it all meant—these took up myriad pages of debate concerning tongues. While doing research for this chapter, the author noted in each source the references which saw speaking in tongues to be the highest-prized and even the normative social behavioral pattern for pentecostals and charismatics. The list of references grew far too long even to be dipped into for citations; the historian grows weary. How much time should be devoted to proving the obvious?

The research did yield need for a distinction not always made in pentecostal observation. It may be suggested that speaking in tongues was qualitatively so different from the other charismatic signs and gifts that it should be thought of as representing "hard" charismatic experience or data. Those who did not see it to be an absolute necessity or as integral to the experience of the Baptism in the Holy Spirit should be seen as "soft" charismatics—vulnerable to being drawn back fully into their host Christian bodies as countless renewal groups have been.

Those who did not speak in tongues or seek the gift might engage in holy rolling, holy dancing, saying "praise the Lord," singing lively songs, looking for signs and wonders, stimulating prayer meetings, healing, tarrying, and the like. The totality of their activities contributed to the drawing of a line between pentecostals and their non-charismatic fellow Christians. But just as belief in the Baptism in the Holy Spirit was absolutely decisive, so *glossolalia* was the "stone of stumbling" that "hard" charismatics and most pentecostals would set in place.

Snakes, Devils, Prophets, Healing

As unfamiliar as glossolalia may have been to the non-pentecostal, it soon became almost taken for granted to the regular observer. For him or her there were more dramatic visibilitations or tangibilitations than tongue-speaking in the further reaches of pentecostalism. For small minorities, snake-handling has served a special behavioral function. Rejected by most pentecostalists, it interpreted literally Mark 16. Devotees considered it their mandate to "take up poisonous serpents" as a sign of their blessing by the Holy Spirit. George Hensley, who was eventually to be condemned by his host denomination, the Church of God, initiated the practice in 1909 near Grasshopper, Tennessee. As colorful and eye-catching as the snake-handling churches have been, they were so consistently repudiated by other Spirit-movement people that it hardly seems charitable to include them here, nor is it necessary for the sake of making the point about the visibility of pentecostal behavior; snake-handlers were of interest for nothing but their practices.[43]

Less dramatic in its ritual but as anomalous in its implication is exorcism. A feature of the movement as far back as the time of the Azusa Street revival in 1906 and employed most by pentecostal healers, exorcism came back into its own through the Roman Catholic charismatic movement. Despite its ancient warrant in Catholicism, some dioceses proscribed the practice.[44] This ancient rite was based upon the idea that the devil was a real person and that his agents could possess persons and even occupy spaces. By a special spiritual act associated usually with specific verbal constructs, the demons could be told to be gone, could be cast out or somehow dealt with. The result was not ordinary, everyday behavior for Americans, and thus it helped constitute the bordering of pentecostal life for some; it was still another demarcating and integrating feature.

As to glossolalia, Paul advised the congregation at Corinth not to permit tongue-speaking without interpretation. "If it is a matter of ecstatic utterance, only two should speak, or at most three, one at a time, and someone must interpret. If there is no interpreter, the speaker had better not address the meeting at all, but speak to himself and to God" (I Cor. 14:26 NEB). Therefore most pentecostals encouraged a special act of interpreting tongues. While this phased over toward ordinary discourse, it was less dramatic than glossolalia, snake-handling, or exorcism, but still served to draw a line for group identification. Visually not too different from other settings for discourse in Christian congregations, it drew its life from its association with the most exotic, speaking in tongues.

Many pentecostals recognized that Paul placed prophesying higher than tongue-speaking among gifts of the Holy Spirit, and therefore those who sought Baptism in the Spirit and a second blessing in their lives characteristically prophesied. Here the group was phased even closer toward conventional preaching, though spontaneity was stressed, and much of what outsiders saw to be the activity of "holy rollers" or "jumpers" was inspired by prophetic speech, not glossolalia. Historian John Nichol provided a comment on one context in which prophesying became distinctive among pentecostals.

> To the Pentecostal, prophecy is entirely supernatural. . . . The gift has strong support for its congregational use in the writings of St. Paul . . . but what happened in the early days of the Pentecostal movement was that many preoccupied themselves with the acquisition and the demonstration of this gift, using it to correct, rebuke, foretell, and direct. Thus functioning as the voice of the Spirit, they placed greater emphasis upon themselves as prophets and upon their utterances than upon the leadership of the appointed pastor or in the instruction which the scriptures give.[45]

In the main pentecostal and charismatic churches' and movements' special claims were made for prophesying, however; as one German advocate put it, "It differs from tongues-speaking only in that it is spoken in understandable speech"; Bruner considered it to occur in "an ecstatic or para-ecstatic condition," just as he saw glossolalia occurring. Therefore it is "not to be confused with preaching or prepared remarks." The Spirit acts directly; this claim added to pentecostal distinctives.[46]

Pentecostals, since they believed in the present and immediate activity of the Holy Spirit, tended to be more open to signs or

wonders and miracles than most non-pentecostal Christians are.
Sometimes resurrections from the dead have been claimed, but
empirical observation behind such claims—needless to say—was
highly limited, and they were not a part of the regular behavioral
expectation in the Spirit movements. Spiritual healing, however,
was among the most publicized and familiar of all pentecostal and
charismatic distinctives; through television, the activities of healers
like Oral Roberts and Kathryn Kuhlman became familiar to
millions. Bruner says "there is an emphasis on healing in many
Pentecostal circles which makes it almost a second Pentecostal
distinctive," and anyone familiar with the literature is likely to
agree with him. The accent led to occasional anti-medical tendencies among pentecostals, but through the years this diminished.

The difference between this "second Pentecostal distinctive" and
speaking in tongues was that it marked a relative and not an
absolute difference from the practices of other Christians. That is,
many who did not seek Baptism in the Holy Spirit believed in and
practiced spiritual healing, and healing was not integral to pentecostal witness. Donald Gee, an apologist for pentecostalism, stated
that

> although not directly and essentially a part of the distinctive
> Pentecostal witness to the Baptism of the Holy Ghost with signs
> following, yet from the beginning of the Pentecostal Movement there
> has been a recognized place for the intimate relationship of faith for
> physical healing arising from the same grace of the risen and glorified
> Christ who bestows the Holy Spirit.[47]

If not unique, the emphasis on healing was still a vivid and
colorful element in the social behavior of charismatic movements.

The Behavioral Gestalt of Charismatic Gatherings

In addition to expecting the spiritual gifts described by early
Christians, pentecostals have made arrangements for circumstances
in which they would occur. These belong to what we have called
the behavioral *Gestalt* of their worship. The old-line pentecostals

cherished "tarrying meetings," prolonged specialized services after ordinary worship. In the context of such meetings, the gifts could be sought, expressed, discerned. These were taken up and transformed in modern charismatic movements, many of which seemed almost to be obsessed by the discussion of circles for Bible study, small cell groups, prayer meetings. They wrote hundreds of pages about setting up situations for spontaneous worship and the receipt of spiritual gifts.

Thus in a book by Roman Catholic charismatics, Kevin Ranaghan called prayer meetings "the principal public manifestation and result of the charismatic renewal in the Church today. . . . Prayer meetings come in all sizes and shapes. . . ." He took pains to show that, despite its superficial similarities to evangelical activity, the prayer meeting could not "possibly be spoken of as a Protestant activity; it is thoroughly rooted in the core of the Catholic worshiping tradition." But "the assembly of Christians led by the Spirit, the prayer meeting, is not just another meeting. It is unique . . . and . . . we are truly unique."

Typical of the scrupulous attention to detail was a subsequent chapter by James Cavnar on the "Dynamics of the Prayer Meeting." Like all his counterparts, he stressed the demarcating character of the event. Leaders were conscious of the unfamiliarity which confronts first-timers: "Jim, the people here aren't ready for the kind of worship you have in your prayer meetings." He distinguished prayer groups from prayer meetings and showed how to produce subspecies of both. "A good prayer meeting has a sense of order in it. . . . There will be good order if there is good leadership and if people are sensitive to that leadership." Out of continuity with older pentecostalism, the newer charismatic event is to have "a definite length of time"; it "can have structure . . . it needs some structure. . . ."

Cavnar and other leaders let there be no mistaking the purpose of their events:

> Let the prayer meeting be explicitly "pentecostal" from the very beginning so that all persons are aware that we are here to seek the

gifts of the Spirit. . . . It is sometimes impossible to move a whole group together to Spirit-filled worship and prayer if they have first grown accustomed to a non-charismatic form of prayer meeting.

An abrasive note or two entered.

When a prayer meeting grows too rapidly, the new people often dominate and set the tone of the meeting. . . . It is important not to allow classical pentecostals to dominate the meeting. Most Catholics are simply unprepared for the style of prayer or theology of classical pentecostals. . . . The problem is mainly cultural, but it is nonetheless a problem.[48]

Paul asked that meetings be handled "decently and in order," and this accent came to prevail over the earlier ecstatic ferments. Denominationalized and half-acculturated pentecostalism also eventually made more of its order than its ecstasy. New-style charismatics stressed their orderliness as much as their enthusiasm. But the attempt to elevate orderliness and order was merely one more kind of concentration on behavioral distancing from run-of-the-mill Christianity, which lacked many of these forms or stressed them less.

The Conduct of Life

If ritual behavior at group meetings was the most visible feature of pentecostalism, it should also be noticed that the personal expression of holy lives could not be slighted in churches with holiness backgrounds. In general it may be said that historic holiness churches which did not turn pentecostal have been more prescriptive and legalistic, more prone to enforcing behavioral expectations. The story of their preoccupations reveals scrupulous attention to personal conduct. The holiness antecedents produced codes forbidding tobacco, theater, lodges, dance, jewelry, many styles of dress, alcohol, secret societies; some forbade wedding rings and neckties in a "no hogmeat, no necktie" religion. Modesty was called for. Until at least 1964, Pentecostal Holiness colleges Emmanuel and Southwestern forced their basketball teams to wear knee-length uniforms in order to keep "holiness standards of dress." [49]

The non-holiness pentecostals had equally high expectations, but because of their free form and spontaneous life, they employed fewer rules and regulations to bring it about. They showed more ability than many modern Christians to forgive sinners and forget sins and lapses—including some by celebrated pentecostal leaders of status as high as that of Aimee Semple McPherson or occasional adulterous ministers. These were often comprehended, dealt with, and then moved beyond. Still, personal behavior away from the group marks many pentecostals. Anthropologist Gary Schwartz, who studied a pentecostal group, generalized that

> Pentecostal ideology lacks an ethically binding, comprehensive pattern for secular conduct. It defines proper behavior but . . . does not direct the believer to specific secular goals. . . . Of course this does not mean that Pentecostal ideology does not invest the boundaries of permissible behavior with considerable import.[50]

The newer charismatics tended to manifest signs of what William James called "the religion of healthy-mindedness," and were often smiling folk who were expected to greet people with phrases like, "Praise the Lord!" Their lives were expected to be radiant and exemplary. In that respect, they were at a quantitative, not a qualitative remove from conventional Christianity, but their association of pentecostal symbols and phrases with such conduct set them aside to some degree.

Spirit-movement people progressively had to confront a whole range of problems which afflicted their Christian counterparts in more staid and acculturated bodies. The most visible change was the decline in a sense that pentecostals were being persecuted and must suffer opprobrium. For many decades, the scorn shown them by other Christians served to unify and add attraction to the group.

In the "good old days" when the movement was young in Tennessee, latter-day historian Vinson Synan reports:

> Heavy persecutions broke out against the people. . . . Several houses were burned as mobs led by "leading Methodist and Baptist

members" ransacked and pillaged the homes of the worshippers. . . .

An important reason for the widespread hostility . . . was the suspicion that everything odd and erroneous was believed and practiced by them. Whenever a pentecostal meeting took place in a community, rumors were rife about "magic powders," "trances," "wild emotion," and "sexual promiscuity." . . . These rumors eventually entered the folklore of the nation and stamped anyone claiming to be "holiness" or "pentecostal" with the epithet "holy roller." Those who engaged in this "religion of knockdown and dragout" were considered to be uncultured and uneducated "poor white trash" who inhabited the outer fringes of society. A member of one of the traditional churches who joined a pentecostal church was generally considered to have "lost his mind" and to have severed his normal social connections. Within this framework, it is not surprising that the relationship of the pentecostals to society has been marked with mutual hostility and even violence.[51]

The colorful David Wilkerson spoke of how change came through the years. His father had been a pentecostal minister.

We were called "holy rollers," and people looked down their spiritual "noses" when they referred to the poor tongue talkers. I grew up feeling like a second-class Christian, unwelcome by quiet, dignified kinds of worshippers who attended nice, quiet, dignified kinds of churches. . . . But now tongues have moved uptown. Orthodox Catholics, staid Presbyterians, dignified Episcopalians, and dispensationalized Baptists are now among those in the middle of the charismatic movement.[52]

Progressive acceptance by non-pentecostals was a complicating feature. In the newer charismatic movements, leaders sometimes almost tried to taunt the establishment in Christianity to express disfavor and rejection, at least to a certain degree. They knew that establishments in moderate and liberal Christianity were otherwise capable of absorbing or co-opting new and at first plaguing alternatives within the church.

Crossroads: Social Action, Respectability, Success

Pentecostalists and charismatics, then, came to a crossroads. Their successes and their compromises in the passage through time progressively eroded the line of visible difference between themselves and other Christians. They could be seen in many ways in continuity with past forms of American piety. They may have to share the fate of their accommodating spiritual ancestors. In seventeenth-century America, New England Puritans, already members of the covenant, had to have an experience of "owning the covenant" in order to become spiritually elite.[53] This act compares to the pentecostal quest for a second blessing. The acculturating fate of those Puritans as they moved toward liberalism, unitarianism, and secularity, frightened some pentecostals. In the eighteenth century, most colonials were thought of as somehow Christian, but the Great Awakening called them to a personal appropriation of the divine call and a visible pattern of consequent holiness. But the heirs of that Awakening often spent their energies on merely becoming better Americans.[54]

The nineteenth-century revivals served, as Jerald C. Brauer has suggested, as a sort of initiation rite for people who were to join a kind of aristocracy of the Spirit in a generalized culture.[55] As years passed, many of them turned toward concerns which led to the social gospel, the kind of expenditure of churchly energy which many pentecostals would not recognize or welcome. Would they also follow on that course?

American religion has been characteristically, if not essentially, experiential, affective, emotive, practical, personal, activist, and behavioral in intent and expression. So was pentecostalism, in a consistent and to a heightened degree. Only through strenuous efforts could charismatics retain some distance from co-optable and absorbable patterns of behavior and keep from being blurred back into the larger mass. The 1960s and 1970s gave many of them reason to seek demarcation. The search for personal identity became ever more intense. All around them, Christians saw other groups stressing particularity: through ethnic and racial assertiveness, through youth and women's movements, through interest groups and non-Christian cults. Their churches did not always serve any longer for these purposes. Many thereupon reached to the experience of old-line pentecostalism to make a new effort. They made no secret of the fact that the extraordinary demarcating Spirit-phenomena were most attractive in their quest.

The charismatic counterpart of the older pentecostals similarly often implied a kind of withdrawal but soon moved back toward some mainstream Christian concerns that could compromise them. Spirit movements had never been characteristically preoccupied, for example, with Christian social action. The new versions in the 1960s and 1970s were in continuity with their ancestors on this point. In the nature of the case, people who sought the experience of the Holy Spirit tended to accent that experience at the expense of other Christian directions.

The demise of numerous Christian social action movements in the late sixties was contemporary with the rise of the new pentecostalisms. But by the summer of 1973, some of the Catholic charismatics who gathered at Notre Dame University for their annual assembly were chiding their colleagues for not having put their new Christian joy and freedom to work in service to others. Father Harold Cohen, S.J., keynoted the event by urging pentecostals to be concerned with war and peace, prison conditions, urban ghettos and slum housing, racial injustice, migrant workers, and every human need and problem. At a seminar, Susan B. Anthony subsequently complained that suggestions of social action were greeted by charismatics with "silence and withdrawal." Father Joseph Fichter, S.J., took a survey which surprised no one: by 1973, pentecostals in Catholicism—and we may presume that their Protestant counterparts differed not at all—"still maintain[ed] their spiritual priorities" and had made few compromising moves toward social action and corporate service in the world.[56]

A move in the direction of action in the world, however valid it may be from the viewpoint of the Christian revelation, was seen by many as a threat to pentecostal integrity. It could lead Spirit-movement people "down" the same path to the social gospel, social Christianity, and other world-engaging emphases which tended to blur the line between the religious and the secular. The result could be blurring of the demarcating principle, a loss of identity.

The possibility of a move toward social action paralleled and symbolized a number of other tendencies which, while rendering pentecostalism more catholic, could also compromise it. Most disturbing to thoughtful prophets within the movement was the obvious trend toward identifying it with middle-class ways of life. The Full Gospel Business Men's Fellowship International, in its very name, showed that pentecostalism had made its way from life among the dispossessed and the people of marginal status to those who were more secure and were climbing. The literature of the pentecostal presses was as devoted to exemplifying and applauding bourgeois styles of living as was the literature of most of the more staid denominations.

Sociologists have had a field day with this feature of pentecostal change, especially when they studied groups which began in a situation of status-deprivation. Emilio Willems' findings concerning members in Chile and Brazil have often been applied to North America, too. The convert *"carefully rids himself of forms of behavior which the society at large holds in disrepute"* if these are "identified with lower class behavior." He saves all his energies for anomalous behavior in the spiritual, not in the secular realm; he is upward-bound in class and status. Gary Schwartz saw this tendency to be operative in the pentecostal group he studied in the United States, though it need not be seen as representative of all such groups and their members.[57]

As late as 1959, the popularizer of sociology Vance Packard could still treat class and status in religion in a chapter title, "The Long Road from Pentecostal to Episcopal."[58] Pentecostalists were proverbially considered to be lowest on the corporate ladders' rungs. That situation was changed somewhat during the 1960s in the midst of the spreading out of the middle class and the development of charismatic movements in standard-brand churches. They made the idea of pentecostalism more familiar and in many ways more respectable in the social sphere. In this respect, as in others, David Wilkerson was correct—pentecostalism had begun to "move uptown." By 1972, William Samarin could pronounce the judgment that "it no longer appears appropriate . . . to characterize Pentecostalism as arising from or being nurtured by sociocultural disruption, low status, and dissatisfaction." He could even say that within the churches "there is now a kind of Pentecostal 'Establishment.' " [59] The behavioral line in the public realm consequently grew ever more vague and thin.

A kind of intellectual anti-intellectualism added to the ambivalence. In order to make way for the primacy of the Spirit, Dennis Bennett half-playfully bragged: "I am personally a crashing intellectual, God help me. I have a Master of Divinity degree from the University of Chicago. I did most of my theological work in psychology and counselling." [60] Oral Roberts, who moved denominationally but not behaviorally out of pentecostalism built a well-financed university in Tulsa, Oklahoma.

Pentecostalism's impressive statistical successes also brought with them their own problems. In the early years, the movement had thrived on the sense of persecution; could it survive on the basis of boasts about growth, however frequently this growth was attributed to the miraculous working of the Holy Spirit? "While one major denomination after another report declining memberships and incomes, and even as their overseas missionary staffs are hit the hardest, Pentecostal churches, to the contrary, have made impressive and even startling gains," wrote a partisan, Steve Durasoff.[61] This kind of reportage appeared in most latter-day pentecostal and charismatic works—in contrast to the literature of the early days, when a kind of certification of pentecostal validity was claimed precisely because not many were gifted with the Spirit's special blessings.

If one were to ask whether pentecostalism's trends were more toward complete standoffishness or (in the language of historic holiness churches) toward come-outism on one hand, or, on the other, toward ecumenical involvement, the answer is simple. They were turning more from absolute demarcation, on the pattern of sects like the Jehovah's Witnesses, and more toward the interactive life of non-charismatic churches. Old-line pentecostalism kept turning ever more churchly and more respectable.

Divisive Belief and Behavior

The respectable turn, however, did not mean that the days of abrasion between Spirit-movements or denominations and the conventional churches were over. The standard-brand churches remained nervous about pentecostal outbreaks and intrusions. From some points of view, the nervousness was well-grounded. From the very first example in I Corinthians, the emphasis on spiritual gifts was seen to be potentially divisive. Spirit movements could breed pride just as they provided distance for their adherents. If the second blessing was a special gift, and Baptism in the Holy Spirit was an extraordinary experience, was it not inevitable that the less Spirit-blessed Christians would be looked down on? In turn, it was just as natural that non-pentecostal Christians who felt that they had experienced religious fullness already would often resent the suggestions that they needed something qualitatively different and obviously "more" than what they already knew. The history of pentecostal schisms bode ill for those who thought that charismatic movements would produce serenity.

Catholic commentator Kieran Quinn looked at charismatics in his church and quoted Ronald Knox, the enemy of enthusiasm: "More and more, by a kind of fatality, you see them draw apart from their coreligionists, a hive ready to swarm." Quinn added, "schism is endemic to enthusiasts." He pointed out, "Become a pentecostal Catholic or stranger still, a Catholic pentecostal. You are no longer primarily a Catholic, rather a pentecostal." [62] John T. Nichol pointed to the long roots of the separatist trend by reference to a southern California pastor who led his congregation in repetitious singing of

> Out of the rubbish heap the Lord lifted me!
> Out of the rubbish heap the Lord lifted me!

"The rubbish heap, as it turned out, was the Baptist Church . . . from which he had been drawn into Pentecostalism." [63] Recognizing the problems pentecostalism produced in even more intimate circles than denominations and congregations, especially in the family, one enterprising publisher put out a book on the care and feeding of a pentecostal in the family. The title was *So Your Wife Came Home Speaking in Tongues? So Did Mine!* [64] The conclusion of the book was ambivalent; for all the help that could be offered, no one could assure serenity because of the special spiritual claims and the behavioral demarcations drawn by the charismatic family member.

While the literature of the mainstream churches was preoccupied chiefly with the question of how to ward off pentecostal divisiveness, charismatic movements of all types tended to advertise themselves ambiguously. "Yes, we are different; our difference is a judgment on the mass of you. You need something you do not have. You must allow us to draw a circle around ourselves for our special meetings, practices, behavior. On the other hand, the gifts of the Spirit should produce unity; give us the chance to spread that unity—by giving us a chance to set up the circumstances wherein the charismatic experience might be realized. Some of us have even joined the ecumenical movement, including the World Council of Churches (though others of us are nervous about such behavior!)."

These ambiguities were born of an inevitable ambivalence: if movements of demarcation are too compromising, they lose distinctiveness and merge back into the mass. If they are too uncompromising, they come to schism. Even the snake-handling cults have experienced schism!

Whatever the ultimate fate of pentecostalism, whether it moves in the northern hemisphere as in the southern, or settles for the slice of the American pie it has come to hold, or sophisticates itself into standard-brand Christianity, by the last quarter of the century, the movement has tended to prove the value of President Van Dusen's contention of 1958. Pentecostalism, he thought, could join ecumenism as the two most impressive Christian growth signs of the twentieth century.

In the complexity and blurring of pluralist American culture religions, the social behavior of pentecostals and charismatics served to postpone if not to prevent permanently an absorption into the generalized patterns of the surrounding world. Meanwhile, they had all the advantages which non-Christian exotic groups and cults had in the society, so far as evoking curiosity and commanding loyalty is concerned. At the same time, they did not seem truly arcane, because with few exceptions they strove to remain in the orthodox Christian fold. However nervously some of them were regarded by non-pentecostal believers, few of them were denied inclusion in the Christian context. Thus their movements could have the best of both worlds. They could grow because they offered identity and did not seem to be shopworn. Yet they could reassure, because their differences appeared within a familiar pattern of beliefs and ideas, however anomalous their behavior.

NOTES

1. David W. Faupel, *The American Pentecostal Movement: A Bibliographical Essay* (Wilmore, Ky: G. L. Fisher Library, 1973), introduces the literature on pentecostalism. Faupel commends, with some qualifications, the following worldwide surveys: John Thomas Nichol, *Pentecostalism* (New York: Harper and Row, 1966); Walter J. Hollenweger, *The Pentecostals: The Charismatic Movement in the Church* (Minneapolis: Augsburg, 1972); Nils Bloch-Hoell, *The Pentecostal Movement: Its Origin, Development and Distinctive Character* (New York: Humanities Press, 1964). I shall refer to adherents both as pentecostals and pentecostalists, because they do. And members of charismatic movements often refer to themselves as charismatics.
2. The account appears in Agnes N. La Berge, *What God Hath Wrought—Life and Work of Mrs. Agnes N. O. La Berge, Nee Miss Agnes Ozman (Chicago: Herald Publishing Co., 1921), pp. 28–39. The Kansas City World* is quoted in Vinson Synan, *The Holiness-Pentecostal Movement in the United States* (Grand Rapids, Mich.: Eerdmans, 1971), p. 102.
3. The literature interpreting Acts 2 is introduced and discussed in an

extensive work by a non-pentecostal, Frederick Dale Bruner: *A Theology of the Holy Spirit: The Pentecostal Experience and the New Testament Witness* (Grand Rapids, Mich.: Eerdmans, 1970), pp. 155 ff.

4. During the years of the newer charismatic movement's rise, the two prophets who most worked with world-reducing metaphors were R. Buckminster Fuller and Marshall McLuhan; see John McHale *The Future of the Future* (New York: Braziller, 1969), pp. 248-50.

5. Walter J. Hollenweger, "Spirituality for the World," *Event* 13, no. 10 (November/December 1973), 9. The remark was first made in an address over Dutch radio.

6. The claim is not made that all contemporary religious movements in Africa are precisely the same as pentecostalism, but that many bear its chief characteristics; see David B. Barrett, *Schism and Renewal in Africa: An Analysis of Six Thousand Contemporary Religious Movements* (New York: Oxford, 1968).

7. Bruner, *op. cit.*, p. 23, comments on the literature having to do with pentecostal growth and statistics; he relies chiefly on Hollenweger's researches.

8. Nichol, *op. cit.*, pp. 25 ff., describes much of this spread in the United States.

9. An account of this "Spirit-filled life" in Catholic pentecostalism appears in Kevin and Dorothy Ranaghan, ed., *As the Spirit Leads Us* (Paramus, N.J.: Paulist/Newman Press, 1971).

10. Henry Pitney Van Dusen, "The Third Force," *Life*, June 9, 1958, pp. 122-24. Methodist Professor D. A. Hayes of Garrett Biblical Institute is quoted by Nichol, *op. cit.*, p. xi. See also J. A. Synan, "The Purpose of God in the Pentecostal Movement for This Hour," *Pentecostal World Conference Messages: Preached at the Fifth Triennial Pentecostal World Conference, Toronto, Canada, 1958*, Donald Gee, etc. (Toronto: Full Gospel Publishing House, 1958), p. 29.

11. Donald L. Gelpi, *Pentecostalism: A Theological Viewpoint* (Paramus, N.J.: Paulist/Newman Press, 1971), pp. 35, 38.

12. Joseph R. Washington, Jr., *Black Sects and Cults* (Garden City, N.Y.: Doubleday, 1973), p. 68.

13. Nichol, *op. cit.*, pp. 94 ff.; Faupel, *op. cit.*, pp. 44 ff.

14. Sydney E. Ahlstrom, *A Religious History of the American People* (New Haven: Yale University Press, 1972), pp. 819-22, 1059f., 1086*n.*; Winthrop S. Hudson, *Religion in America*, 2nd ed. (New York: Scribner's, 1973), pp. 345f., 428-31.

15. Felicitas D. Goodman, *Speaking in Tongues: A Cross-Cultural Study of Glossolalia* (Chicago: University of Chicago Press, 1972), p. 124. The author left open the question of theological validity and personal faith: "I very much hope that in addition to presenting some scientific results, . . . I will be able to convey a little of my wonder at and my reverence for the miracle that is man, which remains awesome whether we postulate a Holy Spirit or not" (p. xi).

16. Morton Kelsey, *Encounter with God* (Minneapolis: Bethany Fellowship, 1972), pp. 38ff., 102ff.

17. William J. Samarin, *Tongues of Men and Angels* (New York: Macmillan, 1972), pp. 227f.

18. Stanley Krippner, "Altered States of Consciousness," in John White, ed., *The Highest State of Consciousness* (Garden City, N.Y.; Doubleday, 1973), pp. 3, 5.

19. The New English Bible translation, used here for purposes of general clarity, has been criticized for translating the term "ecstatic utterance"; given the strictures in the previous paragraph, it can be employed here with a precautious sense.

20. Quoted by Nichol, *op. cit.*, p. 20 from *Ecclesiastical History*, vol. 5: 16, 7: in Philip Schaff, ed., *A Select Library of the Nicene and Post-Nicene Fathers*, 2nd ser. (New York: Scribner's, 1890), vol. 1: 231.

21. V. Synan, *op. cit.*, p. 13.

22. Gelpi, *op. cit.*, pp. 8–34, 39, 126f.

23. Faupel, *op. cit.*, p. 33.

24. Kieran Quinn, "Knox, Me and the Pentecostals," in *National Catholic Reporter*, November 9, 1973, p. 7.

25. David Wilkerson, *David Wilkerson Speaks Out* (Minneapolis: Bethany Fellowship, 1973), p. 21.

26. Hans Jacob Frøen, "What is the Baptism in the Holy Spirit?" in Norris L. Wogen, *Jesus, Where Are You Taking Us?* (Carol Stream, Ill.: Creation House, 1973), p. 129.

27. Bruner, *op. cit.*, p. 59.

28. A condensed summary of the complex attempts at typing church forms is available in Roland Robertson, *The Sociological Interpretation of Religion* (New York: Schocken, 1970), pp. 116ff., where Troeltsch is quoted (p. 116); see also Sidney E. Mead, *The Lively Experiment* (New York: Harper and Row, 1963), chap. 7.

29. Bruner, *op. cit.*, p. 25.

30. Ranaghan, *op. cit.*, pp. 7f.

31. Anthony A. Hoekema, *Holy Spirit Baptism* (Grand Rapids, Mich.: Eerdmans, 1972), pp. 10, 21.

32. Bruner, *op. cit.*, p. 22.

33. *Commonweal*, November 8, 1968, p. 203.

34. See Wayne E. Oates, "A Socio-Psychological Study of Glossolalia," in Frank Stagg, E. Glenn Hinson, and Wayne E. Oates, *Glossolalia: Tongue Speaking in Biblical, Historical, and Psychological Perspective* (Nashville: Abingdon, 1967), p. 77.

35. This catalog of references comes from *The Pentecostal Holiness Manual*, 1969, p. 12; Vinson Synan, *The Old-Time Power: A History of the Pentecostal Holiness Church* (Franklin Springs, Ga.: Advocate Press, 1973), p. 99; Luther P. Gerlach and Virginia H. Hine, "Five Factors Crucial to the Growth and Spread of a Modern Religious

Movement," *Journal for the Scientific Study of Religion*, 7, no. 1 (Spring 1968), pp. 23–40; Donald G. Bloesch, "The Wind of the Spirit: Thoughts on a Doctrinal Controversy," *The Reformed Journal, General Conference, M.E. Church, South*, 1894, pp. 25f.

36. Samarin, *op. cit.*, pp. 212–16.

37. Werner Skibstedt, *Die Geistestaufe im Licht der Bibel*, quoted by Bruner, *op. cit.*, p. 27.

38. Marcus Bach, *Strange Sects and Curious Cults* (New York: Dodd, Mead, 1961), p. 133; Washington, *op. cit.*, p. 118.

39. Gelpi, *op. cit.*, p. 132.

40. Synan, *The Holiness-Pentecostal Movement*, pp. 95f.

41. The source is reprinted by Erling Jorstad, ed., *The Holy Spirit in Today's Church: A Handbook of the New Pentecostalism* (Nashville, Tenn.: Abingdon, 1973), pp. 77–79; it is from Don Basham, *A Handbook on Holy Spirit Baptism* (Monroeville, Penn.: Whitaker Books, 1969).

42. Quoted by Watson E. Mills, *Understanding Speaking in Tongues* (Grand Rapids, Mich.: Eerdmans, 1972), p. 14.

43. See Weston La Barre, *They Shall Take Up Serpents: Psychology of the Southern Snake-Handling Cult* (Minneapolis: University of Minnesota Press, 1962).

44. E. D. O'Connor, *The Pentecostal Movement in the Catholic Church* (Notre Dame: Ave Maria Press, 1971), pp. 168–70.

45. Nichol, *op. cit.*, p. 77.

46. Bruner, *op. cit.*, pp. 142f. He quotes Eddison Mosiman, *Das Zungenreden Geschichtlich und Psychologisch Untersucht* (Tubingen: J. C. B. Mohr, 1911), p. 115.

47. Bruner, *op. cit.* pp. 140f; he quotes Donald Gee, *The Pentecostal Movement: Including the Story of the War Years (1940–47)* (London: Elim Publishing Company, 1949), pp. 40f.

48. Ranaghan and Cavnar in Ranaghan, *op. cit.*, pp. 38, 58f., 61, 70, 71, 75f.

49. Synan, *The Old-Time Power*, pp. 50, 58, 61, 72f., 89, 90, 126, 261.

50. Gary Schwartz, *Sect Ideologies and Social Status* (Chicago: University of Chicago, 1970), p. 180.

51. Synan, *The Holiness-Pentecostal Movement*, pp. 80, 186.

52. Wilkerson, *op. cit.*, pp. 15f.

53. The master chronicler of Puritan accommodation was Perry Miller; his *Errand into the Wilderness* (Cambridge, Mass.: Harvard University Press, 1956) and *Nature's Nation* (Cambridge, Mass.: Harvard University Press, 1967) collect essays which condense much of his life work detailing change in New England religion on the model described here.

54. Alan Heimert and Perry Miller, eds., *The Great Awakening: Documents Illustrating the Crisis and Its Consequences* (Indianapolis: Bobbs-Merrill, 1967) brings together sources on this Awakening and its aftermath, and includes a valuable introductory essay and bibliography.

55. Jerald C. Brauer made this suggestion in "Changing Perspectives on Religion in America," in Brauer, ed., *Reinterpretation in American Church History* (Chicago: University of Chicago, 1968), pp. 25ff. On the trend toward the social gospel, see the controversial thesis of Timothy L. Smith in his *Revivalism and Social Reform* (Nashville, Tenn.: Abingdon, 1957); see also William G. McLoughlin, Jr., *Modern Revivalism: Charles Grandison Finney to Billy Graham* (New York: Ronald, 1959).

56. Joseph H. Fichter, "Pentecostals: Comfort vs. Awareness," *America*, September 1, 1973, pp. 114–16.

57. Emilio Willems, *Followers of the New Faith: Culture Change and the Rise of Protestantism in Brazil and Chile* (Nashville: Vanderbilt University Press, 1967), pp. 129–31; see Schwartz, *op. cit.*, pp. 182ff.

58. Vance Packard, *The Status Seekers* (New York: David McKay, 1959), pp. 194–206.

59. Samarin, *op. cit.*, pp. 6f., 10.

60. Dennis Bennett, "Renewal or Revival," see Wogen, *op. cit.*, p. 83.

61. Steve Durasoff, *Bright Wind of the Spirit: Pentecostalism Today* (Englewood Cliffs, N.J.: Prentice-Hall, 1972), p. 10.

62. Quinn, *op. cit.*, p. 7.

63. Nichol, *op. cit.*, p. 79.

64. Robert Branch (Old Tappan, N.J.: Revell, 1973).

The Theological Opportunity Lying Before the Pentecostal Movement

RUSSELL P. SPITTLER

Russell P. Spittler is Academic Dean of Southern California College, Costa Mesa, California. With an A.B. from Florida Southern College, an M.A. from Wheaton, and a B.D. from Gordon-Conwell Theological Seminary, Spittler earned his Ph.D. in New Testament at Harvard University in 1971. An ordained minister in the Assemblies of God, he also serves as a Lieutenant Commander in the U.S. Naval Reserve.

In 1962 Spittler published Cults and Isms *which has become a standard reference work in its field. Additionally, he has contributed numerous articles to various denominational and interdenominational periodicals. In recent years, Spittler has distinguished himself as a spokesman for classical pentecostalism to the burgeoning world of the charismatic renewal. In 1972 he served on the pentecostal team for the Catholic-Pentecostal Dialogue which convened in Zurich, Switzerland.*

One of the founding spirits of the Society for Pentecostal Studies, Spittler served effectively as the third president of the organization.

The following paper is the text of the presidential address given to the Society for Pentecostal Studies in cooperation with the Tenth World Pentecostal Conference in Seoul, Korea, in September, 1973.

A quotation:

> Some see it as a new Reformation, straining to meet its Luther at a yet undiscovered cathedral door. Some hail it as an evolutionary crisis, with the cells of the old humanity fairly bursting to reassemble into some more spiritual new being. To others it may be a more prosaic phenomenon, the inevitable moving of the pendulum, the return to some forgotten truths—or to dangerous superstitions.
>
> By whatever name, there is an impending sense of change in the world of ideas. The reigning wisdom that informed and compelled the past few decades is under attack—or, at the very least, under cross-examination. That wisdom has been variously called liberalism, rationalism, scientism: concepts certainly not identical but related. But now man's confidence in his power to control his world is at a low ebb. Technology is seen as a dangerous ally, and progress is suspect. Even the evolutionists share this unease: their hope lies not in man as he is, but in some mutant superman.

With these words, *Time* (April 2, 1973) opened a special series recording some "Second Thoughts About Man." The series marshaled impressive documentation to show that in the fields of human behavior, religion, education, and science, there is today a rising tide of opposition to some of the most cherished guiding principles of our modern civilization.

Surely the most firmly established of these modern ideas has been what is called "the scientific method." Our whole modern world is built on it.

For three hundred years, at least, we have lived under the reign of Reason. Early in the seventeenth century, the philosopher René Descartes (1596–1650) taught we must sweep away all superstitious beliefs, doubt everything except our belief that we ourselves exist, then start to think out a new world, accepting as truth only what can be objectively analyzed.

And so began the reign of Reason, the rise of Science. No longer could anything unseen or unproved be accepted as truth. Only what appeared in the scientist's microscope or his telescope, only what suited the demands of logic, could be believed.

There would be no place for religion or revelation. Art and literature might be useful amusements: but only Science and Reason could give us the truth.

So sure were those early moderns of the promise of Reason that in the year 1792 the revolutionary assembly in Paris seriously proposed a new calendar—with the dating of years to begin anew with the year one, thus signifying the firm arrival of the age of rationalism.

A prominent result of this reign of Reason, this lordship of Science, has been modern Technology. Technology is the application of science to make life easy. The "law of gravity" is science: an elevator is technology.

We have seen technology sweep on in massive waves. It seems to have begun in the last century with the discovery of electricity. First the telegraph. Then the telephone. Then the incandescent light. The horseless carriage. The airplane. The radio. Plastics. Television. Styrofoam packaging. And finally, the late great departure of man from this planet and his arrival on the moon.

Technology has made life easier, brought distances closer, opened mass communications. We have come to an age of "experts"—persons who know more and more about less and less.

Someone calculated it would take 400 years to complete all the courses offered in a recent year at a modern university.

In fact, we are victimized by experts. Some scholars speak of the modern world as a "technocracy"—a rule by "technocrats," government by experts: if the people prominent in medicine, foreign policy, or educational theory say this or that is the case, who are we ordinary souls to doubt the "experts"?

We live in the age of Technology, the era in which Science has virtually become a god.

But things are changing. Science has taken us some places we're not so sure we want to go. Our very fruitful Technology has led, as

Time phrased it, "to Hitler and Hiroshima." We *can*—and in this century we *have* done it—use Science to hurt rather than help. Technology it was that facilitated the murder of millions under the Nazis. Technology it was that flashed the devastating atomic bomb at Hiroshima.

Maybe it is time for some second thoughts about man. *And* Science. *And* Technology.

One of the superb recent analyses of the crumbling walls of "scientism" is Theodore Roszak's 1969 book titled *The Making of a Counter Culture.*

As a social historian faced with the rampaging youth on American university campuses in the late 1960s, Dr. Roszak was concerned with what made these youths act like that. He argues that the youth with all their varied beliefs and practices show a consistent pattern of thought that directly opposes our modern technological age. What makes an intelligent middle-class youth walk out of the comfort and affluence of his home, put on hippy-style clothes, let his hair grow long, head for experimental life in communes, take up the use of mind-expanding drugs, and generally discard the material wealth of his parents? The underlying reason, according to Dr. Roszak, is a flat rejection of the scientifically-based, technologically-oriented, and materialistically-flooded modern culture. The youth is protesting the rule of Science his parents have come to accept without question. The youth is expressing, in ways available to him, a hunger for the non-material, spiritual side of life long obscured by our materialism.

Dr. Roszak puts the blame for all this at the feet of Science and Technology. Science taught us always to be "objective," never under any circumstances to be "subjective"—always to *think*, but never to *feel*.

The people doing things today either come from, or speak to the youth—so Dr. Roszak contends. There is the poetry of Allen Ginsberg, the Zen Buddhism of Alan Watts, the blatant drug-religion of Timothy Leary—all these have in common their flat rejection of the choking grip of scientism. There is truth, these various speakers to modern youth agree (and I certainly don't wish to be taken as approving the teachings of any of them!)—there is truth beyond that which is given to us by Science and Reason.

There is truth, these mavericks in modern thought are saying, beyond the reach of the scientific method. There is another side to life and reality besides the realm of the material. There is—and they don't quite use the term in the way we do—an overlooked spiritual side to life.

Most of us have seen the disturbing effects of the use of drugs by youth. But it is also possible to say that the modern youth is attracted by a chemical promise to "expand his consciousness," to let him escape this materialistic culture, to get him into some sort of whole new world where there might be some values other than the ones Science taught him.

The use of drugs, I am saying, has also this implication: it can be, and for many it has been, a part of a basically spiritual search for reality which the youth has not found in the modern world with all its Technology and materialism.

One of the tremendous opportunities lying before the Church today is the thrilling challenge to say to seeking youth that the reality they seek is found not in chemistry but in Christ!

So there is a crack in the wall of Science today. The crack is getting larger. Some stones are crumbling away. The grip of the scientific method has been broken. The modern mind must be remade. There *is*, after all, more to truth than what appears in the scientist's microscope. There is a great reality that is fundamentally spiritual in nature. If searching youth and wise men today use a small "s" for "spiritual," we who have been plunged, immersed, baptized into the Spirit—*capital* "S," the Spirit whose chief characteristic is holiness, the Holy Spirit—we are the ones who have the opportunity to introduce men to the only real God, the Father of our Lord Jesus Christ.

But this decline of Science and fall of Reason are paralleled by equally interesting developments in Religion. In America, at least,

Religion is still an unofficial part of the prevailing culture. But there's not much vitality in the state of things in general in the Church.

The real news is on the fringe. Seven years ago, *Time*'s familiar cover announced "GOD IS DEAD." Two years ago, the same magazine showed a picture of Jesus on its cover and took a long look at the Jesus People.

There is renewed interest these days in Religion—but in rather far-out kinds of Religion. The world of the occult has had a quick rise to prominence. Satanism is a standard option now in that great religious zoo, Southern California.

Pan American Airways offers a "Psychic Tour" of Great Britain, a packaged deal with all meals, hotel, séances, taxis, and witches included. Hare Krishna chanters have brought the exotic saffron religions of the Orient to the streetcorners and bus stations of America.

John F. Kennedy University offered just this summer an eight-week "Institute for the Study of Mysticism and Religion." You could do a course on Yoga, another on Psychedelic Religion, another on Parapsychology.

American astronaut Edgar Mitchell from the cockpit of Apollo 14 conducted some unofficial—and unsuccessful, I may add—experiments with ESP, extrasensory perception. Mitchell now devotes his full time to psychic experimentation: he has, you'd be interested to learn, been in touch with a Spirit-baptized scientist who bears him witness of the true Spirit.

We can't ignore this renewed interest in religion and the supernatural. That the interest shows up in bizarre forms like Satanism, Hare Krishna, and the like—and not in traditional forms of Christianity—I think only shows the bankruptcy of much of the fare offered by powerless traditional forms of Christianity.

There is a spiritual thirst abroad in our modern cultural desert. The Religious News Service pegged as the leading religious story of 1972 what it called "the widespread quest for personal spiritual experience." Pope Paul VI has proclaimed for the Roman Catholic Church a year—and the year began on Pentecost Sunday, 1973—a year in which the interior spiritual life is to be stressed.

We have all thrilled to the recent spread of the pentecostal message among the main-line Christian denominations. I stood spellbound in June 1973, in Notre Dame's football stadium as more than 20,000 Catholics sang in the Spirit, each in his own divinely given tongue. Who would have believed, just twenty years ago, that there would be rapidly growing associations of charismatic clergymen among the Lutherans, the Presbyterians, the Episcopalians?

I sat on a panel recently where newly charismatic ministers raised as their first question, "How can I introduce the life in the Spirit to my church?" What a different question from the days when the same groups were more likely to ask, "How can we rescue the church from these fanatical pentecostals?"

It is even the case that there is a new climate of acceptance of the pentecostal or charismatic message within the Church at large. The most recent book on pentecostalism by a non-pentecostal I've seen is Peter Wagner's book titled, *Look Out, the Pentecostals Are Coming!* And another by Robert Branch with the long but revealing title, *So Your Wife Came Home Speaking in Tongues–So Did Mine.* A far cry these are from something like *The Modern Tongues Movement Exposed* published a few years ago!

So I'm ready to say, brothers and sisters, that we've got two things on our hands: first, the decline of Science, and second, the rise of Religion.

There is, I suggest to you, an unprecedented opportunity lying before the pentecostal movement. On the popular level, there is a world full of men who've had it up to here with science and reason and technology and materialism and liberalism. They thirst for things of the spirit—small "s"—without knowing that God *is* Spirit—capital S. Let those who know what it is to be baptized in the Spirit gird up their loins anew for a boldly renewed evangelistic assault! Whom men seek unknowingly, let us proclaim experientially.

But there is more to do on a theological level, too. In these days of rising education levels of the general public, let us not leave unreached the reflective thinkers who also search for reality.

Pentecostals have always been better at evangelism than at writing theology. We are known more for foreign missions than for theological books. That is as it should be: in my opinion, the theologian must always be the servant of the Church.

But the time has come to pluck a ripened pentecostal theology. The time has come to remind the intellectuals of the day that there are some folk around—not many mighty, not many noble among them—who've been saying long before Roszak, long before the youthful protesters, that life is at its best, man has reached his highest and found God's best, when one not merely discovers truth beyond the material world, but when, more than that, one can by personal and individual experience so encounter that world as to be personally baptized into the Holy Spirit of God.

Let me close with another reference to Theodore Roszak. Decrying the demand of the scientific mentality for strict objectivity, he says: "Scientific culture makes no allowance for 'joy,' since that is an experience of intense personal involvement. Joy is something," he continues, "that is known only to the person: it does not submit to objectification."

We are the only branch of Christendom named after a Jewish feast—the feast of Pentecost. The feast of Pentecost was first and foremost a feast of joy—joy arising from a successful and fruitful harvest.

Let us then make our joy full, as Jesus invited us to do. Let us celebrate a great harvest of pentecostal joy. We have met the Truth in person—the person of Jesus who so boldly declared "I am the truth." So we readily agree with Paul in saying, "I know *whom* [*not* what!] I have believed." If Science is dying and Religion is rising, let's recognize those twin facts for the challenge they are. Say with me as I've been saying to myself in recent months, "Let us go up and keep the feast!"

Index

Acts of the Apostles, 11, 12, 49, 50–52, 72, 94, 103, 112–16, 119, 125, 140, 146, 147, 149, 152–53, 158, 196. See also Bible; New Testament
Adrian College, 44
Ahlstrom, Sydney E., 201
Alliance. See Christian and Missionary Alliance
"Angels," 21
Anti-clericalism, 173
Apostles, 35, 72, 150, 153, 172, 185. See also names of specific apostles
Apostolic Faith Church (Los Angeles), 27
Apostolic Faith Mission, 93
Archbishop of Canterbury, 33
Arminianism, 61, 111
Arthur, William, 42, 46, 65; *The Tongue of Fire*, 42, 45, 65
Assemblies of God, 2, 3, 31, 83–85, 89, 93–96, 129, 154, 165, 200
   1915 General Council, 94
   1916 General Council, 94, 165
Atonement, 8, 10, 48
Autobiography (Mahan), 43
Azusa Street Mission, 2, 11, 12, 17, 26, 27, 29, 52, 59, 71, 73, 74, 87, 91, 93, 102, 125, 126, 131, 133–36, 138, 139, 179, 198, 214, 216

Babylon, 32
Bangs, Nathan, 63
Baptism, in Holy Spirit, 1–2, 9, 17, 30–31, 65–66, 70–71, 93, 101, 127, 140, 145, 185, 209–210, 217–18, 227, 240–41, 243
   evidence of, 27, 49, 51–52, 64, 83, 88–89, 95, 112, 116–17, 129, 157, 212
   history of, 41–45, 48, 72, 107–110
   receiving of, 131–34, 214–15
   See also Tongues, speaking in
Baptism, in water, 112, 152–53, 159, 209
Baptism of the Holy Ghost (Mahan), 46–51, 71
Baptist religion, 1, 32, 61, 90, 95, 127, 200, 228
Bartleman, Frank, 74–75, 92, 102, 106–107, 131
Bauman, Louis, 104
Beecher, Henry Ward, 155
Bell, E.N., 93–95
Bennett, Father Dennis, 3, 198, 201, 215, 226
Bethel Bible School (Topeka, Kansas), 9, 26, 35, 52, 87, 125, 129, 133, 157, 195, 197
Bible, 7, 9, 10, 21, 25, 63, 84, 105, 113, 129, 154–55, 157, 161, 177, 179, 219. See also New Testament; Old Testament
Bible Conference Movement, 84
Boardman, W.E., 68
Book of Acts. See Acts of the Apostles
Book of Common Prayer, 17
Boyd, Frank M., 85, 89
Branch, Robert, 242
Bresee, Phineas, 73, 74

For free information on how to receive
the international magazine

LOGOS JOURNAL

also Book Catalog

Write: Information - LOGOS JOURNAL CATALOG
Box 191
Plainfield, NJ 07061